"One day, you open the ephemeris and there it is: transiting Neptune opposing your Moon taking effect exactly five days before. 'What a coincidence,' you think, as you look down to find your feet are swollen and you're feeling nostalgic about those good old days when you could disco those little feet like crazy all night long. You'll need to read all about what this transit could mean for you now that things are quite different in your life."

—from Introduction

"Neptune [is]...one of the planetary gateways to a 'galactic' consciousness that is free from the limitations of the less-encompassing perspectives of Saturn and all planets inside Saturn's orbital path— especially those personalized realities of the Sun, who acts as head supervisor for Egos Unlimited!"

—from Chapter One

"Neptune loves to see people merge and operate as one unit of consciousness. It's a planet that will try to melt down any formidable barriers between couples that otherwise would keep their hearts and souls from uniting in harmony. Neptune seeks to inspire blissful states of matrimony, even if we doubt that such a thing is feasible in our personal situation."

—from Neptunian Tour of Our Natal Houses

"With tensional aspects involved, transiting Neptune's images often frighten Saturn. We can brood and mistrust our interpretation of situations—true gloom-and-doom artists. We begin to anxiously worry about where to place our faith. Upon whom or what should we depend? Some of us may even sense that we are 'losing it,' becoming unglued on some level, and we probably are."

—from Neptune/Saturn Transits

ABOUT THE AUTHOR

Bil Tierney has been involved with astrology for over thirty-two years. As a full-time professional, he has lectured and given workshops at major astrological conferences throughout the United States and in Canada since the mid-1970s. He has a special interest in studying the birthchart from a practical, psychological level that also encourages spiritual growth. He is a longtime member of the Metropolitan Atlanta Astrological Society (MAAS), and has served as its newsletter/journal editor several times. Bil's work has also been published in astrological publications such as *Aspects* and *The Mercury Hour.* Other books he has written are *Dynamics of Aspect Analysis*, and the Llewellyn publications: *Twelve Faces of Saturn, Alive and Well with Uranus,* and *Alive and Well with Pluto.*

When Bil is not busy with client consultations, lecturing, tutoring, and writing articles and books, his other big passion is computers. Clients enjoy Bil's animated, warm, and easy-going style, and they are impressed with his skillful blend of the intuitive and the analytical. His humorous slant on life is appreciated as well. Readers enjoy his thorough, insightful approach to astrological topics.

TO CONTACT THE AUTHOR

If you would like to contact the author or would like more information about this book, please write to him in care of Llewellyn Worldwide. All mail addressed to the author is forwarded, but the publisher cannot, unless specifically instructed by the author, give out an address or phone number. Please write to:

Bil Tierney
c/o Llewellyn Publications
P.O. Box 64383, Dept. K715–3
St. Paul, MN 55164–0383, U.S.A.

Please enclose a self-addressed, stamped envelope for reply or $1.00 to cover costs. If ordering from outside the U.S.A., please enclose an international postal reply coupon.

Llewellyn Worldwide does not participate in, endorse, or have any authority or responsibility concerning private business transactions between our authors and the public.

Alive and Well with NEPTUNE

Transits of Heart and Soul
Bil Tierney

1999
Llewellyn Publications
St. Paul, MN 55164–0833 U.S.A.

FIRST EDITION
First Printing 1999

Cover design by William Merlin Cannon
Book design by Ken Schubert
Editing by Marguerite Krause
Project Management by Eila Savela

Library of Congress Cataloging-in-Publication Data

Tierney, Bil.
    Alive & well with Neptune : transits of heart and soul / Bil Tierney. — 1st ed.
      p.   cm.
    Includes bibliographical references (p.   ).
    ISBN 1–56718–715–3
    1. Astrology. 2. Neptune (Planet) — Miscellanea. I. Title.
II. Title : Alive and well with Neptune.
BF1724.2.N45T54   1999
133.5 ' 391—dc21   99–32704
                                                    CIP

Printed in the United States of America

Llewellyn Publications
A Division of Llewellyn Worldwide, Ltd.
P.O. Box 64383, Dept. K715–3
St. Paul, MN 55164–0383, U.S.A.
www.llewellyn.com

DEDICATION

I dedicate this book to Donna Van Toen, a
devoted astrologer who has well-navigated
Neptune's deeper waters in good faith.

ACKNOWLEDGEMENTS

A thanks goes to Llewellyn's Acquisitions Manager Nancy Mostad for accepting my Neptune manuscript for publication. I'm also very grateful to Ken Schubert for his fine book design, William Merlin Cannon for the striking cover he created, and hard-working Marguerite Krause for her fine editing skills. Moreover, I really must applaud the efforts of Project Manager and Astrology Editor, Eila Savela (thanks, Eila, for keeping all of my book's offbeat humor intact, and for smoothly handling last-minute details). My thanks also goes to Lisa Braun (Publicity), and Wendy Crowe (Marketing), and everyone else who helped in the production of this book.

And last, I wish to express my gratitude to my colleagues, Jeff Jawer and David Railey, who read pre-publication copies of *Alive and Well with Neptune* and submitted their comments for the back cover.

Oh, and thanks, Neptune, for allowing me to enter your colorful world and for inspiring me to find imaginative ways to describe your wondrous gifts. You enabled me to brag about what a profoundly illuminating planet of heart and soul you really are!

OTHER BOOKS BY BIL TIERNEY

Twelve Faces of Saturn
Alive and Well with Uranus

UPCOMING TITLE

Alive and Well with Pluto

TABLE OF CONTENTS

Chapter Eight

Chapter Nine

Chapter Ten

Chapter Eleven

Chapter Twelve

Chapter Thirteen

Chapter Fourteen

Chapter Fifteen

INTRODUCTION

The Other Side of Neptune

It's no wonder that astrological Neptune rules unsolved mysteries, because it's somewhat a mystery why we traditionally associate this planet with a tempermental sea god known for his stormy personality in Greek and Roman myths—the cultural source of all our planetary symbolism. Isn't Neptune supposed to be the most spiritually sensitive of all the planets—a universal pacifist who wouldn't step on a weed or hurt a fly? Don't we consider it to be a planet that oozes empathy and seduces us to completely merge our consciousness with all else that lives, thereby dissolving the illusion that we possess separate identities?

Neptune would rather feed unlimited divine energy to our souls and inspire us to nourish our bodies with a steady diet of fruits, seeds, nuts, and vegetables. Ideally, Neptune won't kill for meat or endure seeing blood being shed in the name of cruelty or violence. Yet mythological Neptune was no pacifist or peacemaker. He personified the oceanic realm, which is rarely calm or predictable. Its powerful waves crash dramatically against the shoreline's rocks, and sudden storms at sea create turbulent and dangerous waters.

1

The actual planet Neptune wasn't discovered until 1846—a milestone that signalled humanity's readiness to use this planet's energies with greater social awareness. Perhaps it has taken us several millennia to absorb the kinder, gentler side of this planetary archetype. This aspect of Neptune probably got a boost during the development of Piscean water imagery in the earliest stages of Christianity, with Jesus as a living symbol of all those illuminated traits we now expect from the spiritual-savior side of unity-conscious Neptune. This is the side of Neptune all astrologers are familiar with—the one wearing the halo.

The Greeks focused on more "pagan," nature-connected qualities of the Neptune principle with their portrayal of the "wild-eyed" god Poseidon, who was fiery in disposition and driven by elemental instinct, making him temperamental to the point of being a rage-aholic! He certainly didn't have the airy detachment of a typical sky god, nor did he even look serene and mellow (that trendy Neptunian "bliss" look made popular in the late 1960s). Homer's nickname for Poseidon was the "Earth Shaker," which can also describe how we often tremble when we're enraged.

So, how did Poseidon get like this? For one thing, he was traumatized shortly after his birth, as was his brother Hades (Pluto), accused by some of turning out a little twisted as a result. Their father was uptight, paranoid Cronus (better known to us from Roman mythology as Saturn). Cronus got into an obsessive state regarding a bothersome prophecy blurted out by his father Uranus just moments after Cronus castrated him (this was a horrible father-son relationship worthy of any Greek tragedy). The dreaded prophecy warned that Cronus would someday be overthrown by one of his own rebellious kids.

Was saying this just an act of viciousness on wounded Uranus' part, intended to psychologically undermine Cronus, or was this sky god actually foreseeing the future? Whatever the case, Saturnians today still get an anxious, uneasy feeling about the potential for an unknown fate to intervene and upset the status quo of their lives, which is why they make their moves hesitantly and carefully. What Cronus later did to make himself feel safer about his questionable future was to swallow up each of the first five children he fathered immediately after their birth.

Poseidon entered the world only to be thrown into a confusing state of darkness and fear while trapped in the pit of his father's stomach—totally cut off from contact with the outer world and from the loving touch of his mother. This introduced haunting themes of isolation and alienation, a gnawing sense of not being a real part of the outer world, and even of not actually being wanted by one's parents. His other siblings—except for Zeus (Jupiter)—were in the same dire predicament but, for some reason, Poseidon was more hypersensitive than the rest. Touchiness and hostility to rejection continued to plague him even as an adult—you could always count on Poseidon to have a totally subjective and often infantile reaction to any rebuff.

In astrology, Saturn and Neptune are still not on easy speaking terms. Wary Neptune knows full well that Saturn's domineering influence can be stifling and suffocating, especially regarding the process of unfolding one's imagination. Neptune will permit itself only a certain degree of Saturnian structure before it has a panic attack and unravels at the seams. Nevertheless, astrological Saturn is the best agent for the clear manifestation of Neptune's beautiful visions.

After Cronus was forced to vomit forth his kids, releasing them from their prison, Poseidon assisted his brother Zeus—who luckily had never been swallowed—and his other siblings in a victorious revolt against their control-freak father. Cronus was finally ousted from his seat of power, just as predicted. Poseidon had an ax to grind about the psychological abuse he endured. He was troubled by unresolved anger.

After the "War of the Titans" was over and it came time to decide who would rule what particular domain in the new order of gods, the brothers drew lots. Poseidon's realm became the seas and all the waterways of the earth (appropriate Neptunian symbols of interconnectedness). However, although he dwelled with his wife in a splendid golden palace in the ocean's depths, Poseidon never felt he was dealt the best hand. He wanted some of the glory and the perks that came easily to brother Zeus. He felt cheated, and eventually became fixated on the things he didn't have. (Gee, isn't that how some self-pitying Neptunians feel about life, jinxed or cursed right from the start—rotten luck—while also secretly covetous of the so-called glamorous lives of others?)

I bet Poseidon wondered about life's fairness. Destiny had blessed Zeus with a continuously active, exciting social lifestyle that allowed him to live high on a heavenly, sun-drenched mountain at cloud level—while this moody sea god was submerged in a dimly lit, silent region, apart from all the action happening out there in the big world. Hades' domain proved to be an even darker and more remote place, yet somehow that suited him fine. Poseidon, however, had mixed feelings about the life that fate handed him.

He did get to visit and spend time on Mount Olympus now and then, but that only "wetted" his appetite for more. However, every time this sea god tried to seize a chunk of real estate (like the city of Athens or the town of Attica), he lost out to another god or goddess who was vying for the same territory. All of Poseidon's dreams to amass solid land and to attain more worldly power fell through. (Some Neptunians can harbor unconscious, self-defeatist attitudes that lead to repeated failure.)

Whenever he lost out, Poseidon reacted tempestuously and with a sense of revenge. He caused destructive floods (symbolizing tears of rage) and even earthquakes—he could be a real sorehead when he didn't get his way! Actually, these disappointments were how the Cosmos told him that falling for the temptations of the material world (represented by towns and dry land) was not the route he was to take. He had a specific role to play that involved the secret realm of our inner life. High visibility in the external world—always out and about, getting lots of praise and attention—was not to be supported. Yet it's not clear whether or not Poseidon ever understood that message.

Even if this testy water god didn't like it, the archetype he represented found its rightful home in the ocean, symbolizing the depths of the sea of our unconscious. Water is an element of great emotional power that, at times, can flood our waking consciousness and drown all logic and reason, especially when we are provoked and upset. Astrological Neptune has been accused of stirring such responses, especially when we find we cannot contain hidden or repressed feelings any longer—they irrationally come gushing to the surface in a surprisingly uncontrollable manner. That's surely a case of Poseidon rising within us.

During our Neptune transits, we can be worked up when frustration builds to uncomfortable levels. What has been submerged suddenly comes shooting to the surface like a steamy geyser. Poseidon was able to split mountains in two when he was really furious. It's not hard to visualize the havoc created by an exploding avalanche. Therefore, we shouldn't always describe Neptune in dreamy, tranquil terms, because it also has another side that is highly reactive to stress: the hysterical, earth-shaking side, where emotions are like typhoons or those famous Poseidon storms at sea.

Neptune doesn't explode as often as Uranus, a planet better known for its sudden life-altering shake-ups. Nonetheless, when studying certain transits of Neptune, we need to keep in mind the possibility of dramatic emotional outbursts, the stuff that Oscar-winning performances are made of!

For a wonderful, non-astrological portrait of the god Poseidon-Neptune and how this archetype can be expressed in psychological terms (especially by men), I suggest Dr. Jean Shinoda Bolen's *Gods in Everyman*.[1] She also analyzes other gods, such as Ares-Mars, Zeus-Jupiter, and Hades-Pluto.

MAKING THE MOST OF THIS BOOK

One day you open your ephemeris and there it is: transiting Neptune opposing your Moon, taking effect exactly five days ago. "What a coincidence," you think, as you look down to find that your feet are swollen and you're feeling nostalgic about the good old days, when you could disco those little feet like crazy all night long. You'll need to read all about what this transit could mean for you now that things are quite different in your life—see Chapter Nine. In that same chapter, you may also want to read about transiting Neptune going through the Fourth House. The

Moon and the Fourth, along with the sign Cancer, are manifestations of the same life principle—Principle Four—and all share similar themes. There may be a few comments I've made about Neptune passing through the Fourth that will supplement what I've written regarding Neptune/Moon transits.

In addition, think about your natal Neptune's house position—what I've said about this planet's transit of that same house could give you further insights into some of your natal issues. And please read various planet-to-planet transits to gain an extra understanding of any natal aspects you have involving those same planets.

Don't be perplexed if what I've stated about a specific transit doesn't completely fit your current life predicament. It would be uncommon if it did. Transits run the gamut in how they actually manifest for us, something that old-time astrologers didn't suspect to be true, because the range of possible outcomes they envisioned was much more narrow. That gave them the sense of a powerful fate at work having the upper hand. Instead of expecting to read deadly accurate predictions of your personal future events, try to understand the general texture and tone of each transit, and then see how you can custom-tailor the themes to fit your own lifestyle. By keeping all of the above in mind, you should be able to enjoy this book and, hopefully, put what I've said to good use.

TWO-FACED PLANETS: MERCURY AND VENUS

In this book, I will refer to "air Mercury" versus "earth Mercury" or "earth Venus" versus "air Venus." I'm not talking here about the natal element of our Mercury or our Venus, but I am addressing the fact that both of these planets have dual identities. Mercury rules Gemini and Virgo. Its airy face is linked to how Gemini processes experience, while its earthier side—"earth Mercury"—belongs to Virgo. I will cover the transits of Neptune to Mercury's airy and earthy facets in separate chapters, to show how differently each responds to life, regardless of the position of our natal Mercury. Capable of expressing both modes, our

Mercury in any sign can respond according to its underlying air *or* earth orientation. Whether Mercury will more easily relate to either of its two faces is not something we can automatically determine (at least, not by its natal sign alone).

The same holds true for dual-faced Venus—ruler of Taurus and of Libra. Again, an earthy Venus and airy Venus together more broadly define the Venus principle. Some transits bring out Venus' airy nature more readily than do others. Some natal house positions more easily evoke Venus' earthy side. By doing both sides of our Venus and our Mercury, we learn more about how they can, together, enrich our development. Don't waste sleepless nights worrying about whether you're in an earth Venus or air Mercury mode when Neptune or any other Outer Planet transits these natal planets (especially with Neptune, a planet that defies categories and clear-cut definitions). You're doing both sides of these planets all the time.

LAUGHING GAS

I believe that learning astrology from books and articles that teach and amuse us at the same time is a sure-fire way to help us remember more of the material. The amount of data that beginning students must initially absorb can be daunting, so whatever facilitates our memory process is to be encouraged. How fortunate, then, that the behavior of human beings leaves the door wide open for humorous astrological interpretation. We're such a fun bunch of primates—just ask any orangutan who's made it big in show business, and he or she will tell you how comic and entertaining our easily-trained species can be! But sometimes we're just plain "funny" in weird ways.

I believe that Divine Intelligence has a well-developed sense of humor. After all, it created the loony laugh of the smiling kookaburra, made famous in old "Tarzan" movies. Approaching astrology with a straight face and a stiff neck doesn't automatically make it any more relevant. Jupiter would be the first to pitch such an observation to us, of course, while also throwing in a quickie joke or two. Finding the humor in Uranus (see volume one of this series)[2] is easy, because this free-spirited planet enjoys and employs sharp wit and clever social satire that pushes the envelope. However, no matter how outrageous it gets, Uranus never goes for the dumb, cheap laugh—its quickly delivered humor is typically insightful as well as hilarious, giving us a way to look at life from the most unusual of angles.

However, when it came to writing about our Neptune transits, I had a harder time coming up with funny one-liners, probably because this planet deals with so many touchy and delicate emotional issues. Who'd want to laugh at an archetype when it's down and hobbling around on worn-out crutches? All right, I guess some evil Plutonians would! Still, Neptune deals with a lot of "wounding" themes where painful sacrifices are usually demanded. What's so funny about that?

Of course, multi-faceted Neptune also rules Disneyland and other fantasy theme parks, not to mention the giddy effects of champagne and the wonders of Silly Putty, so things here are not all that bleak. Maybe I feared that I would sound too insensitive or mean-spirited if I joked about a planet that already considers itself unfairly persecuted. Still, if any planetary force needs its lighter side to surface more often, besides Saturn, it's Neptune— our expert melodramatist! Even Pluto is easier to poke fun at, because old "Dark Face" is cursed with an extremist disposition, and humor works well when it exaggerates the imperfections of our human condition. I hope that some of my Neptunian material— without the buoyancy provided by a little humor—doesn't sound heavy-hearted enough to sink to the bottom of the sea.

A few other astrologers have already seen the light and are hard at play in keeping astro-humor alive and well. One astrologer who stands out as a dedicated humorist is Kim Rogers-Gallagher,[3] an author of lively astrology books that you'll enjoy. A writer really can't afford to flirt with adding humor to standard astrology unless he or she is also a darn good astrologer, and Kim gets a "thumbs up" from me. As we enter the twenty-first century—with imaginative Neptune now passing through offbeat Aquarius and shaking hands for a spell with wild trickster Uranus in this same oddball sign—I'm sure other astrologers will be willing to experiment by including more fun material in their writings than ever before. At least, I hope so.

NOTES

1. Jean Shinoda Bolen, M.D., *Gods in Everyman*, HarperCollins Publishers, 1989. She also wrote *Goddesses in Everywoman* (which includes an exploration of the psychology of all four major asteroid goddesses). Both are excellent resources for the study of astromythology.

2. Bil Tierney, *Alive and Well with Uranus*, Llewellyn Publications, St. Paul, MN, 1999.

3. Kim Rogers-Gallagher has written *Astrology for the Light Side of the Brain*, ACS Publications, San Diego, CA, 1995; also by the same publisher, *Astrology for the Light Side of the Future*, 1998.

PART ONE

There's Magic in the Air....

CHAPTER ONE

SETTING THE STAGE

NEPTUNE DESCENDING

Astrologers have a field day discussing all sorts of situational possibilities when the subject at hand is planetary transits. The manifestations of transit patterns are highly individualized and seemingly unlimited. Multiply that by the endless variety of planetary configurations to be found in people's natal charts, and it starts to get mind-boggling. It's impossible to write in vivid detail about everything that can happen to us under our powerful Neptune transits, including the subtleties and nuances we experience that cannot adequately be conveyed by even the most poetic words (although music seems to have an uncanny way of capturing the emotive tone of Neptune). Those soul-moving, inarticulate moments of our life when we are overtaken by waves of exquisite feeling definitely belong to this awe-inspiring planet. It's not easy to write about such moments, or about Neptune's "dark night of the soul" episodes, during which we wander through the shadowlands of a troubled psyche.

Therefore, I will focus only on certain themes of transiting Neptune that take into account our capacity for ongoing spiritual development, our psyche's power to entrap or liberate us (depending on its degree of fragmentation or integration), and the assumption that it's best not to avoid any mundane opportunity to manifest a little Neptune in our life on a day-to-day basis. This book deals with Neptune's strange adventures in the here-and-now world, so I won't dwell much on the karmic/past life potential of Neptune transit activity. For those interested in that potential, astrology texts are available that discuss at length the esoteric, evolutionary, and transcendental functions of Neptune, Uranus, and Pluto.[1]

Neptune has been described as one of the planetary gateways to a "galactic" consciousness[2] that is free from the limitations of the less-encompassing perspectives of Saturn and all planets inside Saturn's orbital path—especially those personalized realities of the Sun, who acts as head supervisor for Egos Unlimited! From this galactic outlook, our goal is to step-up or quicken these planetary energies in order to match the higher frequencies of Neptune, Uranus, and Pluto (and beyond). Through a special state of awareness symbolized by Neptune, for instance, we can leave our ordinary ego-consciousness and enter more luminous dimensions of Spirit, levels where we lose our illusionary sense of being separate, ego-centered individuals. By dedicating ourselves to various spiritual practices and mind-altering techniques, we can ascend to greater heights of perception. Neptune acts as a sacred vessel filled with a special spiritualizing energy. From its supernal realm of being, we can become One with the Source of All Life.

This galactic viewpoint embraces the role played by the Outer Planets in helping us acknowledge more than just our material awareness of existence. It implies that Earth is not our place of origin—we are cosmological beings, not merely biological. To add to this perspective, astronomers love to point out that our bodies, and all other physical matter on Earth, originated from the material of dying stars in distant galaxies billions of years ago.

We can also speculate that the Outer Planets themselves, as they descend into matter, need the lessons that only this Earth plane can provide. For example, as Neptune merges its ultra-refined energies with the stepped-down frequencies of the physical dimension, it is forced to define itself within varying degrees of conceptual form, often using the power of our imagination as an initial point of entry—we must first visualize something before we give birth to its material structure in the world. Although it's easier for Neptune to function in an archetypal realm of boundless, continually changing energy, its ongoing earthly challenge is to tackle concrete reality and become humanized and, thereby, more accessible to us. Neptune mirrors what is fundamentally our own experience: a spirit incarnating into a body and learning to use its available energies to skillfully navigate the physical plane.

We humans have our roots in both the heavens and Earth; therefore, we become the prime subjects of this great cosmic experiment. Just as all of nature evolves biologically, we have a chance to evolve in consciousness—a process faster than biological evolution, because Neptunian consciousness, unlike physical matter, is amazingly fluid. Before we succeed in overcoming the facets of our humanness that drag us down and keep us in darkness, we first need to go through a host of psychological and spiritual transitional stages that often result in much Neptunian confusion and ambivalence. That's partly because much of what Neptune stands for goes against our accustomed security needs (Saturn/Moon conditioning).

We also have mixed feelings about any urges to retreat from dynamically asserting ourselves in this ego-driven world. Yet such urges to withdraw from mundane activity are normal and are even the catalyst for deeper psycho-spiritual growth. Such a retreat is best done gradually, not as a desperate act of blind escapism. With Neptune, we must have enough trust to surrender to the unknown in order to grow, and this requires great faith in a loving, supportive Universe. Neptune transits are times when our belief in greater, protective guiding forces is put to the test.

Reflective self-examination, often brought on by our worldly fears and our private emotional pain, can eventually lead us to do some serious soul-searching. However, as we begin to see glimmers of our radiant inner Self—our rainbow within—some of us unfortunately may walk around in a sort of demi-god stage that we find frustrating. We realize we're more than just mammals with extra brain power, but we're still far less than truly divine beings in a state of ultimate inner peace. During key Neptune transits, it's not uncommon for our compelling human desires to be at odds with our strong yearnings to "rise above it all" and claim our true spiritual identity. Still, that's the dilemma we all face. If we are to truly make any real progress here, we must work with our Neptune transits in a self-compassionate manner. This is not the time to harshly judge ourselves for mistakes made on our life-journey, but we do need to quietly reflect on how we can better bring our dreams and ideals to realistic fruition. Do we even have such dreams to inspire us?

It's obvious that Neptune rarely presents us with practical role models to emulate as we embark on our sometimes lonely journey toward self-completion. Certainly, we can *try* to become exalted beings like Jesus or Buddha, or even a channeled high priestess from Atlantis. We could also attempt to live purely spiritual and chaste lives like the saints honored by various religions. However, this journey doesn't come with a clear instruction kit or a money-back guarantee should we go mad instead of attaining enlightenment. It will take courage and emotional strength to live out Neptunian energies, whether natally or by transit. Others may not understand us much when we try to "do" any Outer Planet, and society might even try to stamp some of us out if we seem too subversive in our quest for a direct experience of the Inner Light. Yet that's the chance we take when we realize that *only* being true to our authentic spiritual self will do.

EXPECTING TO FLY

Neptune transits can be times of inflated feelings regarding how we can improve our lives. Our power to believe that no real obstacles block our path can be stronger than usual. If an astrologically aware elephant were to have a Neptune/Jupiter transit, it would probably convince itself it could leap off a high cliff and take to the sky if it wanted to badly enough, while the obvious reality might not sink in until it's too late! Neptune is not particularly mindful of sensible limits, and that can get us in trouble. It's also not a very time-conscious planet, and yet savvy Saturnian timing is often the key to worldly success. Of course, it's success in "otherworldly" realms that Neptune aspires toward. The typical ambitions of earthbound existence become less relevant—but not always. If we greatly value the temptations of this Earth, then we'll put them on a pedestal to be worshipped. Some of us may have little feeling for spiritual matters, and so, during our Neptune transits, we look for material substitutes that can make us feel divinely content. In this case, our ambition to fulfill earthly fantasies may reach unreal heights.

More typically, these transits suggest periods of introspection, even if we also appear quite wrapped up in the affairs of a demanding outer world. Neptune knows that we have to make a living and pay our bills, but we needn't lose our soul or our emotional integrity in doing so. Something deep and wise from within us makes its presence felt, prompting us to cultivate and nourish our sometimes forgotten spiritual needs. Fulfilling such needs helps us to release our latent creative drives.

Indeed, a Neptune transit is a great time to soar creatively. That means we'll have to stop telling ourselves we either have no talent or have little time to feed any potential talent. Our spirit urges us to pick up a paintbrush, immerse our hands in clay, spin the potter's wheel, do a little tie-dyeing, or even put some film in our 35mm camera and go to town—or, more appropriately, to the beach at sunrise! This is a time when all negative expectations need to be put on hold. Let's not anticipate anything, but instead lose ourselves and free-fall into the moment. Let's open up our voice to sing in the church choir, or join a local drama group to learn to act out our passions and satisfy our Neptunian-induced theatrical streak.

If all else fails, let's begin to remodel our house or beautify our natural surroundings. All of these activities have a way of evoking that inner spirit of inspiration that longs for us to stop being so caught up in the drab and dull world of daily routine and economic survival. With Neptune, we can expect to fly high by the power that our faith and imagination affords us, *if* we are willing to first unlock that imagination and faith. Astrologers don't always emphasize enough how colorful our Neptune periods can be.

WHY WORRY?

There may be periods during our Neptune transits when we find that, due to our active imagination, we overdramatize issues in our life that are already a bit worrisome for us. We normally want everything to turn out well more than usual during a Neptune transit, but real life isn't like that. Should we suffer disappointment, we can overreact emotionally and blow these incidents out of proportion. It's usually good not to take immediate action (especially drastic action) when something happens that upsets us. That doesn't mean we should take no action whatsoever, but that we should give ourselves time to mull things over.

For those of us who pay keen attention to our Neptunian process, as impossible as that sounds, we'll find that most of what we worry about seldom happens—all of that emotional churning and insomnia for nothing! People may seem to threaten our security, but there is little actual follow-through on their part—just confusion and heavy drama for the moment.

The more fixed (and earthy) we are, the more we can needlessly suffer during certain Neptune transits. Rigidity can get us in a bind with ourselves during these times because we insist on seeing things one way—our way! However, Neptune is trying to convince us to loosen our tight control over our affairs and surrender to where life wants us to go with this energy. It's amazing to watch how something that appears to be a near disaster one day turns into an unforeseen opportunity the next. People may come in at the last minute to save us from our predicament. When that happens, we need to reflect on how often in the past we have tried to unwisely block the help of others, something that self-sufficient fixed and earthy types tend to do a lot.

Things have marvelously creative ways of working out, if we just get out of the way and allow the Universe to demonstrate real Neptunian magic in our lives. It can be a humbling experience to realize that we are not totally in charge of our destiny. Therefore, don't make a habit of anticipating the worst, especially if we have always been on the good side of Saturn throughout the years and are really trying our best to do the "right" thing at any stage of our life. Individuals who have indulged in self-inflicted failure for most of their lives, and have made things miserable for others by trying to bring everyone's energy down to chaotic levels, should worry the most during a Neptune transit. No magic occurs for these people.

GOOD TRANSIT, BAD TRANSIT?

It's important to apply common sense when we see transits coming up for us that we don't think we're going to enjoy very much. It could be that Saturn's doing this or Pluto's doing that, perhaps simultaneously, and we suspect we'll have a rough time coping with the pressures symbolized for the next several months. But that's not always so. The more we work with astrology, the more we see that transiting squares and oppositions coincide with times when we either feel driven to accomplish something, or when life gives us a kick in the pants and orders us to get going with what we're here to learn. The square or the opposition also advises us to put more motivational fuel in our tank so that our efforts stand a better chance of succeeding. The unsatisfying alternative is to stall and do nothing—a tempting Neptunian option—yet that's when life might turn around and penalize us for our passivity or procrastination (especially with transiting Pluto or Saturn involved).

Even when we get energized and cooperate with a so-called "difficult" transit (Neptune square Saturn), we still might struggle and grit our teeth for a while. However, in the end, we may find we've met our challenges admirably and have even surpassed our own expectations. It's not always going to turn out that well, but when it does, we learn to appreciate what a good tensional transit can do for us once we adopt the right attitude and start tackling our situation with greater determination. With Neptune, we'll always need to follow our inner voice and keep our hope alive.

On the other hand, when a great-looking transiting Neptune trine comes along that we've anticipated for a while (such as one that contacts our Venus/Moon conjunction in Taurus, which we then assume will make our life more serene and content), we may discover instead that nothing very dynamic happens to change things for the better. That's often because we're not feeling energized enough to take opportunity as it comes—or even recognize such opportunity. We expect the environment to unconditionally provide us with divine "goodies" without requiring too much exertion on our part. We depend on our magnetism alone to attract whatever we're wishing for, as if by a miracle. Why? A typical Neptune-inspired rationalization would be, "Because I'm a compassionate, spiritual person who deserves a special break from the Cosmos!" Unfortunately, we're probably too unmotivated or unfocused to make any real miracles happen for us, and that becomes our basic blind spot.

While a few rewards may actually flow down the cosmic pipeline, they are minimal and not appreciated in the long run. Perhaps that lucky break we're wishing for comes along too easily. We just don't take its potential seriously enough to make something big out of it. Whatever the case may be, we can't always count on transiting sextiles and trines to bring us the happiness we long for. Neptune and Jupiter trines, in particular, can instead bring us high bills at the end of the month that reflect those impulse, escapist buying urges we've indulged in—along with a few unwanted pounds from too much mindless snacking. Too often, we don't attract much more than that.

Meanwhile, anxious Saturn and obsessive Pluto, making tenser transits, can urge us to sock away our money in a retirement fund or to buy a few government-secured bonds because we're feeling the pinch to save and invest wisely in our uncertain future. We don't feel as content with life under Saturn's or Pluto's transiting squares and oppositions, yet we can feel driven to take appropriate action to provide valued long-term security for ourselves, even under pressing circumstances.

And so, we need to be careful how we label these transits. For years now, most astrologers have ceased using the terms "good" and "bad" to describe aspects, and I suggest you do the same. Check out the charts of the historically famous and you'll see squares, quincunxes, and oppositions all over the place, natally and especially during transits associated with their finest hours. They apparently even knew how to make the most of their conjunctions, sextiles, and trines, never taking an opportunity for granted or letting one pass them by. That would be a good philosophy for the rest of us to adopt.

NOTES

1. Liz Greene's masterpiece, *The Astrological Neptune and the Quest for Redemption* (Samuel Weiser, Inc.), covers esoteric Neptune and everything else you'd want to know about this planet as well. Llewellyn published Jeffrey Wolf Greene's two books on Pluto, *Pluto: The Evolutionary Journey of the Soul* and *Pluto, Vol. II: The Soul's Evolution Through Relationships.* Also, British astrologer Hadyn Paul has written books that include information on the esoteric side of Neptune, Uranus, and Pluto, as well as the myths associated with each; his book on Neptune is entitled *Visionary Dreamer: Exploring the Astrological Neptune* (published by Element Books).

2. Dane Rudhyar developed this "galactic" view and discussed it in his 1975 edition of *The Sun Is Also a Star—The Galactic Dimension of Astrology,* first published by E.P. Dutton & Co., Inc. This book may be out-of-print (it was last published with its original title and subtitle reversed, by Aurora Press in Santa Fe, New Mexico).

CHAPTER TWO

SWIMMING WITH NEPTUNE

DANCE OF THE TWELVE VEILS

Transiting Neptune is *not* every astrologer's dream to analyze! Astrology is about giving personal, inner meaning to the seemingly impersonal passage of time in the "real" (outer) world. As atomic clocks on Earth tick-tick-tick away in states of incredible micro-precision, each new moment that passes is said to be filled with latent creative potential waiting to be actualized. When someone or something is born in time, to paraphrase psychoanalyst Carl Jung, the "personality" of that exceptional but fleeting instant is indelibly stamped on the newborn entity. No two such moments of birth will ever be exactly alike, suggesting that any emerging potential never repeats in the same way.

Astrologers take this to mean that the complex display of planetary configurations at the precise time of birth—in relation to the birth-locality's angles and to the backdrop of zodiac signs—comprises a timely moment seeking a very special fulfillment. Time, therefore, is the agent that unfolds individualized human destiny and Saturn, as the tireless time-keeper, owns the cosmic clock. So far, so good.

However, when astrologers eagerly hit the fast-forward button to get a quick and clear look at future cycles of unfoldment that await us (which is what transits, ideally, provide), we still want things to work with atomic-clock precision. We want the timing of our predictive techniques to remain reliable and informative. This is why astrologers are such sticklers for making sure everyone's birth time is right on the money. When we suspect that the time is off, some of us will fiddle endlessly with the natal and current chart patterns in question—the proper term is *rectification*—in order to ensure that such patterns activate the appropriate angles of the chart in ways that symbolically reflect actual life events, until at least the most accurate birth time is derived. Doing this sounds like a reasonable task when "time" is of the essence.

What does this all have to do with Neptune and its transits? Even when we have a timed birth chart that we can count on—whether expertly rectified, or from the birth certificate, or straight from the midwife who paid keen attention to the clock—Neptune prefers to live in a world without time, something that Saturn finds inexplicable and maddening. Neptune doesn't even own a clock, and hasn't used a calendar in eons! For example, let's say that Neptune is about to cross over our Ascendant, a process that takes almost two years (it begins to tippy-toe—sleepy-eyed and still in its pajamas—into our First House, but then retreats and hides under the goose-down covers of our Twelfth during its retrograde phase). All slow-moving, transiting planets do this little back-and-forth dance over our angles but, in most cases, we start seeing the results of this contact after a reasonable amount of time has passed.

With Neptune, we can't say that for sure. Has transiting Neptune even entered our First House, we may wonder? Perhaps our unrectified chart's all wrong and is in need of a little fine-tuning, especially because our trusty ephemeris says that Neptune's been hovering around our Ascendant for a while now, but *nothing* seems to be happening! What gives? After all, Saturn and Mars never behave like this when crossing an angle. While we may not care for the results of their transits, we at least can count on them to manifest *something,* even if it's only the Saturnian onset of additional age lines around the eyes, or maybe a nasty Martian outbreak of angry-looking hives. So, what's the problem with Neptune?

A few years may pass before we can go back and make sense out of what most books would call a "powerful" Neptune transit. Powerful? How so, when it seems as if we have a weird case of amnesia when we try to recall what went on? Were we even there, in person, when it all supposedly happened? Actually, blanking out about our past is one way to know that Neptune's deeply at work—we can't remember the faces or the details, but they hardly matter.

Our Neptune transits, however, can really drive the Saturn and Virgo parts of our psyche up the wall (assuming the wall has not dematerialized yet). The earthier and the more fixed we are by nature, the more crazed we feel as Neptune melts and drips all over our otherwise neat and tidy life, making situations sticky and messy for us. If we like things in our world to look sharp and stay crisp at all times, we won't appreciate Neptune bringing along its cosmic humidifier to steam up the place and make everything go a little limp, become wilted, or get damp around the edges. As Neptune begins its seductive dance of the twelve veils— one for each natal house—our vision may cloud over and an unsettling air of mystery may prevail as our focus is directed toward less-acknowledged internal realities. Yet, for a few of us, such a Neptunian period could signal a magical time in life when we've never felt happier or more at peace with the world.

For some of us, however, Neptune transits dredge up ancient emotions from the swamps of our subconscious that have been draining us for years, slowly stealing our vitality and keeping us too passive or weak to break out of chronic patterns of self-defeat. It takes a while for these emotions to surface, so it may not be immediately evident that we're undergoing a slow process of healing old wounds. Neptune deals with breakdowns of all sorts, as things that have been in a hardened state for too long, depleting us or sucking out the life of others, begin to dissolve. Much of the action is concealed or veiled from us (bypassing our ego-awareness), so that we can't interfere with the healing process by playing denial games that would sidetrack crucial matters at hand. Neptune makes sure we cannot sabotage the necessary soul work, as some of us expertly do with our natal Neptune for years on end, until we become tremendously out-of-touch with our real needs in this area of our lives.

Asleep at the Wheel

When it comes to dealing with our transits, it's advisable to remain conscious and alert about what's going on within. However, that's often easier said than done, especially with a tricky planet like Neptune who'd rather slip in through the back door, unnoticed, than meet us face-to-face on the front porch. Neptune prefers to silently creep into the picture and lay low for a while before surfacing. Yet it never pays to be too intellectually objective about matters when Neptune's underfoot, because we'd be tempted to over-analyze issues and fail to really understand or appreciate our emotions during this period.

Our Neptune transits are times when we realize that our intellect can't always help us decode what's happening. Besides, whatever we are analyzing probably has a few missing pieces—we're not playing with a full deck. The cerebral, "gotta know what's up," Mercury part of our nature—always looking for the sensible explanation—will need to take the back seat. Meanwhile Neptune—happily asleep at the wheel—drives us smoothly down the road to self-discovery, thanks to its magical, auto-pilot steering gizmo (and to the various angels who handle traffic flow along life's superhighway).

Actually, Neptune could use a few pointers about earthly living. Neptune can't always dwell in Nirvana and expect to help us earthlings on the ground evolve properly. All of our planets must incarnate on the physical plane—in conscious ways—in order to develop *their* potential further, not just ours. Neptune is no exception. This planet is eager to admit that its power lies not in assertive action, but in non-resistance. That's easy to say, considering that Neptune's favorite place to hang out is on ethereal levels where there's not much to resist! Let's see how Neptune deals with solid matter. Can it materialize itself in tangible form and still remain creatively fluid and adaptable?

Our drowsy Neptunian state, with its characteristic tendency to unfocus, often means that we miss those big, broad road signs along the way that others have no trouble seeing and reading. This can get us in trouble, when the signs we overlook say, "Detour Ahead" or "Slippery When Wet." When we're in such a state of diffused awareness (due to the spreading of our Neptunian sensitivity), we miss the obvious and the immediate. We can become unaccustomedly forgetful, flaky, spaced-out, irrational, or victims of poor judgment in our emotional response to life. Needless to say, this is an undesirably vulnerable condition to be in for long periods of time.

It also appears that, when Neptune is activated by transit, we can snap out of our trance and enter periods of having uncanny insight into people and situations. The right information miraculously comes to us in the nick of time. That's when we sense that this period may be more about developing faith than about applying reason. Neptune always looks out for life's lost babes in the woods and will offer divine protection, if we just believe this to be so and surrender to the flow.

With Neptune, nothing is to be forced on us—unlike the tactics of coercive Pluto or old "take your medicine or else" Saturn. We need to freely wish for what we want and then hope our wish has been heard. We probably need to work on self-forgiveness—realizing that we're not in a state of ultimate perfection—before we can make that wish come true. The power of belief is a major theme during key Neptune transits. If we can believe in something with all our heart, and if what we believe is within our grasp (something only our Saturn knows), then there's no limit to what we can make happen for ourselves. It's always a good idea to check out our transiting Saturn when trying to make sense out of our transiting Neptune phase. We will need Saturn's blessings before we can get our beautiful Neptunian dreams off the ground. Saturn will help us to carefully draft the initial plans and flesh out the details of Neptune's wondrous designs for remodeling our life and to uplift the lives of those around us.

STRANGERS IN THE NIGHT

If natal planets happen to be in the house that Neptune transits, those planets may eventually learn about deep change firsthand. Some planets are more susceptible to the charms of Neptune than others: the Moon may instinctively say no, but her eyes say yes. It's the same for Venus (who never met an archetype she didn't like). Both of these planets seek to make intimate connections so that they can feel *involved* in a relationship (especially one based upon an arousal of *feelings*—something that Neptune can easily provoke). Mercury also is curious enough to want to find out all about how Neptune "thinks," or intuits—or whatever it does—to come by its unusual, otherworldly information. We can expect Mercury to be drawn to this trance-maker for a little extra, out-of-the-ordinary mental stimulation.

Jupiter probably finds Neptune to be good company and even charmingly amusing—but then, Jupiter has a knack for getting along with everyone, stand-offish Pluto included. Jupiter is easily encouraged to gamble on any proposition that Neptune offers. His philosophy is, "How do you know something is lucky or unlucky unless you jump in and try it?" Neptune calmly advises Jupiter to toss aside his inflated life-preserver and jump in from the dark and deep end of the pool. Watch out, Jupiter—Neptune assumes that every planet can effortlessly breathe under water!

It seems that all Outer Planets, especially Neptune, have the allure of tall, dark, fascinating strangers—the sort of people we dream of meeting on a cruise ship during the Full Moon at midnight. We could quickly fall for them, even though we know nothing about their background and little about their true temperament. The sense of the unknown that they provide is part of their appeal. However, if the transit is a square or an opposition rather than a conjunction, sextile, or trine, we can eventually feel threatened by the darker faces that Uranus, Neptune, and Pluto show to us. After a while they don't seem so ideal or fetching. We begin to realize that they can create levels of chaos in our lives that we'll quickly claim not to appreciate or need. By then, however, they've taken us over and we can't seem to return to the normal life we had before we ever meet these spellbinding characters. Darn those seductive sea cruises under a Full Moon!

How Transiting Planets Work

This is a good place to pause and define a few terms. Transiting planets are part of the here-and-now sky that we observe every night. To get a basic sense of transit motion, venture outside every few nights and witness the Moon's gentle path of travel during its monthly phases. Our natal planets (those being transited) make up the symbolic sky we carry inside ourselves right from our moment of birth. We sense, on some subjective level, that these natal planets belong solely to us, as members of our inner family. They grow up with us and become part of our life's ups and downs. We even blame some of these planets for those ups and downs.

Whatever the case, we have plenty of time to learn how to develop our natal planets' expression and thereby shape our character in ways that allow us to feel more self-directed and empowered in the world. After all, our natal planets symbolize necessary parts of our psyche, and so we feel that we possess them and that they sometimes possess us (at least on an unconscious level). However, along with any constructive self-growth to be gained by them comes a good deal of psychological baggage that gets heavier to carry as the years go by.

The transiting planet of any current moment represents changes impinging on our psyche that appear to stem from our external environment and from the people we magnetically draw to us (even those who simply appear out of nowhere, uninvited). We usually don't realize that we pull these factors into our life, but that's what our transited natal planet is symbolically doing, assisted by the power of our subconscious. What comes at us from such external sources may seem all too new and challenging to satisfy our comfort zone, yet such challenges create the tension needed to break our internal status quo. Do we dare let go of our familiar world long enough to significantly alter our perspective? During a Neptune transit, life will let us know how badly we need to do just that at this time.

Especially during the transiting square or opposition phase, the waves of Neptune may turbulently crash against the rocky shores of our normal consciousness, as tidal waters begin to rise and threaten to sink all within us that refuses to budge. Only that which remains flexible and willing to adapt to the current's flow is able to stay afloat—the rest drowns. Ultimately, the needs symbolized by our natal planet being transited must be satisfied by Neptune if this passage is to be deemed fruitful. Using the energy of the natal planet in question, we co-create new patterns of unfolding consciousness and thus strengthen our psyche.

For example: transiting Neptune may be squaring our natal Sun. This suggests that various Neptunian people and situations will come together to make an impact, no matter how subtle at first, on personal facets of our being, symbolized by our natal Sun. Will we seek creative solutions to the challenges of the moment, solutions that always take into account the fundamental needs of the Sun? Or do we recklessly go about drowning our solar urges and losing all sense of solid footing in the world?

After this transit is over and done with, our Sun still has to go out and face the future in all the basic ways that it knows best. Now, however, we've learned distinctly Neptunian ways of getting our positive ego needs met. Our ego is not to disappear into thin air. Hopefully, from now on we'll refuse to use our will to limit our vision of a more ideal life that we can build for ourselves and for the world. The bottom line is that any transit's end results must highlight the nature and needs of the transited planet. That planet has the last word on the matter because it represents a necessary part of us that requires fulfillment.

HAUNTED HOUSES?

A Neptune house transit can seem to linger forever, while we feel stuck in limbo. Neptune itself has little problem with lingering, but *we* may not enjoy this unhurried pace where nothing appears to be resolved. Still, Neptune needs plenty of time to sink into those less-accessible spaces of our subconscious to allow us our visionary moments. Thus, the slower this transit, the more time we have to gain needed, in-depth awareness. The deeper we jour-ney into ourselves, the more complete our internal Neptunian make-over can be. Nothing is to be rushed in Neptune's slow-mov-ing world. Just try racing around at the bottom of the sea—it's impossible to speed about while underwater.

We can feel anxious and unsteady when Neptune makes its surreal atmospheric changes and haunts our transited house, or so it seems. Much of what we thought we took for granted con-cerning the safer harbors of Saturnian reality is now challenged. When situational complications set in, and instability becomes more commonly experienced, we're typically ready to do a little Neptune-bashing. We accuse this planet of unloading a lot of neg-ativity or karma onto us in the form of repeated failures that make our current circumstances seem as treacherous as quick-sand. We are also apt to color these events with our own confused emotionality. Self-pity can take hold like never before, and a sense of victimhood soon follows. Neptune then becomes a slimy monster of the deep, threatening to squeeze the life out of any chance for personal happiness. Indeed, we experience the stormy side of Neptune. Astrologer Liz Greene talks about Neptune sym-bolizing the Babylonian sea-serpent Ti'amat, who devours those realities that our conscious ego has protectively built.[1]

Yet that's only one side of the Neptune experience, and one that fatefully can happen when we've woefully mismanaged this planet's energy for far too long. Life mercifully collapses on us so that we can't do further damage to ourselves—we're forced to sur-render to a higher guiding force. There's another side to Neptune transiting our planets and houses that can be very awe-inspiring. Instead of having disturbing feelings of being haunted, we may feel as if we've exorcised our demons—as if we've been splashed with the most potent of holy waters and miraculously been cleansed of our emotional impurities. It's a transitional state that can border on a religious experience for some. We know this to be so whenever we feel a sense of upliftment that cannot be put into words. Some heaviness that we had kept trapped inside has now vanished. Some fear that has secretly crippled parts of ourselves in the past is now gone. Perhaps, during phases like this, we are truly under a state of divine grace. If so, let's not do anything to discourage us from continuing to give in to this rare feeling of enjoying a little heaven within.

As time unfolds, we may find that we have made peace with many issues of our transiting Neptune house that used to cause us a lot of pain and grief. Neptune's healing waters are always at work in this area of our chart, but we'll have to consciously encourage our own self-healing. Learning to trust both ourselves and the world is a big part of the transformations that can occur here. If we've done our best to *manifest* (with the Cosmos) the finest qualities that Neptune has to offer, we will learn to become expert swimmers in the oceanic world of our unconscious. We won't let any of the darker waters of our psyche ever frighten us again. We now have the compassion needed to embrace with love all those otherwise rejected, unwanted, and seemingly unredeemable parts of our shadow self that have blocked our ability to feel contentment in this house.

Tears may be shed during our most significant Neptune transits, but they can be tears of joy, the welling up of soulful emotion that lets us know that we're all right as we are in the eyes of the Divine (even though some of us have been conditioned to see ourselves as hopeless messes). We'll finally know that we deserve unconditional love, not just a sorry string of baffling but heartbreaking rejections. The love we receive may not always be personal (and rarely is it just romantic), but it can be like the nectar of the gods to those who have hungered and thirsted for so long.

During its transits, Neptune offers us what we'll need to have around us in order to feel at one with our environment and at peace with people who share our space. Because Neptune gets its orders directly from the Great Beyond, we'll need to let life rearrange itself on our behalf as it begins to open a few unrealized doors of amazing possibility for us. The scenery and the script are now in the hands of a Greater Intelligence. All we have to do is calmly make our entrance onstage and let Neptune's magic show begin.

NOTE

1. See Liz Greene's *The Astrological Neptune and the Quest for Redemption,* Samuel Weiser, Inc., 1996, pp. 7-14. Liz has many things to say about the complex dual function of primordial mother-monster Ti'amat, an important deity crucial to the Babylonian myth of creation.

CHAPTER THREE

A NEPTUNIAN TOUR OF OUR NATAL PLANETS

THE USUAL SUSPECTS

Before exploring the details of the hypnotic world of our Neptune transits, it might be wise to first preview each planet and every house that Neptune will contact—and perhaps inspire—during its pilgrimage around our birth chart. Astrologers call one such complete Neptune cycle a "Neptune Return," which takes about 165 years to occur. No one will live long enough to celebrate that occasion, but some of us can make it all the way to the opposition point of the cycle and perhaps even a little beyond that. Neptune opposes our natal Neptune during our early eighties, just before our Uranus Return occurs at approximately age eighty-four.

It's no wonder, then, that we associate Neptune with unfinished business or unresolved matters, because our Neptune cycle is never fully completed in just one incarnation. Is this the planet of no return? Of course, transiting Pluto does the same thing. Both planets hint at evolutionary developments "to be continued" in a future lifetime. In an attempt to touch our heart so that we may feel all around us the presence of the Divine, this cosmic dream-maker slowly drifts through our houses until, at best, we arrive at Neptune's opposition point less weighed down by bitterness, resentment, guilt, and feelings of self-disgust—all of which are quite deadly to us at this age. Such attitudes need to be dissolved if we value the health of our body and soul.

Being an Outer Planet, Neptune will seem pretty strange to all of the planets that lie within Saturn's orbit, although Neptune at times will also appear very captivating as well. Neptune tempts each planet to become less physical in its orientation, less into material attachments, less bound by rationality, and less in need of ego-attention. Neptune will whisper into any receptive planet's ear a few inspiring words about vaster, invisible worlds of pure light and boundless energy—worlds beyond anything our five senses can fully perceive. That sounds both fantastic and terrifying to most of our personal planets, but it may also seem more marvelous than frightening to those of us already on a conscious path of enlightenment.

Let us begin with a look at our birth chart's planetary cast of colorful characters—especially when seen from Neptune's uncommon perspective. This may give us a better feel for just what's at stake during our major and most memorable Neptune transits.

THE SUN

As a symbol of our ego and its drive to attain central, conscious power, our natal Sun wants us to feel alive and well all the time. Life is to be a vital experience for this beamingly energetic planet. We are to radiate all that we are in ways that directly impact our surroundings. Pessimism and self-doubt are not part of the Sun's psychological profile. This planet is always eager to pump us up and strengthen our will to achieve in this world. Ambition is deemed a healthy thing, highly valued by the Sun. Taking the lead in life and not ever being dependent on others are also to be applauded, because it means that we have complete confidence in our ability to be self-sufficient. It also allows us more control over our actions. The Sun doesn't need to hire cheerleaders or publicity agents—it has itself to pep up and promote! However, due to its unabashed display of ego-assertion at times, this solar part of our inner nature can go overboard when basking in its "me" consciousness. Neptune finds that troubling.

Of course, there are other solar traits that Neptune finds initially appealing. The Sun wants life to be a full-bodied mix of color and drama. Neptune can be dramatic, and it certainly has a love of unlimited color. In fact, neither planet can stand to see life become too plain and dull—which is why they once declined to attend Saturn's thirtieth birthday party! Both planets encourage "larger than life" experiences, and each enjoys a good amount of glamour. At its best, the Sun can be warm and generous in spirit. Neptune, brimming with sensitivity and empathy, can also be warm and generous in giving freely to those in need. Both planets can find themselves playing heroic roles, saving people in perilous conditions, and generally protecting the weak and the defenseless from harm. The difference, however, is that Neptune doesn't need the praise and the pat on the back for its heroic acts that the Sun eagerly anticipates. The Sun is always performance-conscious, proof that our ego happily is symbolized by it.

Both planets, especially when interacting, can also reinforce a temperamental streak. We know about the Sun's potential to flame out when disturbed (those hot solar flares), but Neptune under stress can unexpectedly shoot steamy geysers from deep below its deceptively calm exterior, in hysterical or panic-stricken moments when emotional hurricanes suddenly form over Poseidon's inner seas. It's not easy for these planets to remain cool, restrained, or detached once triggered by certain situational stresses, especially those involving people. Therefore, Neptune transiting our Sun can be a period when some of us will have a hard time keeping up the dignified air of regal command that we've so relied on in the past. Our composure can break down under Neptune's influence as hyper-sensitivity takes over.

Actually, transiting Neptune looks for strong-willed archetypes to latch onto when it wants something important to emerge from the Collective Unconscious, especially something that can play a major influence in inspiring the human heart on a mass level. Neptune senses that the Sun (certainly no quitter) has a better than average chance at succeeding in any project it enthusiastically tackles. Neptune is fascinated by the indomitable will of the Sun (and of Mars). Neptune doesn't really comprehend why any planet would feel it must exercise such force of will, and yet, without sufficient will power applied to physical expression, no beautiful dreams are allowed to manifest and endure, although those same dreams and visions effortlessly come alive in Neptune's intangible realm of the spirit.

The Sun can provide the necessary determination to not give up on an ideal that Neptune wants to turn into a universal "reality" in a humanized sense. The Sun loves to create things with a sense of flair, while Neptune is blessed with an inspired ability to let its imagination soar to great heights. This transit can be a wonderful time to magically transform major areas of our life—with a little help from unseen but benevolent forces employed by the Cosmos. The downside of a mismanaged union of the Sun and Neptune is the danger of losing our center (the Sun), our primary purpose in life, and even all sensible or protective boundaries. Here we can let powerful, destructive images from "the deep" flood our ego, and either bloat it grotesquely or else weaken its structure so seriously that malformation results, keeping us in a state of disability on some level. It's best that we cooperate with Neptune's gentler side so that we keep all energies flowing creatively. Read more about this in Chapter Ten.

THE MOON

Neptune knows that it can easily influence the Moon, up to a point, because this naturally receptive planet is less resistant to subliminal messages than is the Sun, and also because the Moon already has one foot in the door that leads to our mysterious subconscious. (The other foot is smack dab in the vulnerable world of everyday human experience.) Although the Moon typically has its front entrance well-bolted during the day for security reasons, it has an unconscious habit of leaving its windows open while it's asleep at night, thus inviting in whatever wants to enter unnoticed. The Moon is not always able to keep out such intruders. It's instinctively defensive, but inconsistently so. This explains why it's easily put upon by the other planets. They each get to make a deep impression—a psychological crater—on our vulnerable Moon. Neptune has a special talent for secretly invading the space of any unsuspecting planet, asleep or otherwise. Neptune is the planet of sneak attack. The Moon is an easy target for Neptunian seduction.

Since these are both "water" planets, they share in the development of our feeling nature. Both are highly atmospheric and responsive to even the subtlest influences in the environment. Transiting Neptune doesn't expect the Moon to pose any major difficulties, because our lunar nature allows us to flow with change when we're feeling secure and well-adjusted. Yet how many of us are always emotionally secure and well-adjusted? We're more likely to have a closet full of insecurities that prompt us to tightly attach ourselves to people and objects. When those security symbols that we've carefully collected dissolve, we may panic or suffer anxiety.

Some of us have powerful feelings of neediness or fears of abandonment. Such feelings perplex Neptune, who knows first-hand that all life is eternally protected by the tranquil, unifying waters of the Cosmic Mother; therefore, why fear being left alone in the cold and empty void? During Neptune's transit to our Moon, we may need to reflect on where ideal maternal support is to be found—we may discover that it has to come from within us. Neptune will also teach us about handling our safety issues with a greater sense of faith in a protective Universe.

Neptune craves to be fed divine inspiration in the same way that an infant hungrily seeks mother's milk. For that reason, Neptune is somewhat sympathetic to the Moon's possessive instincts. Neptune itself wants to possess or be possessed by a blissful state of Oneness. Yet, because it's an Outer Planet, Neptune is determined to wean us away from clinging too dearly to any one person or thing that belongs to this earthly plane.

However, Neptune's not especially interested in emotional detachment (that's Uranus). It just wants us to intimately feel ourselves to be a part of everything that is—the whole of life.

While our Moon feels very connected to living life in a body subject to mood-altering rhythms, Neptune asks, "Who needs a body? Who needs these limiting flesh-and-blood experiences?" Such a question unnerves our lunar sensibilities. Giving in to dramatic but often confused emotions versus "rising above them" in that classic sense of Neptunian inspiration—or blind denial—will be our dilemma during our Neptune/Moon transits, especially during the square and the opposition phases.

These water planets help us to develop a vivid imagination, suggesting that we are apt to go more deeply inside ourselves during these transit periods in order to explore images far below the surface. The more artistic or musical we are, the better we can channel such combined energies. Neptune adds a touch of idealism to our perceptions, which could lead us to overdo our lunar side and misread it as the only valid way to process our life experience. If our feelings aren't aroused, then the experience must not be of much worth—at least, that's our assumption. It won't be an easy task to pull back and objectively evaluate ourselves at this time, and this alone can be a source of many personal blind spots.

Both planets act like sponges, enabling us to soak up the environment and absorb the wide range of personalities with whom we interact. However, all water-logged sponges periodically need to be squeezed and allowed to dry out to avoid getting that rotten smell. The same goes for us: we cannot immerse ourselves in wave upon wave of emotion without eventually suffering some degree of psychic deterioration. We may not smell rotten, but we feeling that way. We'll need the ventilating qualities of an airy but disciplined intellect to ensure a healthy sense of inner balance.

For the most part, Neptune shares a lot with our Moon, except that it wants us to experience such qualities on a more universal level of understanding. Neptune simply wants lunar energy to expand for us and become more inclusive, so that we feel truly at home with all beings on the planet. Is our emotional framework ready for this? This transit encourages us to explore that question. See Chapter Nine for more on this subject.

MERCURY

Neptune has heard rumors that Mercury is just as adaptable as the Moon, which sounds like good news, because Neptune doesn't deal well with rigidity. It's true that Mercury can be as elastic as a rubber band *if* that serves its purpose. However, Mercury lives in a perceptual world very different from that of the Moon. For one thing, it's no impressionable pushover, easily manipulated on the emotional level by others.

In fact, Mercury is not used to responding to life with any depth of feeling, although it can mimic such response if need be (usually as a result of mirroring someone else's emotions). Mercury is uncomfortable with owning up to its feelings, until after it has analyzed them to death or has completely talked them out—but by then, what real, raw feelings are left? Certainly none of the more unpleasant, unmanageable ones. Mercury also doesn't rely on gut instinct to gather information about its environment. Its tactic is to convince us to innocently but directly ask nosy questions, rather than quietly and perceptively "feel" out the atmosphere and wait for answers to gradually drift our way, Neptunian-style.

Still, Neptune is sure it can work its magic on Mercury and make this planet forget just what a "mental" case it really is—a confirmed brain-aholic, that is! However, doing so is not going to be easy. Neptunian expectations sometimes have a delusional quality about them. While it's true that Mercury is open to all kinds of data, because it delights in being educated about life, Mercury is also quick to reject what it thinks is pure hogwash!

Neptune rambles on in a way that seems much too fanciful to Mercury, who instead demands organized facts and requires clear proof that those facts are reliable. When Mercury confronts Neptune—especially the earthy, Virgo side of Mercury—it expects to be presented with supportive documentation that will back this mystical planet's "far-out" theories and speculations. However, instead of offering hard facts, Neptune can go blank, become tongue-tied, suddenly forget, or act as if the need for such "proof" is quite irrelevant and surely a sad symptom of being spiritually out-of-touch with the Universe. But Mercury is no dope and won't easily be side-tracked in this evasive manner. Off the record, Mercury thinks that Neptune's a real quack, although a fascinating one.

Actually, Mercury needs to take a breather now and then from operating like a computer that processes complex, multi-threaded data at rapid speeds. Neptune tries to convince Mercury that its beloved brain has whole sectors of unexplored, untapped potential that cannot be triggered in purely linear, logical ways. Neptune also wants Mercury to consider that the mind and the brain may not be one and the same, and that our mind most likely doesn't even reside in the brain. It may exist a bit outside of our body as part of our unseen auric field, which uses our physical brain only when waking consciousness and rational functioning are absolutely necessary (which for Mercury would be *all* of the time).

Obviously, this Neptunian explanation of mind versus brain won't be an easy sell, because Mercury can't deal well with such vague and dubious definitions about issues it deems critical to the understanding of how perceptual reality operates. Yet such questionable definitions are the ones to be found most often in Neptune's dictionary, where pictures are actually more descriptive than words.

Mercury has a childlike inquisitiveness that Neptune finds appealing. Mercury's ability to look at anything from many different angles also works well with the ever-changing expression of Neptune. Thus, our imagination and our versatility can be highly stimulated during this period. Neptune often gets us so wrapped up in our beautiful, internal visions that we're not paying attention to outer-world realities, especially the minor details around us. Mercury, a planet that's used to being highly alert to its surroundings, could end up feeling like it's *always* retrograde when Neptune's in town! That means we need to look below the surface of life more often for answers and not accept everything at face value. Mercury actually doesn't mind being exposed to wondrous concepts that challenge existing ideas, which is something Neptune can provide. For more, read Chapters Eight and Eleven.

VENUS

Out of the foam of Poseidon's wave-tossed sea, poised on a huge half-shell, came Aphrodite (a.k.a. Venus, a planet that's traditionally exalted—given preferential treatment—in Neptune's watery sign Pisces). In astrology, Neptune has been dubbed the "higher octave" of Venus, suggesting that it's a spiritually stepped-up version of this "love" planet. These two seem to have connections that go way back! It's true that Venus loves beauty, kindness, and the gentle and sweet ways of considerate people. Venus gives, but it also needs others to give back in return. Venus also can be passive, wants to be pampered, and has bouts with laziness. It easily overdoes a good thing but makes sure it has someone else to blame. Still, it's a peacemaker at heart.

Unfortunately, transiting Neptune does nothing to whip Venus into the lean and mean energy machine that Mars likes to be. Mars is a planet of spartan appetites, which is how it's physically able to stay all muscle and zero flab. If self-restraint and appetite-control are what Venus needs, Neptune seems to encourage permissiveness instead. Transiting Neptune overlooks self-indulgent behavior and may even help us to come up with more imaginative ways to enjoy the Venusian comforts of sensuous living.

Actually, that's not entirely true, because Neptune secretly battles the trappings of the flesh. It believes that physical desire is the number one enemy that has kept humankind from directly knowing its true spiritual identity. In addition, Venusian sensuality can get entirely too lusty for pure Neptunian sensibilities. After all, when it comes to desired bedmates, Mars, not Saturn, is Venus' first pick! Neptune has mixed feelings about joining up with Venus, whether for purposes of physical pleasure or for reeling in the "perfect" lover. Venus intends to own whatever is the object of its desires, and it doesn't plan to let go once it has succeeded. Neptune, a non-possessive planet, considers that to be a selfish and unacceptable trait. It will take a few soul-testing experiences in the world of attachment before Venus can develop spiritual depth, and Neptune will make sure those experiences involve a sense of loss and sacrifice, if need be.

Neptune tries to persuade Venus to consider other ways of evoking a little heaven on earth, ways less harmful than those life-threatening pleasure-addictions that eventually turn destructive. Venus has much talent in the arts and in music, with an eye for color and design, plus an ear for melody and rhythm. Neptune loves working with any planet willing to artistically express itself without self-imposed limits (which means it finds Saturn to be too fussy and self-critical in this area). When well-managed, Neptune/Venus transits can awaken our latent abilities in ways that fulfill our Venusian needs along highly imaginative Neptunian paths. This brings a magical sense of depth and breadth to our creative expression. If Venus can use its talent to uplift and inspire the world, then Neptune is even more satisfied.

Both planets have trouble handling fights and arguments—they'd rather run away from tense confrontations than stand firm and defend themselves. States of tranquillity suit them better. Transiting Neptune knows that Venus will be cooperative for the most part, while Venus is comforted to know that Neptune usually likes things mellow, even placid. Neither wish to ruffle feathers and hurt people's feelings.

During such transits, we can unite with others in greater harmony due to our stronger than average sense of being interconnected. Some of us enter a powerful state of unity-consciousness. We'll just have to make sure that we're not merging with others too indiscriminately, for then we may risk losing a chunk of our identity as we become over-accommodating. We may assume "peace at any price" as our ultimate objective in all our one-on-one relationships. That sounds lovely, but let's make sure that others who are less selfless do not take advantage of our yielding nature at this time. Read more on this in Chapters Seven and Twelve.

Mars

The thought of pairing Neptune with Mars at first seems like a cruel cosmic prank. What could they possibly have in common? The fighting animal spirit and the exclusive self-interest in Mars seem much too alien of an ego-orientation for Neptune to ever comprehend, much less work with comfortably. However, the Universe demands that these planets come together every so often to manifest something of evolutionary value for us. Besides, Neptune doesn't believe in totally shunning any planet just because its disposition is difficult to like. Remember, Neptune believes that "all is eternally one" in a Cosmos held together primarily by the principle of love. Neptune aspires to manifest that love principle as much as possible. Still, Mars can be a handful to deal with and is clearly one of the toughest earthly challenges Neptune will ever face.

At least Mars has the courage to pioneer uncharted territory. This is one Martian trait that Neptune needs to take advantage of, because everything about Neptune's world seems like "uncharted territory" to those of us struggling to survive in the gritty, material realm of here-and-now reality. Neptune may have extraordinary vision, but it lacks the required guts and stamina to make dreams come true in the physical world. It will try to chant or pray with great devotion in an attempt to make its visions miraculously appear—but in Saturn's domain, much of what manifests for us comes through applied effort and the steady determination to not give up on our goals.

Mars knows that success is more than just wish-fulfillment and the reward we deserve for being a kind soul—it also involves hard and sometimes sweaty work, suggesting that a degree of physical force is necessary. Mars makes Neptune feel that it really doesn't know a heck of a lot about living life in a body, but this Neptune transit is a time to bring more of the spiritual dimension into physical form through the power of our inspired actions.

Mars is a colorful planet that sees life in vivid shades of blood-pumping red. It can't handle too much dull beige or other anemic hues. Mars likes life to be vigorous and in motion—alive and well and raring to go! Neptune doesn't enjoy such a fast and robust pace, yet it, too, wants life to be more colorful and vibrant with energy—although a refined level of energy. Mars may not be subtle enough to suit Neptune, but Neptune knows that Mars is straightforward and honest about its intentions. What a relief, because others have unfairly taken advantage of gullible Neptune for as long as it can remember. In this transit, Neptune is dealing with a planet that rarely is ambivalent or confused about what action to take when impulse or inspiration hits. This puts the pressure on Neptune to stay focused and steadily deliver the creative power that keeps Mars highly energized and motivated.

One thing that Mars is sure to like is Neptune's lack of boundaries. Mars hates being caged or boxed in, and Neptune doesn't like to put up brick walls. Under Neptune's spell, Mars can feel like there's nothing that can stop it in its tracks. However, this may not be the best way for us to handle our Martian energies, because eventually we run out of gas, even though the road ahead seems to continue forever. There's also a tendency to not know where to direct our attention.

Neptune periodically knocks the wind out of Mars' sails, leaving us inexplicably tired or exhausted in ways that force us to periodically rest. Neptune seems to know that being on the go too much can get an over-active Mars in trouble; even illness becomes one "creative" way to slow us down. The biggest hurdle to overcome is to get Mars to stop looking for constant external stimuli to act on, because that's really not what Neptune's about. Mars tends to be too easily triggered—it's a hormonal thing. On the other hand, Neptune feels that a little quiet down time would be greatly appreciated. With Neptune/Mars transits, we'll need to pay attention to our uneven energy surges and make the most of our day when the tide is high, then perhaps get a full-body massage, followed by a good catnap, when we've run out of steam! Read Chapter Six for more.

JUPITER

Up to this point, all of the planets I've mentioned fall under the "personal" category because they each have a special interest in their own ego-fulfillment and in directly obtaining personal satisfaction from worldly experiences. Even though Venus and the Moon seem to do things for others, they eagerly wait to see if their kindness will be reciprocated—this is even how they judge the character of others. When the personal planets urge us to attend to the needs of others, it's usually only those folks we personally know or wish to relate to—like family, lovers, and friends.

However, by the time we get to a "social" planet like Jupiter, we are dealing with societal functions that go beyond family ties and close alliances. With Jupiter, we become aware of larger collective realities that help to shape our individual interpretation of life, that give it a broader, long-range meaning, perhaps within a historical context. Merely surviving in the world by applying brute strength and raw instinct is not what Jupiter is about (that's Mars/Moon energy). Instead, Jupiter supports the establishment of cultural frameworks through any form of group cooperation that embodies the uplifting qualities of the human spirit. It's the stuff of which time-honored social rituals are made (with the added input and approval of Saturn).

Boundless Neptune feels an immediate kinship with expansive Jupiter. The fact that they both share rulership over Pisces underscores their sense of camaraderie. Of course, Neptune most relates to the watery side of Jupiter—the gentler, more compassionate Piscean Jupiter with humanitarian aspirations. Jupiter's loud and fiery Sagittarian side, acting at times like an unstoppable one-planet promotional campaign, is less easy for Neptune to absorb. Self-aggrandizement is not a basic Neptunian talent, although Neptune, like the fire side of Jupiter, shares a few traits that are a must for selling older-model used cars—number one being the gift of hype. Fire Jupiter is certainly filled with a crusading spirit, but it can be expressed in almost too militant a manner to satisfy the pacifist in Neptune. In addition, this Sagittarian facet of Jupiter has all of the delicacy of a blast of trombones, compared to the gentle, otherworldly tinkling of Neptune's wind chimes. Therefore, Neptune senses that it won't enjoy many quiet, reflective moments when joining forces with boisterous Jupiter. At least it has a companion it knows it can trust, as it did with Mars, only with a greater sense of ease.

Actually, Jupiter has one thing that most planets do not: a big heart that generously pours out to those in need without letting ego control the show (unlike the Sun). That becomes one of its most attractive features, according to Neptune, who also places a high value on showing a heartfelt response to the needs of the social underdog. During these transits, Neptune is doing everything it can to inspire Jupiter to give of itself unconditionally and to help to heal society on some level, usually by offering people a little optimism about their future.

Although that sounds nice and spiritual, Jupiter is one planet that cannot afford to give away anything blindly and *un*conditionally, because that's when it typically finds itself penalized for using poor judgment. Old Saturn is forever taking meticulous notes on the misbehavior of the other planets, and it doesn't take kindly to senseless expansion or the unwise waste of energy. It doesn't find the naiveté of some planets sweet or charming. What Saturn says goes, because it's the planet that establishes the rules of the game that apply to this earthly realm.

Still, Neptune loves the fact that Jupiter is also a bit of a dreamer, with great expectations about better tomorrows for all. Both planets love to give hope to those in despair. They seem to have just the right amount of buoyancy to nurse "the walking wounded" back to health. Without these planets, we wouldn't look toward the heavens and wonder about what great things the future may hold for us. Therefore, Neptune/Jupiter transits will be times of positive speculation about what awaits us in life. We may learn that our faith can move mountains. Read more on this in Chapter Fourteen.

Saturn

Greek mythology tells us that Saturn (as Cronus) was the daddy of Neptune (Poseidon), but here was a father who didn't spend one minute getting to know and love his son. He simply swallowed Neptune whole immediately after the baby god's birth. No wonder claustrophobic Neptune is still traumatized by fears of confinement and abandonment!

Actually, to ensure its power to rule over the manifest world, the archetype of earthly time (Saturn) manages to consume the archetype of cosmic timelessness (Neptune), which sounds symbolically like what happens when we each incarnate in a physical realm that immediately swallows up our memory of our spiritual origin. Realize, too, that Saturn castrated his own daddy, Uranus—an archetype of the abstract heavens—and thereby pretty much accomplished the same thing. It sounds as if mythological Saturn did whatever it took to destroy the power of that which is eternal and universal in essence. For these and other reasons, Neptune has forever been wary of Saturn's devouring energy, and will only work with the Ringed One as long as it doesn't ever again become trapped in the dark pit of this planet's stomach.

Greek myths aside, transiting Neptune marvels at Saturn's ability to not only create form, but to keep that form intact. Being another "social" planet, Saturn uses its form-building talent to keep society from falling apart. Neptune itself doesn't have such binding power and wonders where Saturn obtained its cosmic glue! Neptune can quickly see how truly enchanting it would be to be able to focus on its own exquisitely beautiful designs for an appreciable length of time. Humanity would enjoy this, too. Imagine having something awe-inspiring *not* disappear for a change, the way our Neptunian dreams vanish the moment we wake up in the morning! Actually, Neptune is ill-equipped to navigate the physical world, but appreciates that Saturn is an expert at this. Therefore, if Neptune wants to bring down its rarefied energy to levels that our human senses can really enjoy, it will need the assistance of the qualified master of earthly materialization—Saturn.

Unfortunately, Saturn can be such a worrywart and partypooper, not ever wanting to relax and enjoy the lightness and whimsy that Neptune can provide to a world-weary soul. Imagination is Neptune's best remedy for loosening congestion caused by too much tedious, uninspired reality. We need an occasional escape and our lapses of "reality" to avoid that dreaded, swallowed-up feeling that we get from being knee-deep in Saturn's slow-to-change world. This transit can make us feel as if a wondrous light has illuminated the dark places of our fragmented psyche; think of an iridescent aurora borealis painting the cold, black nighttime sky. Embracing faith becomes our big challenge. We will learn to put our trust into the hands of unseen, guiding forces and watch how we gently attract situations that enhance more meaningful Saturnian life structures.

It's not always going to be easy to pull these two energies together, because Saturn instinctively feels a need to contain Neptune to keep it from becoming undermining. In addition, Saturn has heard about Neptune's chameleon-like abilities to change colors and blend with just about anything, and that makes Saturn quite nervous, because it doesn't like things to change their appearance that easily. However, when Neptune transits our Saturn, our life is at a stage when everything has a chance to look quite different—and, frankly, quite beautiful. Our skies may still be somber with shades of gray but, with Neptune in command, a few rainbows pop up here and there.

Nonetheless, transiting Neptune works to dissolve walls and barriers that we have built around us through our self-ignorance. Our internalized Saturn may have been too imprisoned by its own limited, material framework for much too long. Neptune slowly works to release us. Neptune has us in a protective and enlightening flow. We semi-consciously swim in a river that will lead us to a vast ocean of expanded opportunity for self-expression, if we stop swimming against the current. On some days, though, Neptune wants to give uptight Saturn a powerful sedative and tell it to go take a long, long nap—*anything* so that Neptune can continue do its work without hitting unnecessary Saturnian roadblocks! See Chapter Fifteen for more on this topic.

URANUS

Will Neptune meet its match in Uranus? After all, these two planets fall in the "transpersonal" category, which they share with Pluto. Our ego cannot as easily gum up the works and interfere with needed development when two or more transpersonal planets join forces. We'll find we're less able to directly control what occurs in the outer world during these transit periods. What we can control is our reaction to the changes and upheavals we witness, although even that's debatable, should our untamed unconscious decide to simultaneously explode with destablizing images that overwhelm us.

Uranus symbolizes a part of us that is quite different from Neptune. Uranus shows zero interest in merging with anything else in order to lose a sense of itself. In fact, to be lost in a sea of conformity or have its highly-individualistic identity evaporate is its one fear. On the other hand, Neptune can't imagine existing in a world where everyone is an isolated unit of consciousness, an entity made to feel even more separate and distinct from others by over-identifying with a body and a brain—two purely biological creations subject to the ravages of time. Neptune cannot even conceive of death in the sober, no-nonsense, finalizing way that Saturn can. Uranus, at least, agrees that there's more to existence than just what our consciousness can perceive. Uranus theorizes that our brain can't handle very much to begin with, because it represents obsolete hardware that is woefully behind the times compared to the more advanced, revolutionary software our intuitive mind can churn out when inspired (quick—more memory chips!).

Uranus is not a planet that is moved on the emotional level. Despite this, Neptune is determined to teach Uranus about heart and soul, not just about mind and theory, no matter how brilliantly presented. For those of us who are already using Uranus on a personal level—where Uranus is not just some collective, impersonal force—we realize that slowing down to listen to others is not an easy feat, because we typically intuit what they're trying to say and are ready with a quick response. Transiting Neptune helps us to incorporate the ability to be a more empathetic listener, which is the best way to deeply absorb another's reality. ("Deeply absorb?" gasps Uranus, "Where's the exit? I can't breathe...")

Astrological Uranus knows a lot—thanks to its flashes of insight—but it doesn't really "know" human suffering first hand. Neptune is eager to remedy this ignorance. Compassion needs to be part of the greater awareness that Uranus within us seeks to have about life. Otherwise, we'll live in our heads too much and arrogantly believe that we've figured out all of humanity's complexities. We may think that we know exactly how life's complications can be ideally eliminated. However, rarely does Uranus volunteer to sit in another's wheelchair long enough to emotionally feel that individual's reality. Uranus runs away from feeling another's pain and anguish. Neptune wishes to work on this major oversight in Uranus' make-up.

Therefore, these planets hold much promise regarding our ability to see the world in a radically different way. In the process, we may be surprised to find out just how enlightened we aren't! Both planets have been associated with earth-shaking developments and with the toppling of suffocating worldly structures. Perhaps a few of our time-honored, sacred cows must die so that we are freer to explore for ourselves—with eyes wide open—this puzzle called existence.

Neptune loves Uranus' willingness to daringly plunge into the unknown, but Uranus is too often sold on the educational value of shocking people out of their complacency. Although this "technique" works, it's an approach that's too jarring at times—it can frighten more than enlighten. Transiting Neptune believes that its mission is not to zap us with a stun gun or scare the pants off of us. It just wants to peel off a few layers of illusion that have covered up the inner truth about our authentic self. It senses that Uranus is on a similar mission, although Uranus shows little patience for and understanding of others who are "less advanced" intellectually. (Its "genius" doesn't appreciate slow-wittedness.) Transiting Neptune slowly infuses us with levels of universal love, so that we awaken to our need to be more compassionate about human imperfections. Our Uranian attitudes soften, helping us to become more humane. Read Chapter Sixteen for more.

NEPTUNE

When transiting Neptune meets our natal Neptune, there is nothing to stop this planet from behaving in its most natural state—deeply unconscious and totally subjective. If any planet is in a position to understand the otherwise easily misunderstood intentions of Neptune, it's Neptune! This is an archetype that most often feels quite out-of-sync with modern materialistic values. This is especially true when the emphasis is placed on aggressively stockpiling consumer goods that will supposedly bring us lasting happiness and inner peace—forget about the credit card debt involved, just keep on buying more expensive "toys" that we can't afford.

However, lest we think that Neptune is naturally to be found deeply meditating on the meaning of life while secluded in some isolated mountain temple, realize that this is one planet that can get sucked into the world of commercial enterprise quite easily. Why we addictively buy what we really don't need often depends on the illusionary allure of glamour created by slick advertising and marketing (Neptune-inspired), as much as it does on impractical shoppers. Such consumers purchase certain products in record amounts and unwittingly create consumer fads (Tickle Me Neptune), thus inflating business profits.

Like it or not, hype sells, especially when it also, coincidentally, happens to promote an ultimate cultural dream that many value, such as defying the aging process. In the long run, it's this all-too-human level of Neptune that seldom satisfies us, because it's founded on artificial highs devoid of real soul-content, highs that cannot be sustained. Fads come and go, and megastars in the media eventually fade away (unless they're first rocked by scandals). When our fantasies evaporate, we come out of our Neptunian trance feeling a little down and plenty disappointed.

During the few Neptune/Neptune transits we'll have in our lifetime, we become more aware of what has transient worth versus timeless value. Perhaps this is because some of us initially chase after fool's gold and get burned and very disillusioned in the process, only to regret our shallowness and our spiritual bankruptcy. While feeling remorse for squandering the gifts that life has given us, we may eventually begin to "see the light" and learn to put our temporal stay on this often frustrating planet in proper perspective. Neptune deals with surrendering our self-will and our ego-resistance so that we may be led back to our spiritual roots in a state of fuller inner awareness. This, however, is something our ego is scared to experience for fear that it will be dissolved once and for all in the process—never to be seen again!

In the real, day-to-day world, these Neptune cycles are usually too subtle for most people to register, except for the square phase during our so-called "mid-life crisis" years. Still, we may at least feel a twinge of phoniness during these times, knowing that we are obediently playing society's game while wearing our smiley face. However, deep inside we pray that higher forms of collective consciousness exist somewhere in the Universe. While some of us may yearn to be lifted off this planet and transported to a better place, Neptune/Neptune phases put the pressure on us to make things more beautiful and transcendent in this very physical dimension we inhabit—this mundane realm of incarnation. More on this subject is covered in Chapter Seventeen.

PLUTO

Mythological Neptune and Pluto (as Poseidon and Hades) were brothers who shared the traumatizing experience of being swallowed whole by their father Saturn (Cronus) right after birth. Each knows first hand how dark and cramped it can be inside the belly of an archetype that symbolizes the constraints of time and space. Once Jupiter (Zeus) rescued them from their prison, fate entered the picture when the brothers chose lots to determine their futures. Neptune was to rule the ocean depths while Pluto ruled the Underworld. Neither of these realms was above the ground, continuing the theme of confinement. With Neptune and Pluto, we associate penetrating depth and the mysteries of darker, unseen forces at work below our threshold of consciousness. Anything in a deeply submerged state corresponds to these planets.

Astrological Neptune knows that Pluto is an eternal enigma and quite a loner in temperament. Of course, Neptune hates for anyone to be so isolated and inaccessible, and feels tempted to reach out and touch Pluto's heart whenever these two come together by transit (which is not that often). Touch Pluto's heart? It's not too clear, even in myth, how much heart Pluto really has. Of the two brothers, he was the child apparently most scarred by the cruel experience of rejection and near annihilation by his cold-blooded father. Astrological Pluto still has not forgotten that terrible incident, and rages against any and all authority figures who dare to dominate through the absolute expression of power and control. Pluto wants to grab all of that power for itself.

Wise Neptune, feeling compassion for obsessive-compulsive Pluto, understands that we can unconsciously become that which we despise. Neptune would love to say "forgive and forget," because that's its standard solution to just about everything that it otherwise finds disturbing. Rumor has it that Neptune once tried to convince Pluto that old man Saturn was just a pathetic, dysfunctional mess rather than some heartless monster—after all, just look at *his* daddy and the dynamics of *their* difficult relationship! However, Neptune chickened out at the last minute, sensing that such psycho-babble wouldn't sit well with a pent-up planet ruling lava-spewing volcanoes.

Nevertheless, transiting Neptune knows that a lot of unprocessed buried pain and boiling anger seethes within Pluto's psyche. There is also much trapped, libidinal energy in need of an opportunity to find release in some intensely creative manner. Neptune is on a mercy mission to unearth the hidden treasure that our inner Pluto refuses to expose to the light of day. Pluto affords us the power and the stamina to undertake a big project that can rejuvenate both us and our social environment; all that is needed is the right kind of inspiration. This is what Neptune hopes to provide in a non-intrusive way that won't turn Pluto off, although sometimes Pluto only responds well to something that's equally forceful and intense.

It's true that many of us are not going to pick up on these subterranean energies, at least not with any real sense of conscious command and comprehension. However, they may express for us in smaller situational ways (other than plumbing problems!) that help us feel powerful little rushes of inspiration. We may also become enthralled by some big scientific or medical breakthrough in the world—in this case, the broader social environment regenerates for us in some wondrous manner. More on this subject is found in Chapter Thirteen.

Now that the planets of our life's drama have been introduced, it is time to preview the twelve houses. The actual natal atmosphere of each house depends on how accurately we know our birth time. The birth time is a piece of data that no astrology student can afford to treat casually—you can't do a chart properly for someone who only tells you that they were born "sometime in the early morning!" Track down the source of that time of birth, especially before trying to interpret a Neptune transit—which can already seem nebulous enough. Let's move on to the next chapter for a detailed look at each natal house and how Neptune might feel about transiting it.

CHAPTER FOUR

A Neptunian Tour of Our Natal Houses

The Usual Places

The following is a preview of transiting house themes and life issues that will be covered at length starting in Part Two, Chapter Six. In our transited house, we'll find most of the Neptunian action taking place. Our environment sets up just the right conditions for us to learn how to better incorporate constructive Neptunian values once we deal squarely with a few nagging blind spots, doubts, and fears.

Our First House

This is a house that pushes for all planetary and sign energies to surface and propel us to confront immediate challenges in our here-and-now world. Often, the issues at hand deal with our simple survival in life through the development of a strong, separate identity that helps us to fend for ourselves. Sometimes, fighting for our right to exist, free from the influence of others, is part of this challenge. Neptune transiting the First House can feel like a fish out of water in many respects, because its instincts tell it to remain silent, lay low, and camouflage itself so as not to become too dominant in its environment.

However, learning how to stand out in a crowd is something that the First House promotes, not so much for attention as for the freedom to act apart from others. In this life zone of our chart, a direct and assertive approach is typically the winning one. Although self-assertion is something very difficult for Neptune, that's what our surroundings expect and at times demand. We'll have to generate self-seeking traits that will enable us to face the world with courage.

Transiting Neptune, still feeling either quite inspired or subdued from its ponderous passage through our Twelfth House, is not in a state of real momentum by the time it crosses over our Ascendant. In contrast, Mars passing over our First House cusp is ready to burst on the scene, because it's so glad to be out of the murky swamplands it typically finds in our Twelfth House. At this eastern angle of our chart, people will see us going through our Neptunian adjustment period, for better or worse. Things usually look a little messy at first, until we realize that a new self-image is trying to be born that will help us to feel more connected to the rest of humanity. A new personal identity may emerge, once we abandon socially-programmed character traits in favor of learning to be more ourselves, while we gently absorb the essence of people and things around us. This is how we learn to feel more unified with all forms of life and how we become more empathetic.

Our First House is about new cycles of self-development. If we've dissolved most of our emotional debris from the past in our Twelfth, then transiting Neptune has more power to build a beautiful vision of what we can become as our future unfolds. Personal hang-ups that have previously stopped us from attaining true self-recognition may now disappear through the healing magic of self-love. However, things are not always rosy for us during this lengthy transit, and there will be pitfalls to avoid if our goal is truly to stay alive and well with Neptune.

The First House puts this planet through a reality test, because Neptune would rather remain invisible, or at least do its work quietly. Other houses will be available for that (such as the Eighth and the Twelfth), but not this house of surface exposure.

Here is where our Neptunian aspirations are to be put into forward motion and allowed to start something fresh and deeply fulfilling for us. We'll have to go with the flow courageously and in good faith, if we wish to experience the best this transit has to offer.

There will be moments when we'll have to act alone to promote our vision. The First House doesn't like to see too many other people in charge of our pet projects. We alone are to be the main focus—it's our action here that counts the most, not someone else's. Self-leadership is the way to go. It's unlikely, when this transit is over, that we'll convert or revert to any lifestyle that emphasizes heavy earthly ambition. We won't feel a need to aggressively conquer the world and secure a commanding seat of power. Some of us, though, will show much enthusiasm for dreaming big, wonderful dreams of spiritual enrichment for ourselves and for everyone else on the planet! Read Chapter Six for more.

OUR SECOND HOUSE

Once we have envisioned ourselves as someone dedicated to allowing more of our inner light to shine forth, and as somebody who will help others to better know and love themselves as they struggle to make sense of their lives (because people in need are attracted to our aura of serenity and the wisdom we appear to possess), our next challenge is to bring more of this peaceful quality and deeper understanding into the practical experience of living. Learning to make it in the world in very physical terms is of great interest to the Second House.

Actually, this is a house that can make ethereal Neptune a little nervous, for here is where concrete manifestation is seen as a prerequisite for worldly success and stability. Here we learn to build life-sustaining form from the basic elements of the material realm. We also are to find reliable ways to ground ourselves so that we can sure-footedly shape our life. We must have something real and valuable to show for our enduring efforts. Otherwise, long-lasting security will not be ours to enjoy. Neptune finds this emphasis on solid form-building to be intimidating, and it wonders if this is another symbolic instance where it will end up in Saturn's belly, hemmed in by the physical limits of a concrete world.

This Neptune transit, however, can be a time to heal wounded feelings that we've held inside that involve a lack of self-worth. If we've developed a sour attitude about attracting material comfort in the world, or if we're forever uncertain about how to capitalize on our bankable talents, could it be because our self-value has been too low for too long? If there is a blind spot that is keeping us from consciously appreciating ourselves, perhaps as we financially struggle to make ends meet, Neptune will bring this to our attention in a way that will have the greatest emotional impact on us. Neptune never trusts that we'll get the message through merely an intellectual analysis of our dilemma. Our feelings must first be provoked before true self-realization occurs.

It could be, at least for some of us, that Neptune will help to uncover the mystery of why a few of us deny ourselves the joys of material abundance, or perhaps why some of us blindly live for nothing but material gratification. Although Neptune doesn't want us to become slaves to our endless appetite for material consumption, neither can this planet sit back and watch us suffer economic deprivations that are the result of hidden self-hatred or confused feelings of unworthiness.

Interestingly enough, we may instead experience the miracle of financial enrichment, thanks to abundance-believer Neptune, as we enjoy the pleasure of being materially well-supplied during this period. After all, receiving gratification from what we attract and possess is a part of this house's experience. Yet later on, just before Neptune is about to exit this sector, we may find that we've satisfied those tangible needs that we had long rejected, and have even made peace with ourselves financially. Now we realize that we can be truly happier with owning less.

Although we have healed ourselves by realizing that we do deserve the best the Universe has to offer, we also understand that we don't need an excess of worldly goods to feel safe and content. Maybe any moneymaking pursuits are now geared toward fulfilling Neptunian visions of helping the sick or the down-and-out in society, those less-fortunate individuals who have special survival needs. Neptune will show us how a little imagination and a big heart can make our Second House experience a soul-enriching one—in the process, Neptune learns that immersion in earthly affairs doesn't have to feel so confining after all. Chapter Seven will explore this transit further.

Our Third House

At this point on the tour, Neptune is probably secretly relieved that—no matter how enlightening our material affairs may have turned out—its official Second House assignment is over. It was not as oppressive of an experience as Neptune had anticipated. In fact, many hidden Neptunian talents were unearthed and used in practical ways. New insights were gained in the area of finance that allow for a more intuitive flow of money-management. Still, our enjoyment of buying and owning physical objects, no matter how beautiful and comforting they may be, has its limits. We realize that there's more to life than just shopping.

We can eventually feel stuck, surrounded by all of those nice things that now must be maintained. In addition, we can't merge our soul with such inanimate items—their tangible nature will always be a reminder that we're still locked into a very dense world of manifestation. It's really not anything like the heavenly realms, Neptune notes. Therefore, as Neptune enters our Third House, it starts to feel free to take to the clear skies—an ocean of sorts—of a less-restricted mental world. Neptune now has a chance to spread its energy far and wide (although not as expansively as it will during its passage through our Ninth).

In our Third House, Neptune creates mental images that allow and even encourage us to change so that we better adapt to the needs of the moment. Thoughts can spring forth that inspire us to tackle everyday tasks in sensitive, imaginative ways, but we'll have to follow our inner voice more consistently. This might be a challenge in itself, because the Third House typically looks to the outside world for instant information on how to deal with everything—this house figures that somebody smart and well-educated out there can accurately answer our specific questions, and that whatever we need to know immediately is not expected to come from our subjective self. Transiting Neptune is here to defy that notion.

It may take years, but eventually we will learn to trust that quiet, knowing part of ourselves that leads us to the facts we need in a subtle, introspective manner. We can sense an invisible, protective presence that guides us along our path of self-education regarding the busy world around us. What fluid Neptune and the mutable Third House have in common is that they don't care for rigid, one-sided thinking. Both promote our ability to view issues from many angles, which helps to keep our developing assumptions tentative and open-ended until we see how things change. Staying mentally flexible is good advice during this transit, because Neptune will often show us that situations are not quite what they appear to be at first. Let's not take drastic action based on incomplete data.

Communication is a big Third House theme. Ordinary verbal communication—sticking to the objective facts—is not something that Neptune enjoys. That approach is too plain, dry, and unimaginative. Neptune is a fabulous storyteller, able to embellish reality with fantastic tales that enchant our mind and inspire our heart. Neptune has the power to feed our soul by making words and concepts appetizing, tantalizing, and filled with a rare and poetic beauty. It's also a planet that understands how to read life in an uncommonly symbolic way, where even the simplest things hide deeper spiritual meaning. Neptune wants us to interpret any secret message that we find in our local surroundings. We obviously need to be careful not to read too much into things, because our Third House wants us to stick to the surface of life for the most part. We can save all that mystical "mumbo-jumbo" for Neptune's Twelfth House assignment.

Yet Neptune is not satisfied with going along with the game plan set up by our conscious mind. We will need to make room for our intuitive side to come forth, scan the environment, and see what it can sense. We may surprise ourselves regarding how uncanny our feelings can be about people once we learn to trust these feelings. After all, they're just another form of communication—in this case, our inner self trying to inform us about less obvious matters at work within our Third House circumstantial affairs. Read more on this in Chapter Eight.

Our Fourth House

By the time Neptune transits this next house, we hopefully have learned to trust that our instincts and hunches can further educate us about life. They can train us to recognize subtleties in human communication. Our mind may have also learned the value of introspection, which will now come in handy in this house of subjective concerns. Many astrologers don't mind calling the Fourth a "water" house, meaning that many of the things symbolized by this element relate to our feelings about our close surroundings and how we go about establishing psychological security in this house. In addition, at least for many North American astrologers, this house is associated with our maternal experience of life, typically, our relationship with our mother.

These issues reinforce the underlying watery nature of the Fourth House. Neptune is a water planet; therefore, its slow journey through this house should have a pervasive—although not too outwardly apparent—effect on our emotional development. Neptune loves to work with any house as sensitive as the Fourth, because this planet also is attuned to the fluid, inner, feeling world of people. Transiting Neptune anticipates that it will have great influence in this house.

However, there's a problem here. Our Fourth also deals with how we anchor ourselves deeply in subjective reality. It encourages the development of strong, underground roots that help to secure a nearly unshakable psychological foundation for us. It's from this well-entrenched, unconscious bedrock of identity (symbolized in part by the sign at our astrological Nadir[1]—the angle opposite our Midheaven) that we first instinctively respond to life, even before we adopt the Ascendant persona that we use to deal with our societal framework. Our Nadir suggests a less socially-adapted part of ourselves.

If, for some reason, our roots are unhealthy—perhaps we've inherited a dysfunctional, generational family trait—it will be harder for us to take an unbiased look at our condition and attempt to alter it for the better. Planets that prefer to stay close to life's surface (the Sun, Mercury, Venus, Mars, Jupiter, and even the fraidy-cat Moon at times) won't wish to take the plunge to find out what's lurking at the dark bottom of the well of our subconscious. Neptune, however, will sink to any level it takes in order to start a cleansing and healing process.

Neptune is adept at eroding already-weakened structures, so it feels right at home in our Fourth, plumbing our depths and sensitizing itself to spotting anything that's ready to give way and collapse. If we are in good psychological shape—suggesting that we've emotionally adapted to change for quite some time and have engaged in honest, inner work—Neptune encourages us to become even more resilient at our psyche's roots, which enables us to handle life's rough waves without capsizing and drowning.

Besides prompting us to engage in introspective soul searching, transiting Neptune is interested in our family relationships and in how we feel about the home environment we've created for ourselves. Having an ideal nest (our surrogate womb) is important to Neptune. This planet will enable us to be very sensitive to the atmosphere of our home and to the immediate feeling we get when we walk in the door. However, with Neptune, some of us might feel like space aliens who yearn to return to our true galaxy of origin—nothing on Earth feels like familiar turf.

During this transit, we will have to develop a better sense of our real home. This can result in a nagging inner restlessness that leads us to move to new and sometimes foreign locales based essentially on faith, not reason. With Neptune calling the shots, we can feel as if we've never seen a clear road map pointing us in the right direction. Instead, life tells us to follow our heart. See Chapter Nine for more on this transit.

OUR FIFTH HOUSE

During Neptune's transit of our Fourth House, we may sadly have had to pull away from powerful but unhealthy emotional bonds that kept underdeveloped parts of our nature trapped and suffocated. As a result, a few co-dependent ties may have been broken. Close family relationships that kept us in an unrecognized state of immaturity may have dissolved. Maybe we've sacrificed too much of ourselves to those who have done little to spark our sense of self-assurance. Perhaps our sense of personal autonomy didn't have a chance to develop in this house until Neptune came along to make a few tidal waves.

Many of us are ready to surface once again and explore a life zone known for its bright lights and sparkling opportunities for self-extension. No more tears will be shed—as we leave our psychological scuba gear behind—because now it's time to become the awe-filled, golden child most favored by the gods! We are to release our youthful spirit in ways that honor our imagination's key role in helping us to grow further. The Fifth House may seem too frivolous and light-hearted for any transiting Outer Planet to be taken seriously, but actually it's an area where we can learn to follow the wisdom of our heart—a very important lesson for those on a conscious path of self-realization. Remember, the Fifth House trines the Ninth of spiritual journeying, suggesting a harmonious alliance between these two sectors. As we open our heart center, we feel a great love for life, something the Fifth House very much supports.

Neptune doesn't always create its "sacred space" in the holy and reverential manner often portrayed. We shouldn't assume that Atlantean temple priests and priestesses were too spiritually elevated to crack a smile. If we note the fun that little kids have playing "make-believe," we will realize that it's possible for Neptune—the blessed saint of make-believe—to provide us with its own brand of cosmic entertainment. There is a fanciful side to Neptune that the Fifth House will bring out with great flair.

Our Fifth is where we let our hair down and demand to have a good time. Neptune, not being such a workaholic anyway, likes to indulge in leisure activity. This planet is an escapist at heart who feels it's not here on Earth just to toil the hours away. Getting lost in enjoyable Fifth House affairs is not a problem for Neptune. However, becoming addicted to this recreational approach to better living can become a serious issue at some point.

Still, in this house, creativity wants to burst at the seams, something that Neptune finds motivating. Healthy Fifth House expression is quite uplifting and self-affirming. During this transit, we'll need to do what it takes to bring more color and even a touch of glamour into our lives. Doing so may help us to not grow too old too quickly, which will please ageless Neptune. This planet already feels like an innocent but protected babe of the Cosmos. It just so happens that our Fifth deals with how we relate to our "inner" child. This child within us is given a grand opportunity to liberate his or her glorious ability to come alive in almost boundless ways.

Neptune is a romanticist rather than a realist when it comes to matters of the heart. Our Fifth House describes how we invest ourselves in love affairs. Things can look rosy here when Neptune begins to paint our lovers—or would-be lovers—with its magic brush. Yet there is little about the Fifth itself that is prepared for disappointment and rejection—this is super-confident Leo's favorite hangout. Here we can expect life to roll out the red carpet and show us nothing but first-class treatment; that is, if our self-esteem is high. If we blend this planet and house together, it's easy to see how such expectations of fulfillment through special treatment may reach inflationary degrees. They also fan the flames of unbridled ego. Therefore, during this transit, we'll need to kindly remind ourselves that there are limits to everything. Not all we touch will turn to gold. Besides, the gods are less kind to those filled with hubris. More about this transit is covered in Chapter Ten.

Our Sixth House

The joyous celebration that life magically became in our Fifth House—especially for some of us hyper-creative types—is unfortunately not to continue in the sober, reality-focused Sixth. In this house, we are to get back to the business of practical living. We may not want to accept this fact at first, but if we don't snap out of our Fifth House mania, we'll be accused of "being in denial" by those who warn us to stop playing games and start developing a stronger work ethic. We'll need to face it—the party's over!

Actually, one thing that Neptune hopes to accomplish in our Sixth is to teach us to love one another through selfless service. This may seem to be a simple but saintly message, yet it's one that resonates very well with the Sixth House. Service done willingly will not only help to heal a world in disorder, it will also keep our health in good shape. Many of the techniques we can use on the road to wellness can be found in this house. If we've had too good of a Neptunian time indulging ourselves in our Fifth, we probably need the quick relief that only our Sixth House can provide. To get the best results, we must be a willing patient, although Neptune's not too sure at first that it really wants to be cured. We may still be on a Fifth House high and don't want to come down to boring "reality."

However, if we bring any of our Neptunian vices with us into our Sixth, we may not be able to begin our new assignment. (This is a possibility, because undue self-indulgence is one of the pitfalls of mismanaging transiting Neptune in our Fifth), We first must clean up our act. Therefore, the early years of this house transit are often spent learning to make necessary self-adjustments, correcting any health imbalances created by our bad habits before we can tackle the serious life-tasks awaiting us. Staying fit is important to this house. Neptune allows us plenty of time to make amends where needed, but let's not take advantage of such a lenient planet and repeatedly put off the self-disciplined measures required. That's when our problems set in deeper and deeper, making them harder to fix as we begin to suffer "mysterious" ailments.

A badly-handled Sixth House experience can make us feel as if our life is falling apart. Nothing we do seems to work—not even the small stuff. Neptune can, unfortunately, magnify our sense of internal disorder and outer turmoil. It may take years for us to get to this disorganized point in our lives, but when it finally happens, we may feel too weakened in spirit to turn things around. Self-defeatism can take its toll. Why wait until we are at the doorstep of a crisis that leaves us desperate for relief?

Transiting Neptune will show us a better way to deal with our inner stresses and our troublesome shadow parts. We can't continue to act in ways that only render us chronically non-functional (the Sixth House's worst nightmare). Therefore, the environment will provide people who have special talents for healing us on different levels. These folks are usually wise enough to know that we first must be willing to be healed before they can show us how to best facilitate that process ourselves.

A major preoccupation of any slow-moving Sixth House transit is job-hunting, which for Neptune means the search for ideal employment. Many of the mundane work situations offered by our environment are simply not appealing to us, especially as our Neptunian sensitivity to our surroundings increases. We can easily feel discontented with what's available on the job market. Should this transit last for fourteen years or even a bit longer, some of us may feel impelled to try different ways to make a living, in the hope that we'll find work that speaks to our soul. Sadly, a few of us may remain in dead-end jobs that require personal sacrifices and that become less and less satisfying as the years slowly grind on. See Chapter Eleven for more on this topic.

OUR SEVENTH HOUSE

This is a major transit, because Neptune is crossing over the Descendant—one of the four angles our chart—and simultaneously opposes our Ascendant. Before we can handle the challenge that awaits us in our closest Seventh House partnerships, we need to ask ourselves if we are clear about why we want any relationships. Are we committing ourselves to the type of person who can help us to get in touch with our partnership needs? All of the Outer Planets, when moving into our Seventh, prompt us to ponder deeper issues regarding unions. In contrast, "personal" planets transiting this house would never think it necessary to rack our brains to figure out this motivational stuff.

In the long run, Neptune will feel comfortable influencing the matters of this house, because our Seventh involves themes of sharing. Neptune loves to see people merge and operate as one unit of consciousness. It's a planet that will try to melt away any formidable barriers between couples that otherwise would keep their hearts and souls from uniting in harmony. Neptune seeks to inspire blissful states of matrimony, even if we doubt that such a thing is feasible in our personal situation.

For those of us who are married, we'll need to assess whether or not a shaky union that has sprung a few leaks is worth saving. Since our Seventh House supports our ability to deliberate and to weigh all sides of any marital issue, it helps us to appreciate the many ways of viewing our problems. Therefore, Neptune's tendency to not rush into taking final action is encouraged. We can vacillate under Neptune's influence, waiting to "feel" when the moment is right to do something that triggers major change—this is not a decisive planet. As a result, years of buried frustration can pass before we tackle what needs to be confronted face-to-face.

Even the best of marriages have a few touchy areas that would benefit from mature, straightforward dialogue between the partners. Knowing Neptune's inclination to be indirect about such issues, we'll need to convince ourselves that open confrontation is "good" for the soul of this union. Otherwise, we can waste valuable time playing non-productive avoidance games. Even if we aren't married or with a partner, we seem have our own psychological denial routines to address. We'll need to understand why we side-track any attempt on life's part to get us intimately involved with another.

What Neptune probably appreciates most about this house is the likelihood that we won't have to experience it alone. It takes two to tango, and Neptune can be a very smooth and graceful dancer. Part of our growth at this point will involve how well we closely cooperate with another human being. On the up side, we may have many periods of feeling inspired and blessed precisely because we have a high-quality partnership, and because it's held together by genuine love and mutual respect.

Neptune's voice struggles to be heard in these cynical times of ours, but its message is and always has been that true love conquers all obstacles in its path. Much of what Neptune beneficially provides for any intimate union may sound corny to hard-nosed, practical types. Things can seem artificially ultra-romantic in a delusional, Hollywood-style way to those critics who believe the glass is always half empty at best, if not totally empty due to leakage from numerous tiny cracks. Still, Neptune and the Seventh House share the warming belief that two hearts beat stronger than one, especially when they are in perfect sync.

In general, this transit will force us to look at the people with whom we are most intimate as merely human, not as perfect saints. Natal Neptune in our Seventh may take illusionary routes when dealing with people, but transiting Neptune tries to illuminate us regarding those with whom we want to share our life. We're learning not to have unrealistic partnership expectations. Read more on this in Chapter Twelve.

OUR EIGHTH HOUSE

Here's another water house for Neptune, but this one contains dangerous sharks and dark whirlpools. The waters are definitely murkier and the undertow can be treacherous in the Eighth House, making navigating trickier for a planet already known for not having a clear direction. However, transiting Neptune does aim to heal any deeply conflicted issues by opening our heart rather just energizing our mind and our will. Problems are resolved once we've had a transformation of feeling and a purging of suppressed, negative emotion. Yet Neptune doesn't have to resort to drastic measures to get us to transmute our feelings, even while touring this natural domain of intense Pluto.

Whatever didn't get addressed in our Seventh House regarding our partnership dilemmas has a good chance of being permanently healed in this house. Depth awareness is something that both Neptune and the Eighth share in common, as well as a love of mystery and a talent for unearthing secret information. Neptune is adept at healing the wounded, and the Eighth House is famous for its experiences with reviving those who are nearly dead on some level. No troubled marital condition is totally deemed hopeless here. However, much work needs to be done to fix whatever may have been seriously damaged—trust in one another, for example. Couples caught up in the throes of an ongoing Eighth House love-hate relationship is capable of tossing derogatory innuendoes back and forth or of casting aspersions that further destroy mutual respect. Neptune sensitizes us to this tendency.

In our Eighth House, we normally suffer when we refuse to come clean by honestly seeing things as they really are. This house is hard on those who don't want to let go of cherished illusions, or who deliberately cloud matters and dodge thorny issues as a manipulative ploy. Neptune is not known for the cold clarity that we typically associate with Uranus, nor for the stark, gritty realism that comes easily to Pluto. Thus, during this transit, we'll feel an urge to uncover the truth about our most intimate unions as well as about our darker self—but only a little bit at a time. We know that we have to digest the sometimes shattering emotional changes that truth-seeking demands when we probe deeply into our committed relationships.

There is a chance that we'll spend a few lost years trying to fool ourselves about our marital situation, even if that's what we did when Neptune transited our Seventh. While stalling acts are tolerated in our Seventh—fairly weighing all sides of an issue takes time—our less-patient Eighth House will push for an ultimatum if that's what it takes to release the stranglehold that a bad union has on us. Although transiting Neptune can be excellent at showing us what's been mouldering in our inner basement, we will have to develop the guts and self-respect needed to make decisive moves that will bring ugly marital matters to a head. It's also important that we learn to live with whatever permanent life-alterations such a critical showdown has set into motion.

Wherever it transits, poor Neptune wants us to have a little peace of mind and sense of hope. It tries to show us a spiritual dimension of our essential Self that is conflict-free and eternally ours. However, the Eighth House knows that warfare is the natural state of the less-enlightened human condition. This house's natural rulers are Pluto and Mars—two militant energies. It may be a struggle to reach the sublime, internal states of tranquillity and bliss that Neptune promises, but our Eighth offers a steely psychological strength that Neptune lacks. There is something valuable to be gained by enduring our trials-by-fire in this house. Hopefully, we eventually will surrender to Neptune's positive flow and drop our guarded emotional defenses once and for all. Read more about this transit in Chapter Thirteen.

OUR NINTH HOUSE

Life can put us through hell when an Outer Planet (or *any* planet) moves through our Eighth, even if we do end up significantly transformed once our internal battle is over. Actually, Eighth-House inner work prepares us to receive the universal revelations to be found in our Ninth. The harder we dig to uncover hidden parts of ourselves in our Eighth, the more we understand and appreciate the growth-expanding potentials of our Ninth House. Entering this new house can make us feel as if we've finally left Hades and are now journeying to Mount Olympus, where the cool air is fresh and the sun shines forever!

Neptune loves the soaring sense of spirit that plays a major role in this house. This life zone encourages unrestricted physical and mental travel. We find wide open spaces that are begging to be intellectually and philosophically explored. Neptune, being the claustrophobic type, can't handle the thought of anything or anybody trapped in cages (although wombs are a different story), so "wide open spaces" of any sort appeal to this naturally-expansive planet. It also helps that this is a house of widespread interests and global concerns, especially because Neptune shows a compassionate interest in collective development along humanitarian lines.

In the Ninth House, broadly applied ideas and ideals can be widely distributed for the benefit and inspiration of all. This stimulates Neptune, a planet that also likes to disperse its energies far and wide. This transit is often a time when we feel moved to seek an education in areas that have long-range growth potential, not just for our sake, but also to benefit society. The Ninth is a house of future speculation that works well with Neptune, a planet as comfortable with dreaming about an idealized, faraway future as it is with exploring the ancient but forgotten past. It's living in the present that Neptune can't always handle.

It's the Ninth House's freedom to engage in endless "what ifs?" that comforts Neptune, also a planet of extraordinary possibility. Mental speculation about a better world for tomorrow—a favorite Ninth House pastime—ties in very well with Neptunian longings for a future in which universal understanding abounds. Neptune supports unifying belief systems that leave no one feeling like an alienated outsider. Both planet and house ask, "Why can't we all just get along?" They'd also both agree that it takes all kinds of people to make up a big, beautiful world! Lessons in tolerance that result in the breaking down of unjust social barriers are part of this transit.

The Ninth House also enjoys reaching out to make international connections. It insists on protecting diversity of thought, because there are many theoretical paths (religious and otherwise) followed by many cultures that help us understand life's ultimate purpose. What such paths have in common is that they require a powerful sense of faith and trust on our part. We need to keep in mind that, when mishandled, unbridled faith promotes a zealous "true believer" approach whereby only one path to God is recognized—just ask any "born-again" convert under Neptune's spell. For the most part, however, Neptune looks at our Ninth House and sees nothing but a vast field of dreams that can raise our consciousness.

This is the first house in our chart in which we encounter the masses, where we ponder what might be right for society's overall development. It's hard to use the abundant resources of this house for strictly self-serving interests although, historically, it's been done before by power-crazed monarchs and dictators. Everything about our Ninth encourages us to enthusiastically share what we have or what we know with many others, some of whom reciprocate by expanding our view of the world. The concept of freely exchanging spiritual and cultural enrichment for all to enjoy is very strong in the Ninth House.

People with many natal planets here are very concerned about society's challenge to find noble ways to upgrade itself and to inspire its citizens to bring out their best. This is a house of high social standards and of civic pride. Culture matters a lot for these folks. Transiting Neptune will spend many years here trying to convince us that humanity's collective mind is worth elevating, and that we can play an active and highly creative role in this process if we set our sights high and follow a grander social vision. See Chapter Fourteen for more about this transit.

OUR TENTH HOUSE

Now that we've gotten our hopes high about Life itself in our Ninth House, Neptune wants to make sure that most of that "feel-good" attitude is carried over into our Tenth, where we really get to practice what we preach. The Ninth deals with intellectual, theoretical speculation regarding society and how it can better remodel itself. In the Tenth House, what truly has a realistic chance to work often becomes codified as enforceable law—it's one more thing we have to conform to on a mass level to ensure collective sanity (and that's debatable, as is everything else coming from the Ninth).

In our Ninth, transiting Neptune felt the freedom to swim in the ideological waters of its choice, without running up against obstacles it couldn't circumnavigate. In the Tenth, things are not as flexible. Conditions are already set up for us so that we obey orders more than question them. The powers that be like things structured the way they are—safely traditional and conventional—and don't take too kindly to any planet, seemingly coming out of nowhere, that's hell-bent on shaking up the System!

However, that is precisely what all of the Outer Planets seem to have on their minds when they crash the guarded iron gates of the Tenth House. The Old Establishment must be toppled if it's turning us all into obedient sheep and killing our collective spirit—the part of us we were so careful to honor throughout our Ninth House transit. At least, this is how we start to see things.

This Neptune transit isn't about overthrowing a nation or about turning against lawful society. It's about overcoming our fear to alter the status quo of our public image. The System we are to fight is as much an internal reality—due to years of societal conditioning—as it is an impersonal, external structure that rules how we are to live. How much of this System's outer packaging have we bought without question? How little of it resembles our personal ideals and dreams? Neptune is most interested in unfolding these private dreams at this time.

The Tenth House demands that whatever is to manifest must to be made of substance, not hot air. If we think we have something of solid worth to offer the world, something that's also very inspirational in nature, Neptune is ready to protect and guide us on our path to success. Our Tenth House is more than just a place to establish a brilliant career that allows personal gains and privileges. It's also where we are obligated to be an upstanding member of society, and give back our finest contributions. Neptune has a strong social conscience as well, and is an irresistible force that encourages us to give more than we take from our community. This Neptune experience is no joy when we're in the public spotlight and, therefore, vulnerable to judgment, because we can be overly sensitive to attacks on our reputation. Nonetheless, it's important that we don't hide from the limelight that fateful timing, via the workings of a mysterious Universe, ushers into our life.

If the Tenth House is that place where our experiences of our father can be found, transiting Neptune tries to break down any walls built many years ago through misunderstandings between parent and child. Whenever Neptune is transiting a "people" house (the Third, Fourth, Fifth, Seventh, Tenth, or Eleventh), it works up a bit of magic to get everyone involved to bond a little closer by first overcoming difficulties of the past. Neptune can melt hearts that have been in a state of chronic deep freeze.

If we've had nothing but warm and loving contact with our dad, then Neptune just deepens our relationship. On a more profound level, Neptune here can help us make peace with all symbols of authority—probably because we have learned to stop fighting and instead start trusting our own inner sense of authority. More about this transit is found in Chapter Fifteen.

OUR ELEVENTH HOUSE

The one thing that Neptune quickly realizes during its tour of our Tenth is that, in that house, society seriously takes hold of our individual lives in concrete ways, and in a manner more committed to shaping and to controlling mass consciousness than in the Ninth. In the Ninth House our beliefs don't stand a chance to change the world if our message has no basis in reality; they certainly won't get the attention of society's true movers-and-shakers—in other words, Tenth-House types in power positions.

Neptune is a planet very much made for the broadest, collective application of its persuasive energy. Rare souls throughout every century have been able to effectively tap into Neptune's power to fulfill their intensely personal drives—even to satisfy their inner demons. The inspired, creative results in many instances made a lasting impact on humanity's collective psyche. Neptune somehow knows that its gifts are much too fantastic to selfishly hoard. I suspect that any attempt to bottle up Neptune's essence for obsessively egocentric purposes has probably led many on a downward spiral to madness and self-destruction, as in the case of "tortured" geniuses in history, whose chaotic lives implied that they were cursed by their extraordinary talents (too much Neptune for one person to internalize and safely contain).

As Neptune moves into our Eleventh House, we're probably well aware that we cannot benefit ourselves by using this planet's energy in exclusively self-seeking ways. Hopefully, this was a soul-lesson we vividly learned during Neptune's lengthy Tenth-House assignment. The need to make greater, selfless contributions to the collective experience becomes stronger in this house. Here, all walks of life can be found, a situation which challenges us to accept a wide range of humanity. The Eleventh also supports full-fledged individualists who work within group structures that allow for plenty of room to grow. Neptune is especially interested in getting us hooked up with groups that are creative and visionary.

During this transit, we may be looking for ideal camaraderie—not just for the joys of socially bonding with like minds, but for the potential to stir a quiet, cultural revolution within society. Neptune is a planet that has little trouble undermining structures that straightjacket the spirit, although it never attempts to do this in an abrupt, explosive manner. There is much in our current society that suffocates our collective soul— the daily grind of the business world alone can be deadly—and this transit inspires us to add new elements that uplift and emotionally elevate the lives of others. Under Neptune's gentle guidance, our intent is usually humane and compassionate.

Neptune senses that it can loosen up and experiment freely in our Eleventh, which is good, because this planet doesn't handle set rules and regulations very well. Here, at least, Neptune won't have to wear some type of dumb uniform! It's not a planet that can accept regimentation. Luckily, in our Eleventh, we're shown a world of constant social change, because the people associated with this house casually come and go in our lives. Steady, reliable relationships are not to be found here, especially with Neptune transiting the sector. Because of this, we learn to develop a friendly detachment regarding everyone we meet—we cannot afford to be possessive. Neptune certainly supports such an approach. Our connections can feel deep on an emotional level that's hard to describe, but life still demands that these relationships enjoy a lot of breathing room.

This can also be a wonderful time to feel free to pursue any colorful lifestyle that we wish to create for ourselves, as long as we remain within the law. There is a bohemian quality about Neptune in the Eleventh. We may find ourselves less willing to follow the conventions of the times, basically because we feel like

futurists who are far ahead of our contemporaries. It's an orientation that brings out the eccentric in us in ways that may baffle
others. Still, we'll probably come off as a kind and gentle oddball—not as a truly subversive threat to society. Check out
Chapter Sixteen for more on this.

Our Twelfth House

"It's so good to be back home," says Neptune. Of course, this house is
still a part of our earthly experience, not Neptune's actual place of
origin. However, compared to all of the other houses of our chart,
the Twelfth House feels the most Neptunian. For one thing,
there's not a lot of outside busyness or worldly demands to deal
with—all of that pretty much peaked in our Tenth House. In fact,
it's relatively shady, calm, and quiet in the Twelfth, and the volume is turned down low. Thankfully, Neptune never has a problem making its way through the silent dark, because it is a nocturnal creature, like Pluto.

During this transit, we may feel increasingly removed from the
day-to-day pressures and dramas of the outer, mundane world. We
cannot get caught up in them on strictly superficial levels. This is
a time to take stock of ourselves in terms of our spiritual identity,
rather than get hung up on the identification labels that society
has slapped on us. However, we can easily feel alone as we go
through this soul-searching life phase, because both planet and
house emphasize solitude. In this house, for once, Neptune can go
at its naturally slow and dreamy pace, even if that tempo proved
problematic for this planet several houses ago. Here, the expert
trance-maker is itself in a deep trance, and it feels wonderful—at
least, from Neptune's mist-shrouded perspective.

However, some of us during this transit may wonder if we're
losing touch with "reality," which is usually defined for us by others in very Tenth-House terms. Our culture does not encourage
lone-wolf lifestyles, because it sees them as warning signs of dangerous, anti-social behavior in the making. Of course, if we become
reclusive in a traditional, institutionalized way (such as isolated
monks in a hard-to-reach monastery), it usually would be deemed

acceptable, if a bit odd in today's world. Although a monastic life may not be what we wish to experience at this time, some of us cocooned in our home are already playing out a similar role.

During this transit, there will be many years to delve into our inner world in order to find out if we still have hidden pockets of unresolved pain or sadness that need to be addressed and healed. These are the parts of our psyche that have always felt disenfranchised and rejected by our ego. Transiting Neptune now plays Mother Teresa, wandering through the wretched slums of our unconscious, looking to rescue whatever still lingers in a pitiful state. Neptune also tries to dissolve the weakest or sickest parts of any structure, even if that structure is part of our most internal being.

For those of us who have previously done a lot of successful inner work and are less troubled within, this Neptune transit can plug us directly into the most creative energy the Cosmos can offer—those bright lights shining far away on the transcendental side of town, where the mystics and the angels get to play! This transit signals a time to surrender to the artistic impulse within us and to start composing beauty in any form that feels comfortable to create. We also will need to work on loving our body as much as we claim to love our spirit and our Divine Source. Any planet moving through our Twelfth opposes our Sixth House, so health symptoms may arise due to emotional energy imbalances.

Our Twelfth House is associated with the ending of cycles and with our need for closure. Any transiting planet here tries to help us to wrap up loose ends and unfinished business before that planet prepares us for the new start awaiting in our First House. Here, we are to unburden ourselves of psychological baggage that we no longer need (all of that weighty stuff that has kept us feeling suppressed for years). In this house, Neptune can be an illuminating force for our greatest good. Self-forgiveness seems critical to the overall success of this transit. We wash away those troubled inner parts that have kept us feeling less at peace with ourselves and with the world around us. See Chapter Seventeen for more on this transit.

NOTE

1. A technical note: Steven Forrest uses the term "astrological nadir" in his books (see *The Changing Sky* in the bibilography at the end of this book), probably to differentiate it from that point on the celestial sphere directly beneath the observer—also called the Nadir—used in horizontal coordinate systems; it is this Nadir that is always found opposite the Zenith. The astrological Nadir, instead, belongs to the ecliptic coordinate system and is exactly the same northernmost point also known as the Imum Coeli, also known to astrologers as the IC. The astrological Nadir, then, as always opposite the Midheaven and is not to be confused with the other Nadir. Whenever I use the term "Nadir," I'm referring solely to the "astrological" one.

PART TWO

OUR WONDROUS NEPTUNE TRANSITS

CHAPTER FIVE

DREAMS AND VISIONS OF ONENESS

UP IN SMOKE

Neptune can be very difficult to pin down and define. Think of trying to hold on to smoke. It cannot be done—even smoke trapped in a closed jar eventually disappears. Smoke is fluid and ever-changing. It easily demonstrates some of the traits of this structure-defying planet. In addition, too much smoke impairs vision, analogous to the blinding faith of some overzealous Neptunians.

The unmanifest world is Neptune's natural realm of expression. This planet's special power lies in its weblike ability to invisibly link everything on the inner planes, something that literally sounds much like the Internet's World Wide Web. This mega-phenomenon really exploded in the public's imagination when transiting Neptune and Uranus conjunct several times in the early 1990s. Neptune's dreamlike domain is an intangible dimension, devoid of clear-cut boundaries and any awareness of time. It's easy to get lost in Neptune's formless world, where nothing remains solid or permanent, where shapes and images are always blending, or changing into something else, or inexplicably vanishing like a mirage.

Neptune's vast, magnetic network enables meaningful connections (even synchronicities) to be made that seldom appear logical or rational. For the Neptunian, the wind-blown feather of a white dove landing near one's shoe could be assumed to signal the protection of a nearby angelic presence. The feather's symbolic meaning, something deeply felt, would be accepted without question, because Neptune does not motivate us to take things apart and objectively analyze the pieces. If we did, we'd destroy the magic at work. It's like putting hot spotlights on fallen snowflakes to get a better look at how exquisitely they are formed—they quickly dissolve.

Representing the unseen and less-knowable depths of the Collective Unconscious, Neptune underscores our free-floating capacity to visualize images. Indeed, Neptune creates the colorful and sometimes nightmarish scripts and landscapes of our nocturnal dream track. Apparently, at the core of our Inner Self, we are each the brilliant actors and directors of our own surrealistic "Fellini" movies. Neptune's rich inner imagery and vivid sensory response enables us to view life as a kaleidoscopic mass of intense colors, sounds, and morphing forms. Neptune paints powerful pictures in our psyche that are mesmerizing, hard to categorize, and yet powerfully seductive. Still, we recognize the deeper symbolism involved at a soul level.

Without access to nightly dream activity, we would eventually suffer psychological disintegration. To stay sane and functional, we don't necessarily need to remember our dreams—we just need to have them. Even if we were to be deprived of sleep for days on end, and "going bonkers" due to it, we would eventually enter the dream state in the form of waking hallucinations and other sensory-driven distortions. This suggests how strongly we must have those unearthly experiences in altered consciousness that only Neptune can provide. Of course, when we're up and about, Neptune also tries to speak to us in the form of daydreams, those brief moments when our mind wanders. Such musings and reveries allow us to take a dip in Neptune's quiet waters to reflect on our inner world of private dreams.

POOL OF INSPIRATION

Perhaps Neptune best represents the Collective Unconscious' emotional memory bank, as well as our human ability to creatively use that reservoir of pooled energy whenever inspirational avenues of expression are made available. This may sound too ethereal and otherworldly for some, but that's the way Neptune would have it. Unspoiled Nature has absolutely no trouble formatting Neptunian energy through its complex palette of colors and its unlimited variations of beautiful forms. When we view any natural setting, everything seems to fit together in a unified state of diversity. Gorgeous natural scenery triggers inspiration in poets, photographers, and artists due to Neptunian elements subtly at work on the senses. This is not an intellectual response.

However, for us earthlings, confined by the Saturnian limits of physicality and ego, it's often a different story—Neptune becomes difficult to skillfully handle. Most of its available outlets are downplayed by materialistic societies and earthbound cultures, devalued as being too "impractical" to be taken seriously. Therefore, we don't get to spread our Neptunian wings well enough to fly high while growing up, because this misunderstood planet's expression is deemed to be immature or out of sync with reality—perhaps it's okay to be immersed in playful fantasy during our pre-school and kindergarten years, but that's about it! We typically tend to abandon our imaginative Neptunian ways of being in the world by the time we are "responsible" adults.

MANNA FROM HEAVEN

Neptune symbolizes a fervent and sometimes quasi-conscious degree of hope. It sincerely believes that any and all human misery can be rendered painless and scar-free by acts of miraculous conversion. Neptunians, wanting to make people's character flaws melt away, yearn to save the "wretches" of the world by the amazing grace of God. We may totally and willingly place full faith in the almighty but unseen powers of divine healing and soul restoration. In an effort to transcend the brutish world of selfish, earth-trapped souls, under Neptune's influence we attempt to tap into the compassionate and all-forgiving Heart of the Divine for unconditional relief and solace. We seek to find everlasting comfort in the embrace of an all-knowing, all-accepting, and all-loving Higher Consciousness. Transiting Neptune stirs these feelings in the most emotional of ways, probably because we pay closest attention to our life situation when deep feelings are aroused.

We even find ourselves willing to create day-to-day rituals (symbolically meaningful to nobody else) that facilitate all things magical and awe-inspiring. Prayer, with hopes that all prayers will be heard and answered, is one of the most common of these rituals. Coming up with ordinary solutions or pragmatic approaches to mundane problems is less appealing. Neptune believes in manna from heaven, in mystical linkings, and in the possibility that impossible dreams can come true. Neptunians often put all of their unwavering faith into such yearnings with complete confidence and non-resistance. No other planet appears to completely surrender to a vision or an ideal as does Neptune. Under Neptune's influence, we can also fully give in to our greatest psychological weaknesses, letting them paralyze us on some level.

FLOOD SWEPT

Traditional astrology views Neptune as "watery" and "passive-receptive," even though mystic Poseidon wasn't described as a calm and tranquil god. Indeed, Neptune has a side to its nature that is passionate. It arouses our human capacity for powerful emotions that sometime overwhelm us, flooding our consciousness and drowning our ego. Neptune enraptures and enthralls. When inspired under Neptune's spell, we can be possessed of an almost fanatical degree of certainty regarding our beliefs and actions. Neptunian concepts and images often completely enchant us. In turn, we use them to captivate the world.

It's easy to imagine how all-pervasive our perceptions of life can become when a transpersonal planet as unbounded as

Neptune is involved. Coupled with logic-resistant emotional conviction, we can become defiantly unshakable in our Neptune-inspired beliefs, even when they are also emphatically self-delusional. No one can break us from this trance while we are in the throes of total inner commitment to our ideal, dream, or vision.

Those touched by Neptune often have a visionary sense of universality that they apply to life in an attempt to ensure the unity in consciousness they seek. Such can be the stuff that religious fundamentalism and other social "isms" are made of. For Neptune, dreams and visions of oneness are to benefit all people. No one is to ever be left out, abandoned, or exiled as a pariah. Experiencing total unification becomes the primary goal. However, those who are heavily Neptune-identified during this planet's powerful transits will need a cold splash of objectivity and levelheadedness to avoid being handicapped by their often-distorted interpretations of the environment.

Transiting Neptune readily "colorizes" relationships and events with highly subjective tones and shades. Here we run the risk of overgeneralizing and indiscriminately applying our beliefs, especially when powerfully redemptive feelings concerning humanitarian issues are aroused. For Neptune, the needs of the many override the needs of the individual. Unlike separatist Uranus, Neptune protects undifferentiated "mass consciousness." It seeks cohesion and homogeneity on the collective level.

TRUE BELIEVER

Neptune is known for its mesmerizing, evangelistic ways—resembling fiery Jupiter in action—and is blessed with a charisma that can capture wide audience attention. When Neptunians believe in anyone or anything, they believe 110 percent. However, transiting Neptune, like Jupiter, can easily overdo a good thing. We may not only believe in what we do wholeheartedly, but we also emotively reach out to others to inspire them to adopt and disseminate our beliefs—as long as they don't alter anything. The initial vision must remain pure and uncorrupted—an overly idealistic and unconsciously authoritarian requirement that most Uranians would have problems accepting.

With Neptune, some of us can hang on to thoughts, emotions, people, and situations for too long and for the wrong reasons. This becomes especially apparent during more stressful Neptune transits. We are usually the last to know or to acknowledge the underlying issues that feed our troubling situations or escapist behavior, even though such issues seem transparently obvious to anyone who closely observes and analyzes us. Regardless of how heartfelt our emotion-based assumptions can be, they can blind or numb us regarding the "truth" of any matter. Even our attempt to shield ourselves from realizing our illusions becomes less successful during challenging Neptune transits (the square, quincunx, and opposition). The ultimate truth has a way of spilling out, making a real mess of our life. The truth, however, forces us to grow, especially if we already have a history of operating under false premises because we fail to ground ourselves in reality.

A few of us undergoing tensional Neptune's transits (perhaps involving our Moon or Mercury) accept both white lies and deliberate deceits as viable ways to bypass pain and critical self-review. Chameleon-like Neptune has a talent for avoiding open exposure whenever possible, preferring to either hide in the shadows or constantly change colors to suit its immediate survival needs. Concealment becomes a well-developed but often misused strategy, especially regarding one's natal Neptune dynamics. Transiting Neptune is less willing to go along with any charades that we may have long used to avoid honest and direct self-encounter. It instead adopts a more aggressive role (the Poseidon factor?) in flushing out our secrets, if keeping such secrets and self-deceptions would further damage our emotional development or enslave us in a vulnerable fantasy world. Neptunian "flushings" are less harsh and merciless than are Pluto's purges, but they're equally potent over time. That which is unreal must be fully dissolved so that we finally see ourselves and others in the clearest light possible. Neptune works to undermine those accumulated distortions that have managed to overwhelm us.

THE WONDER OF LOVE

In the long run, we are forced to "fess" up when dealing with matters of the house that Neptune transits. Just how dirty is our laundry, anyway? These transits allow us the option of renewed vision and revived hope. Self-deception sometimes becomes an addiction that we need to address squarely. When we do, the fog we have helped to create eventually lifts. Neptune erodes faulty, crumbling structures, not sound ones; it renders them less stifling and frustrating. Why would we wish to continue putting our emotional energy and faith into something or someone so defective? If we don't love ourselves enough to completely let go of someone who is not good for us, then the love we attempt to pour into that person is misplaced and will never fill them up or be appreciated. Meanwhile, we're drained until we're running on empty. Even if it takes tragedy to break up our most unhealthy relationships, transiting Neptune will make sure that our soul is protected from further abuse. Neptune will offer sanctuary to the emotionally wounded in any way it can.

Our Neptune transits assist us in the process of spiritual recovery by helping us to forsake self-destructive paths, even though the pull to go down those seductive roads can be great. We are going to learn what a selfless act self-love can be. This is important because, under Neptune's spell, some of us can have a problem with allowing ourselves to be "selfish" or even self-preoccupied. By making peace within, we find that we have the abundant energy needed to give more to others. Self-love also means that we don't anticipate rejection. We can embrace a broader range of relationships without fear. Like any Outer Planet on the right track, we don't take things too personally once we have come home to our spiritual self. Defensiveness is not the problem it once was for us. In addition, with a well-handled Neptune transit, our tendency is to try to bring more beauty into the world. Dormant artistic talents can emerge and be put to use in quietly self-rewarding ways.

NEPTUNE TRANSITING A NATAL HOUSE

Neptune's transit through a house shows us where we are to learn about the pros and cons of putting an almost-godlike value on people and situations. Here is where our capacity for faith and trust can seem boundless, and be expressed in impersonal and sometimes transcendental ways. Still, we can be so psychically "open" that we may end up feeling defenseless and nakedly vulnerable to a wide range of questionable external forces. Neptune can weaken our usual ego-defenses. Of course, such a level of sensitivity may take many years of transit influence to develop. Neptune needs at least a decade to move through a house in most charts, and even longer when entering an intercepted house.

On the other hand, we might attempt to unwisely resist Neptune's dissolving power. Our ego typically abhors losing those protective Saturnian structures that block Outer Planet energies before they become invasive and dangerously destabilizing—energies that can enforce radical change beyond our control. Both the ego and Saturn cringe at hearing that something is "beyond our control." Therefore, we might fight the urge to go with Neptune's flow, unwittingly frustrating ourselves on the soul level. Without such accustomed ego boundaries, we can become ultra-sensitized and vaguely confused about issues to be dealt with in a transited house. Our potential to misinterpret life's situational signals runs high. Some of us scramble incoming data and blindly react based on incomplete or distorted information, often with an unquestioned sense of assurance and hope. We embrace what is false while rejecting the truth that underlies the issue in question, something that only serves to hurt us deeply in the long run.

At times, however, our openness allows for tremendously uplifting, awe-inspiring experiences that enrich our spiritual identity and enable us to feel unified with Life. Neptune can take our soul to rarefied levels of awareness regarding universal realities. This is a very lofty way to process any Neptune transit, but it's a path we can successfully take once we develop sufficient self-awareness (first earned the hard, Saturnian way). However, if we are the only ones to feel unified with everyone in our immediate environment, while they in turn regard us as just "strange," the results can be isolating and disillusioning. Some of us, in the process, may unintentionally scare others, who may view us as mentally unbalanced. This suggests that much inner work needs to be done during our key Neptune transits before we can afford to go out and effectively share our visionary enlightenment with the world.

Neptune symbolizes an egoless state—a reluctance or an inability to center around even appropriate self-interest for consistent periods of time. No wonder it's hard for some of us in our natal or transiting Neptune house to firmly experience any lasting sense of measurable growth or worth. We may not sense that we are building anything of solid value, at least in ways that any materialistic society would typically approve of and support. Even setting reasonable limits for ourselves can be a challenge, especially when that involves shutting out people who would otherwise drain us of our time and energy. We can easily be drawn into the web of those in dire need, in a state of calamity, or at a very low point in their lives. We'll need to pull away and learn to refresh our soul, as well as dig into the real motivation for why we expend ourselves so fully and, at times, so foolishly.

Neptune transits describe periods when we sometimes wish to have total immunity from the drudgery of daily living. This planet does not do well with the many dull, colorless facets of daily existence. It doesn't handle routines easily. Our natal and transited Neptune houses can be areas of unexamined illusion and escapism. Here, our innocent, naive expectations seldom are fulfilled by the harsher, uncompromising realities in our environment. We anticipate receiving more than we actually attract. These houses need a periodic dose of unbiased objectivity (Mercury) and no-nonsense reality-testing (Saturn/Pluto). Neptune seeks a better way to experience life, but our actual situation often fails to respond favorably to our unrealistic, inner hopes. The big letdown that can occur when the bubble bursts can be quite disheartening.

We often sense the ideal *potentiality* of our transiting Neptune house while we overlook or minimize the strength of this house's existing limitations. Neptune is forever eager to soar up, up, and away to giddy heights or else dive down to dramatic, all-encompassing depths. Our transiting Neptune house can reveal any ongoing blind spots, where we have been more heart-focused than head-smart. However, it becomes almost too easy for our "higher emotions," our spiritual goodness, and even our humane sense of decency to be manipulated. Ironically, sometimes we are done in by other Neptunians who are emotionally out-of-touch with their inner selves. We will learn, usually the hard way, not to operate solely based on our first impressions. In this house, we need more clarifying facts in order to carefully digest the issues in question; overlooking vital details can be hazardous.

NEPTUNE TRANSITING A NATAL PLANET

Both powerfully romantic and easily heart-flooded, Neptune suggests that we are also open and vulnerable to the downside of dark human emotion. Deep hurt and even deeper, unspoken pain are two very real Neptunian "realities." Neptune initially "sees" what it already believes, but often refuses to believe what it first sees, maybe because this planet just doesn't want to see *anything* after a certain point—it prefers to feel blissfully connected. The natal planet that Neptune transits can indicate where our attempts to lose our sense of self may be put through tests that are both soul-uplifting and agonizing. In some scenarios, even the angels cannot save us from ourselves as we dive, eyes closed, into a personal whirlpool of self-neglect.

Regarding the planet that Neptune transits, we need to ask ourselves whether we feel clean, or tainted on some level? Slow poisoning is a Neptunian potential. Are there skeletons rattling in our psyche's secret closets? Have we wallowed in destructively covert activity for too long? Will we permit ourselves to remove our masks and take off our disguises long enough to see what's always been inside us, waiting for a chance to fly? Most importantly, will an honorable degree of self-love prevail as we painfully expose ourselves to any confusion we feel about expressing this natal planet? Can we forgive our past mistakes long enough to catch sight of our beautiful inner light? If so, then this Neptune transit can truly put us on a path toward spiritual liberation.

Any natal planet contacted by transiting Neptune will find that it is able to tolerate long periods of being left alone, detached from the complexities of social stress. We begin to yearn for solitude, where we can be free from negative emotional stress. Neptune is the "mute" button on Life's universal remote control. However, we can also be receptive to brief but intensely spiritual interchanges that miraculously happen in the busy outer world. The inspiration that these experiences arouse is a vital life fluid to Neptune.

However, it is our daily struggle with the raw earthiness of living (including the confines of time, space, and the body itself) that prompts some of us to seek alternative, fantasy-filled escape routes according to our natal planet's needs. Energy is often lacking regarding this planet's expression—our transited Moon may not be concerned, because it likes to nap, but imagine our how Mars feels when it has so much work to do, yet so little get up and go? We might start off like (spirit-filled) gangbusters, only to fizzle out and lose focus for no apparent reason. We come to an unexplained halt at a point where we're tempted to abandon our objectives.

We might generally feel drained by the weight of mundane responsibilities and the pressing details involved. This may be because our spirit yearns to go home—to Heaven, Paradise, Nirvana, the Cosmic Womb, or to any place far removed from the heavy gravity of worldliness. As we attempt to withdraw from conscious body centeredness, our physical energy periodically wanes. We can become mysteriously devitalized, not only physically but mentally, if Neptune contacts our Mercury. Some blame this on a "leaky" aura, but it can also feel like an attack of low blood sugar. World-weary Neptune is simply trying to render us sleepy or unconscious so that we may better enter its intangible dimension in a proper state of acceptance.

Our transited planet is ready to find a special state of inner peace. We may pray here for varying degrees of protection from the storm clouds of life. We are inclined to seek serenity, quiet, and a private place to contemplate, meditate, go within, rest, or to simply be left alone—unfettered by the constant movement of a hectic, material world. For example, Neptune transiting our Venus and evoking its earthy side might mean that we are *unconsciously* drawn to the things we currently purchase, things that are often best enjoyed when we are alone. These items may often remain hidden in our closets or bedroom drawers, perhaps rarely used or seldom seen by others. Yet when we do remove them from their special hiding places to gaze at them, they can transport us into another, more peaceful world. Deep emotion and nostalgia are triggered. This is obviously a good transit for finding old treasures from another social era at yard sales and flea markets.

One more thing: our natal planet may learn to empathize. How does it *feel* to be in someone else's shoes? At times, we run the risk of *over-feeling*. We can become so emotionally overwhelmed that we shut down or dissociate ourselves from life's sadder realities—a natural water planet defense. Usually, however, we find that our heart leads our head as we seek more meaningful human contact. We could try to offer others this unearthly energy we're plugging into without any sense of ego demand or material payback. Neptune is trying to get us to feel that All is One! Boundaries are illusional and separateness does not exist. With this sense of universal bonding, Neptune helps us to sustain our compassion and allows us to tap into expansive Neptunian realizations about life.

IN DEEPEST WATERS

At this point, you've been well briefed about transiting Neptune, but let me add that your approaching assignment will require you to have your protective nautical gear on at all times. Make certain that your ultra-light, dual oxygen tanks are in proper working order—check for leaks! Above all, have the tremendous courage that all "psychonauts" need when diving below the familiar waves of waking awareness and into the mysterious, but often enchanting, waterworlds of the unconscious. You may start off feeling unsettled and a little woozy from the pull of powerful but invisible currents, which could put your emotional orientation at risk. You've been provided with just enough concentrated Saturnian stabilizing-solution to ward off most panic attacks. However, use this sparingly and only when absolutely necessary, because you cannot afford to remain too numb on this inner journey.

You'll see and feel things beyond your wildest dreams. The strangest creatures of your imagination may loom right before your eyes. Look, but don't overreact. Your surroundings, however exotic, will disappear without warning, and reappear in intoxicating new forms. Absorb, but don't try to analyze the experience immediately. In Neptune's world, nothing keeps its shape. The time has come to jump into the swirling, moonlit, dark purple waters and say goodbye to solid, dry land for a while. Plunge into the depths with faith and hope that this trip will reveal valuable hidden treasures along the way. And for Pete's sake, take off that waterproof watch—it's useless in Neptune's timeless realm!

CHAPTER SIX

NEPTUNE TRANSITING THE FIRST HOUSE

PARTLY CLOUDY

Neptune in our First House can start off as an ultra-subtle influence, so imperceptible that we may not register its effects for quite a while. It just oozes in, slowly and silently. Unlike noise-maker Uranus—which strikes like lightning and blasts us with startling new conditions—behind-the-scenes Neptune initially operates without much event-oriented drama. It stealthily works on our psyche, in murky realms far beneath the surface of our conscious, daily self-expression. Nobody witnesses Neptune's chemistry in action at this early stage.

Without calling attention to itself, Neptune invisibly uses its potent energy to dissolve whatever has become psychologically over-crystallized within us (especially nagging fears, doubts, and secret self-rejections). We have no reliable clue as to what's going on during this phase of the transit, except that we may feel vaguely off-centered, strangely discontent, or emotionally unclear about our life focus. Although we may not be able to put our finger on just what's bothering us about our lives at the moment, we feel that something is not right with this picture. A few years may pass before we have the courage to find out what's really troubling us. Things looks cloudy now, but that's not necessary bad.

A HEALING VISION

One problem is that we can't sharply define what we currently want for ourselves. Things are starting to blur, creating uncertainties about our future direction. We don't seem to be moving forward, at least not very fast. We're not invigorating our new cycles with confidence and power, often because we are out-of-focus regarding our immediate objectives. Perhaps we're mysteriously running out of steam, inexplicably abandoning seemingly ideal goals that we were sincerely pursuing before this transit took hold. Fresh dreams may take their place, although they don't seem likely, at the moment, to get off the ground. They also appear impractical and far-fetched to others. All of this uncertainty mystifies us as much as it does those close to us, who may wonder if we're unraveling at the seams.

Nothing looks clear and definite to us. There's no need for an eye-doctor, but maybe it's time to see a spiritual therapist. Our surface self-projection (symbolized in part by our Rising Sign) will undergo gradual but pervasive changes during the next several years. Certain facets of the aging persona we still semi-consciously display to the world are now ready to fall apart and dissolve. This persona might be on its last legs anyway, unbeknownst to us. Our accustomed ways of moving out into our environment are becoming obsolete and unrealistic, even damaging, to the broader development of our soul. Therefore, certain rigid behaviors and blind spots are now to melt away and make room for more adaptable and better-integrated qualities that demonstrate a tuned-in level of selflessness in action.

Neptune, our key to the power of self-healing, can urge us to undo whatever is unhealthy to our unfolding self-awareness. This planet attacks fundamental, inner weaknesses that, if left untreated, could sabotage and insidiously destroy existing frameworks (just as termites, hidden for years, eventually threaten to collapse a home's foundation). Ironically, also ruled by Neptune are those very same weaknesses that erode existing faulty structures. The problem and the solution are both contained within the planet itself. Our Neptune transit helps dislodge whatever is defective within us, those unredeemed parts that we have failed to honestly address in the past. We now have a chance to reveal and heal the self-sabotaging elements of our First-House identity. Meanwhile, the finest traits of our Ascendant are now to be repackaged in a more appealing, even charismatic way.

BAD KARMA?

In this house of self-starting activity, we are to deal with how we project ourselves into the here-and-now to meet the environment that we attract—sometimes to initiate independent action and sometimes to defend our autonomy. Neptune doesn't appear to put its best foot forward at first, although sometimes we can act as though everything is wonderful and conflict-free in our world. We can seem flaky to people who watch us slowly become unglued, lose our center, or appear plagued by contradictory moods. Although we can seem less solid and reliable to others in our closest relationships, because Neptune also opposes our Descendant, imagine how *we're* feeling—not too secure with our self-definition. Therefore, if we are not acting like "our old selves" during this time, that's perfectly all right. That old act is getting stale anyway. This is just Neptune doing its preliminary metamorphic magic on us. We're caught in a yucky transitional stage, feeling a bit ego-woozy and shapeless.

Initially, we may not feel at all alive and well during this transit, but with a little faith and trust in a Cosmos that knows exactly what it's doing, we will eventually be able to present more of our spiritual, humane self to the world. However, nothing is to be rushed in Neptune's timeless dimension. There are no pressing deadlines to meet. Some of our personal problems may seem to drag on endlessly and unfairly, making us wonder if "bad karma" or plain old rotten luck is finally catching up with us. This is partly due to our inner insecurities concerning personal change, and partly to general feelings of lethargy. Neptune on the Ascendant commonly coincides with low physical energy and a lack of initiative. We don't feel that we have our usual body's vitality at our beck and call. Worse, life could seem like one big yawn.

Saturation Point

If Neptune slows things down, it's because—as a force enabling our ultimate self-illumination—it needs to be exceedingly thorough in its purging and purifying process. For optimum results, it must completely saturate whatever it contacts with its lubricating, cosmic essences. One interesting point is that Neptune rules oil, and oil prevents things from rusting, or from becoming brittle or cracking due to too much dryness. Similarly, Neptune tries to keep our soul sufficiently moisturized. We'll need to be philosophically patient and hopeful that any presently muddled outlook on life will someday give way to greater vision, clarity, and deeper self-understanding—especially as our identity surrenders to and merges with higher (divine) consciousness.

Meanwhile, we look in the mirror and don't care for what we see. Who is this weary, confused-looking person staring back at us, who's having one too many "bad hair" days? Who is this part-time phony who daily shows to the world a personality that prevents others from getting a real glimpse of the hidden self within? That's just one side of the coin. Neptune transits, although often tied to self-deception, also teach us about trusting the gentle, benevolent flow of the universal process. Such trust means no longer having to hide behind glamorous facades that camouflage our human vulnerabilities. We need not paint the outside world as a cold and uncaring place. Self-acceptance, leading to true self-love, becomes a dynamic lesson of this transit.

That Light Within

Through the gateway of our Ascendant—regardless of what sign is involved—we can present a personalized identity that keeps its focus on surface appearances. That includes anything from how we look to the idiosyncratic body language we use. These are the behavioral signals that we first send out to others, who then develop their initial impressions about us. Our Ascendant (a.k.a. Rising Sign) is a real part of our total make-up, despite its label as the "mask" we wear in society (a term that unnecessarily makes it sound like it's something we fake). Unlike our Moon, our Rising Sign does not show deeply ingrained facets of our being. Its qualities are more open to being modified, given the right stimuli. In any case, our Ascendant is certainly a visible part of who we seem to be, and what we are willing to display day in and day out. It describes what's readily "rising" out of us in our daily surface interactions with life.

Neptune transiting this natal angle suggests that it's now time to go far below the surface and tap into less-obvious layers of our Ascendant sign's potential. We are never to abandon the qualities of our Rising Sign—we simply need to find better ways to universalize them and to allow for a fuller experience of their transpersonal power. After all, each zodiac sign symbolizes a mighty archetype that describes a process of being. However, this implies a challenge to alter our waking consciousness. The Ascendant is a separative point in the birthchart, where themes of self-focus and self-interest are strong; therefore, Neptune can help us soften our sense of boundaries, our sense of "me-versus-them." Neptune, as the antidote to duality, will erase sharp lines of division whenever possible.

As Neptune moves through our First, we eventually feel as if more of our inner self can flow out into the world, while more of humanity simultaneously pours itself into us. Neptunian energy is inclusive and all-encompassing. This may sound wonderfully spiritual, but learning to discriminate regarding what we will absorb will be important, because what could also pour in might be some of the Collective Unconscious' conflictive energies—the stuff of social maladjustment. Of course, if some of us are already too unstable or ego-depleted before this transit kicks in, any further destabilizing of our tenuous personal parameters could prove dangerous to our mental health. The rest of the chart needs to provide clues: for example, does natal Neptune already square or quincunx our Ascendant or the ruler of the Ascendant? If so, this Neptune transit might flood some of us with an overwhelming urge to lose our identity completely, leaving our psyche totally fragmented and leading us into oblivion with a one-way ticket in our hand. You may wish to read Liz Greene's book on Neptune[1] to understand why this may happen to some folks more than others. My point here is that Neptune acts as a destabilizer, making an already shaky psychological condition even shakier.

CLOSET CLEANING

Astrologers don't know everything about Neptune—not yet—but we do know that, during this planet's major transits, we may be required to confront pain and hurt that's been buried for years. We don't go immediately from "unenlightenment" to "bliss consciousness" until we have done some deep-sea diving through the turbulent transitional stages—exactly where some of the scariest sea monsters of our psyche dwell.

Neptune going through our First (and also through our Fourth, as we shall see) can trigger some unpleasant psychological material to float like scum to the surface—or furiously gush out like a steamy geyser, in true Poseidon style. In question here is intense emotional material that we have masterfully repressed. Some of us can have traumatic memories of scarring events from long ago—even from past lives—that have not, as we had assumed, sufficiently healed. Therefore, we relive some of these forgotten images, but with new people who are part of our current life situation. We finally get to feel our pain more fully in a non-denial state, which can make things temporarily agonizing, until Neptune helps us gain a broader perspective on these highly sensitive issues.

We are to get a better sense of the evolutionary lessons that such difficult early conditions have provided. We don't necessarily have to forgive the perpetrators from our past (although true Neptunians probably would want to do so in order to feel completely healed), but we are, at least, to finally stop harboring these toxic wounds. Some of us will face unfinished business of a serious nature through the bubbling up of long-submerged feelings.

SOULSCAPE

It's inspiring to state that Neptune passing through this house can make us more aware of artistic beauty—and filled with a yearning to create it—as well as more spiritually uplifted or uplifting to others. It's cool to read that we may start to see auras, develop the healing touch, and even have out-of-body experiences. All of these are within the realm of Neptune's domain and its cornucopia of infinite possibilities. However, these may not be the most important goals to first aim for during this soul-searching transit.

Our more urgent need is to get real with ourselves in a non-judgmental way. We have a lot of clearing out to do, and maybe some tears and fears to shed. This is not because we are funda-mentally "bad" people, or innately messed-up, or born to attract tons of karmic punishment. Living in today's harsh, coarse world can be very tough on the soul because society's junkiest messages are too easily implanted in our heads, preventing us from moving confidently closer to our spiritual center. It's hard to find our way back Home, considering that the media bombards us with so many chaotic images.

We are also told that it's a rat race out there, and we've seen examples of a dog-eat-dog mentality where the aggressive and the ruthless seem to thrive and enjoy worldly rewards. All of this craziness makes less and less sense to many of us while Neptune moves through our First. It becomes unreal to the suppressed soul inside of us who is tired of keeping up false appearances. We need to discover how we can be beautiful to ourselves, how we can develop an inner sense of calm, and how we can attain real love without the struggles and uncertainties we've known before. We are also to learn how to achieve deeper levels of everlasting inter-nal security. As clichéd as it sounds, the kingdom of heaven first comes from within, with just a little help from the angels.

Neptune comes alive when our faith is strong. This is an excellent time to hold on to a progressive, loving self-image that can be translated into an enriching soul experience. Whatever we can do to bring out our goodness—while helping others to realize their inner light and accept their greater social obligation to serve humanity—can be joyously fulfilling during this Neptune transit. It all sounds a bit saintly, but so be it. We need to let this spiritual energy flow and help us to embark on new and wondrous beginnings!

KALEIDOSCOPE EYES

We can go through strange and hard-to-describe periods, during which we feel lighter than air, as if not entirely in our bodies. Vibrating at Neptune's frequency means that we open ourselves to receiving an abundance of universal love and joy. This may mean feeling elated for no particular reason, even a bit floaty. However, Neptunian highs are not easily sustained, especially if we've cheated to get them (with, for instance, a six-pack or two of beer on a lazy, lost weekend). Any mystic will tell you that an artificial Neptunian high is nothing compared to the real thing! We'll need to act on any fresh, uplifting visions we've been granted. Even if we wake up some mornings feeling a little disoriented, this is a life period during which we can be in awe of how beautifully the Universe's special plans unfold for us, when we choose to place our full faith in the divine process at hand.

NEPTUNE/MARS TRANSITS
NOT SO PUSHY

Neptune must seem so weird to Mars: it has no muscles, doesn't like to be perpetually awake doing things, and often cries, or else hugs strangers for no reason—sometimes both at the same time. Mars is also a bit baffling to Neptune: it runs on sheer brute force, cannot deal with silence, sees people or things as objects to attack or exploit, and only cries when angry—after it first throws a wicked punch! With Mars, it's others who usually end up crying. How are these two ever going to get along during the lengthy duration of a Neptune transit? Well, Neptune does have the upper hand because it's the one orchestrating this transit. Realizing this can make our Mars squirm, because we may feel that we're less able to be fully in charge of our actions during this crazy period.

Our natal Mars can symbolize many qualities, but one thing Neptune would like to dissolve as soon as possible is this fiery planet's selfish streak. Mars (unmodified by its sign) typically supports exclusively self-centered interests, which it deems essential to its immediate fulfillment. Its desires are not collective in orientation, and not even *other*-oriented on a one-to-one level. Mars has animal-savvy instincts that ensure earthy survival, yet its actions often can be based on raw aggression and on a "Who cares about you, what about *me*?" policy. Mars, whether on the offense or on the defense, will bite first and ask questions later. This planet's a born taker, not a giver, even though we try our best to domesticate such a wild dog.

Neptune is hardly an assertive planet, much less aggressive. Its metaphysics lead it to believe that things will either flow to us effortlessly if they are meant to or, if not, they'll just drift out of reach for someone else to deal with. We really don't have to be pushy or grabby to get what we want. A little prayer and visualization might help, but getting our desires met is ultimately not up to us. Benevolent, guiding forces of the Cosmos are in charge of our destiny. At least, that's Neptune's assumption. The message here for Mars is, "Don't rush to stir up hasty action at this time. Wait for subtle signals that will let you intuit when to do something. Go within and be still." If we have our Mars in Pisces or in Taurus, that advice could sound perfect. However, if we have Mars in frisky Aries or in jumpy Gemini, we'll have a problem with this "go within and be still" business!

FOGGY ROAD AHEAD?

In our culture, taking action is valued more highly than just sitting around, contemplating action (which Uranians would rather call "brainstorming"). Action gets situations going in the physical world (Mars' domain). Wanting to start something *now* instead of later feels natural to Mars. However, at this time we get mixed messages. Our current environment, colored by transiting Neptune projected onto our world, is not allowing for well-defined beginnings. The energy to initiate new plans can be weak, especially with the square, quincunx, or opposition involved. Mars likes things to be sharp and crisp—in black or white—but Neptune dulls the edges and makes the colors appear less distinct. We may feel that our actions are not getting off the ground for some mysterious reason, especially if we are trying to launch something bold and new, backed up by a lot of Mars-approved self-absorption.

We may feel inspired by what we are trying to accomplish, whether it's fighting for a big social cause or just setting into motion some hare-brained scheme to quickly and effortlessly get whatever we desire. With the square or the opposition, transiting Neptune suggests that some of our moves, from a practical perspective, are not smart ones. We could be wasting more time and energy than we realize, with little to show for our efforts. However, with that comforting sense of hopefulness that Neptune is known for, we still may dedicatedly apply our energies to immediate goals even as things fail to gel. We can take on a stupid, "What, me worry?" attitude as we gamble ever more deeply with our fate and fortune.

Transiting Saturn would have stopped such ill-planned activity long ago, usually after noticing a few, tell-tale signs confirming that the timing is bad and that we need to go back to the drawing board. Not Neptune, which instead lures us on to further botch our plans of action. This is especially so if what we wish to do is highly egocentric or is too steeped in self-absorbed fantasy. However, Mars loves a challenge and doesn't want to give up and quit just because a project may have sprung a few leaks. That would sound gutless and weak to this daring planet. Therefore, some of us may continue along a shaky path that demonstrates to others how well a mix of blind will and lack of common sense leads to confusing fiascoes.

BRAKE FAILURE

If we are already true Neptunians at heart—check for natal clues—we probably don't understand or appreciate the wisdom of limits. We could view our earthly incarnation as doing time in jail for unknown crimes we did not commit (perhaps due to all of that "original sin" business). To hear some of them tell it, Neptunians have been set up by cruel fate. Throw in a rotten natal T-Square plus too many retrograde planets, and they feel certain that they've been framed and found guilty by a cosmic kangaroo court. Experiencing the personal and pain-producing limitations that life sometimes demands simply underscores this unconscious belief. For some of us, Neptune transiting our Mars does not recognize the need for safety brakes. Escapist spontaneity can be glorified, and the power of our self-will appears to be unlimited. Therefore, during a Neptune/Mars transit, be warned that any impractical action we take can blow a tire and cause us to veer off the road to success, only to end up stuck in the mud—or worse, to sink deep in quicksand!

DISAPPEARING ACT

This doesn't mean that we are not to do *anything* of vital personal interest during this almost two-year transit. That would be crazy-talk astrology, as well as unworkable in today's busy world. Simple, miscalculated actions can result in minor but forgettable disappointments. It's the bigger, more elaborate affairs that we'll have to watch out for, such as relocating because of a career transfer, or getting married, or flirting with risky, addictive behavior. The more complex the activity, the more likely that complications may creep into the picture and rain on our parade. This is not voodoo at work. It's usually the result of ignoring significant details and not paying attention to minor but solvable problems *as they arise*. Neptune rules blindness, and here we are taking bold action with our eyes closed to certain harsh, "in our face" realities. We may try to sweep a few things under our magic carpet and pray they disappear, but they don't. That's when we wish we could disappear, but we can't. Things we choose to overlook now conspire to trip us up later, during periods of even greater vulnerability.

So, what's the big lesson? Are we to suffer defeat, sacrifice a dream, or get paranoid about losing our autonomy and retaliate by creating little disaster scenes wherever we go? None of the above is necessary. The way to be alive and well with our Neptune/Mars transit is to listen more carefully to our inner voice—as well as to people we trust—when the message is, "Stop working, you're tired. Get some rest and refocus energy for a while. Listen to some music, or take a nap. Don't force action." Or maybe the message is, "You're angry but you're also confused and emotional right now. Back off from direct confrontation. It's not the right time to lock horns with another. Reflect on your grievances in private, but wait for a more conducive environment to share feelings with whomever has upset you." That's the inner voice of wise old Neptune whispering to us.

EASY DOES IT

Mars needs to know that gentle actions in life can be more effective than slam-dunks. Less-forceful approaches can do the trick. Even not taking certain actions at the moment can set up a better timetable for getting the results we want later, when the tide is high and the fish are practically jumping into the boat. Remember, Neptune rules manna—even tuna!—from heaven. If we feel as if we're in a state of limbo—more than just indecisiveness— it's probably for a good reason. The message is: don't fight it. Lay low or do little bits at a time, at a stress-free pace, but save the rest to tackle at some future date when it feels right and when Neptune gives us the affirmative nod.

Neptune is not trying to punish us for following our Martian impulses. It's trying to teach us that misapplied energy is a time-waster that can slow us down in the long run, something that Mars would especially hate to have happen. It's better to be poised and ready to act, but to also wait quietly until the situation is ripe, rather than be too quick to take big plunges at this moment. We'll need to hold back a little more than usual to reserve our energies. We don't have that much energy to burn right now anyway, including our sexual energy. Oooh, did somebody say sex?

EROTIC SPELL

Sex is big on Mars' list of favorite activities—even when alone! However, drowning in a hot romance is not the best idea when Neptune aspects our Mars in stressful ways. Even with the sextile and the trine, the experience may be strangely unfulfilling, because pure sex is too wantonly physical and unsatisfying for ethereal Neptune, who'd rather just cuddle and doze off. Mars, usually able to separate from the influence of other planets, now finds itself easily seduced. Our guard may be down, allowing a strangely passive quality to emerge, passive but a little reckless. Certain natal Mars signs (Pisces and Libra) are more vulnerable in this regard than others (Virgo and Aquarius).

What's so bad about being seduced once in a while? Perhaps nothing, if we can emotionally detach from the experience long enough to resist getting hung up on what's happening. Sex becomes a grand escape, offering exotic pleasures that make our ordinary, humdrum life more bearable. Therefore, it holds a special enchantment for us, and we don't necessarily have to be deeply in love with our partner-in-play. However, that's not how things turn out for some, because Neptune can fool us. We can be swept head-over-heels in a kind of lust that masquerades as the rare expression of soul love. Sex becomes an intoxicating drug. We want more and more of it, even as we find ourselves becoming weaker and weaker in terms of our autonomy and self-will.

Before Neptune came along, we used to be better at fending for ourselves. We were less susceptible to letting others break down our defenses. Can we still resist? What if our alluring new partner is married with children? What if that sounds like our situation at home? What if there are other things that are socially inappropriate about this affair, explaining why we choose not to go public with it? It may make no difference after a while, because we crave our magical fix with our dream lover. This can be an insidious Neptune at work, as Mars becomes a sucker for such stimulation. Mars isn't particularly sensitive to the pain it can cause others. This planet will encourage us to keep illicit affairs alive as long as we are thoroughly wrapped up in the experience. Once the thrill is gone, however, our Martian urge is to dump our partner with no regrets.

Later, should this relationship fall apart because it was built on weak threads of fantasy, our Mars response is to suddenly snap out of it and detach as if nothing had happened. Perhaps we will claim to have been the victim of animal magnetism and hormonal frenzy. We may start to believe our own hype—that we were enticed into the situation, entrapped against our will and better judgment. It's somewhat true that, under Neptune's influence, we can feel as if we are in a trance, possessed by an alien entity who plays by looser rules of moral conduct. In the end, however, we need to own up to our Neptune/Mars experience and not to come off as such a pitiful pawn of tempting circumstance.

It's probably best not to overly encourage too much sexual adventure when transiting Neptune aspects our Mars. Maybe Mars transiting our natal Neptune might stir up delicate romantic feelings that can transcend typical carnal appetites. Tender love-making during this brief time period could take on spiritual overtones. However, with Neptune doing the transiting, it's Mars that becomes activated, and Mars doesn't spiritualize energy easily. It fights Neptune's essence: the experience of just letting things flow without forcing action on something or someone.

FLIPPING OUT

What about anger? We can relate to that basic Martian emotion. However, astrological Neptune is not used to dealing with that feeling—apparently the poor thing was archetyped without an anger-reflex muscle! Here's where we could run into problems, because pacifist Neptune will try to put out the fires that Mars generates when feeling upset or threatened. Mars naturally flames out, scorching its adversaries, as its quickest way of protecting itself. At the very least, it will make enough noise to frighten away potentially dangerous foes. If we look fierce, wear red paint, and bang drums loudly all night, the evil spirits will not visit us. If they do, we'll just have to fight back and destroy them, even at the risk that they might demolish us first. It is this pit-bull mentality of Mars that Neptune finds so incomprehensible. Neptune wonders what's so bad about first trying to merge with these so-called "evil" spirits in an attempt to become one with them and thereby dissolve enmity. Of course, this New Age approach sounds totally nutty to Mars, who'd love to hurl blissed-out Neptune into a tar pit!

How does this play out in the course of a Neptune transit? Neptune attempts to dilute the passions of Mars, especially when they turn ugly and self-destructive. We're prompted to find more creative, non-violent ways to harness our temper. Neptune believes in re-channeling frustrated energy, taking it to higher and more sublime frequencies. However, it can also erode the safe boundaries that have kept our disturbing Martian conflicts in check.

If we're already known to flip our lids over ridiculous stuff ("Hey, who the hell reprogrammed the remote?"), then Neptune can open up the floodgates of barely contained hostility and rage. Turbulent Poseidon takes over in all of his sea-swept fury and stirs up a little mayhem. Most of us won't process this transit in such an upsetting way (what a relief), but there are a few of us who may literally feel beside ourselves with anger, as that alien entity takes over. We're now talking about being alive and well *over the edge!*

Some of us, for whatever reason, refuse to contact our inner Mars, just as we avoid our inner Pluto. However, during this transit we may have to face up to our denial of angry feelings and emotional injury. Neptune, realizing that a healing is overdue, will help us to spew out buried emotions that reveal the depth and extent of any long-held pain. Once we bring our repressed, vitality-sucking anger out into the open, there is a better chance that it will cease to have power over us, instead of festering in the dank chambers of our psyche. Neptune, not just Pluto, deals with ejecting toxic substances that could poison our body and mind. From this catharsis, more energy is made available, and we discover a healthier ability to directly express those stormy feelings that otherwise could create internal havoc.

NOTE

1. Liz Greene, *The Astrological Neptune and the Quest for Redemption,* Samuel Weiser, Inc., 1996.

CHAPTER SEVEN

NEPTUNE TRANSITING THE SECOND HOUSE

INTANGIBLES

Now here's an unusual challenge: Neptune spending the next fourteen years or so of our life on stable, dry land in a realm that values that which is tangible and well-formed. Anything less is considered immaterial. Our Second House is a life zone where we normally want things to be rock solid, firm, and reliable, like the ground we walk on—even if some of those things are fundamentally abstract in nature (as they might be with Aquarius or Pisces on the cusp of the Second). Regardless, they must feel real to us to be appreciated and deemed of worth.

Obviously, the Second House is interested in securing possessions that seldom resonate with ethereal Neptune—a planet associated with the incomprehensible state of "nothingness." This house would rather be well-stocked with lots of "somethingness" at all times! Neptune doesn't understand our attachment to things that remain intact, as if immune to the evolutionary, form-altering flow of existence. Why should we value anything trapped in a frozen state of permanence? Neptune is generally unimpressed by the relatively lifeless properties of matter.

In Neptune's rarefied world, pure consciousness can effortlessly create beautiful, complex, intangible images that seem more real than anything of earthly origin. Magical Neptune can always manifest whatever it needs instantly, as well as create quick disappearing acts. However, all images born of Neptune on this level constantly transmute their form. Energy does not become imprisoned within Neptune's fluid, ephemeral structures. Supposedly, this is what the scenery will be like in the afterlife. Neptune also describes the colorful but changeable stage settings of our dream world.

THE MATERIAL TRAP

This transit may be about learning to recognize how our material desires and possessions, while necessary for functioning on the physical plane, can also trap our energies and stifle our inner being. Our Second House is where we attract and gather objects that fortify our worldly awareness, while also shielding us from invisible, otherworldly planes of consciousness. We have a better chance of connecting with those realms in Neptune's favorite retreat, the Twelfth House. Transiting Neptune entering this house presents unfamiliar conditions that may be once-in-a-lifetime experiences. Nothing in our past has prepared us for what's about to happen here.

How old we are when this transit begins makes a difference, because our material values often change with age and worldly experience. How we view this transit at the idealistic age of twenty-three will be different from how we interpret it at seventy-three, when we are perhaps wisely more accepting of the outer world on its own terms. Still, what can be commonly felt is that Second-House matters, especially financial ones, are less able to offer us reliable security. Although we attach ourselves to solid ground, it slowly shifts due to internal rumbles and to the outer collapse of support systems. Things can feel shaky, uncertain, and confusing regarding long-range plans to build sound financial structures. This can become quite a challenge to the part of us that wants to magnetize and hang on to whatever attracts us emotionally.

Neptune tells us to not become so fixated on firm guarantees of material fortification in the years to come, especially if we are already amassing wealth or possessions for the wrong reasons. Our Second House is usually not a status-oriented area (unlike our Tenth House), but we may be surrounded by prized objects that do not help us to reveal who we really are, deep down inside. Is that snazzy Porsche in the garage a true symbol of our inner self? How about the opulent ten-bedroom mansion in the ritziest neighborhood we can afford? Actually, this sounds more like transiting Neptune's Second-House fantasies of winning the lottery than it does our current condition. Some additional questions to consider are: Do the items that we own and value help us to make contact with a more profound sense of eternal being? Do the things we have around us touch our soul? Do they raise our consciousness? Most importantly, can we fully love owning such things but also live without them if necessary, or do they enslave us on some level? Do our possessions possess us? This transit will help us to answer these questions.

CRAVING BEAUTY

Neptune favors beautiful objects like artwork, exquisitely designed furnishings, and picturesque landscapes outside of one's bedroom window—in fact, anything that's rich in color and texture. Neptune doesn't do well with squalor, although some out-of-touch Neptunians seem to gravitate toward trashy, seedy environments devoid of beauty as a result of being on a severe, self-deprecating binge. Anything that inspires our sense of aesthetics and visual wonderment can be well-supported by this transit, because this draws us closer to our spiritual center. That can mean enjoying the simple but awesome beauties of nature, or anything with a calming quality that helps us to relax and go within ourselves.

I'm not about to present a shopping list of Neptunian items to purchase for the next decade or so, even though buying and setting up an aquarium in our den might be a nice touch. The slow meanderings of colorful fish amid swaying aquatic plants can be very soul soothing, not to mention hypnotic to watch. We will all need to explore on our own what works for us, listening to our inner voice for wise guidance on future spending. However, it's a good idea to be more selective and realistic with our purchases, because our self-discipline may be weaker than usual.

SPIRITUAL EXPENSES

Sometimes what we might really learn to value is not anything manufactured, but that which comes straight from the heart of another being—for instance, a deep, full-body massage by someone who possesses true healing talents. Neptune is coaxing us to spend money on whatever get us in touch with ourselves, and that can include resources that help us to navigate our inner space. If the body is the temple of the soul, it's going to need its periodic tune-ups to prevent self-created blockages that make it impossible for our soul to thrive and make its presence known. Spending our hard-earned money on yoga, aura cleansing, tai chi lessons, or even ballroom dancing could show us new ways of viewing money's therapeutic function in our lives. Paying for art lessons or musical training, perhaps learning to breathe and thus sing better in the process, would also be a great way to work with this transit.

We may not become another Michelangelo or a big hit on Broadway, but that's not what Neptune's trying to evoke. It is merely helping us to reclaim an awareness that dormant, less ego-driven talents exist within us that need our tender cultivation. Not everything of true worth is to be found outside of us, to be had for the right price in a consumer's paradise. Eternal assets exist that can better ground us on Earth, while they also enable us to feel anchored to transcendent realities. As in most of Neptune's transits, what is changing inside us at this time can be very subtle, and invisible on the surface. The culture we live in usually gets in the way of the unfolding of less materialistic yearnings. We could even feel a troubling degree of guilt for not being as hungry and eager as others to make the big bucks and show the world the power of our prosperity.

This can become a huge issue for some of us. How we make our money and support ourselves can be shown by our Second House. With Neptune, we begin to sense that our ambition is waning when it comes to earning a fat income and having the finer things that money can buy. These objectives become less relevant to the person we are discovering ourselves to be. Remember, we just experienced some major, soul-searching lessons regarding our self-image, when Neptune was in our First. We could still make a ton of money, but we're less desirous of owning costly things that merely enhance our social status.

WHO NEEDS IT?

It no longer seems reasonable that we should be killing ourselves for the almighty dollar. We realize that it's okay to own a car that's more than seven years old, as long as we don't neglect its upkeep. We don't need to spend our vacation at an expensive Palm Beach resort when driving to the Smoky Mountains for the weekend will do, *especially* if we witness the eerie, primal-looking, mist-shrouded Smokies at dawn. We wonder, "How many Armani suits does a career person need, anyway?" What we could actually be feeling is consumer burn-out. It starts to become a drain to buy stuff, particularly because whatever we buy these days is never enough to make us feel content, or confident that we have it all. There's always someone else who has bigger and better toys. True material happiness starts to seems like a grand illusion, foisted on us by advertisers and other social propagandists!

What are we to do? How about taking a break and detaching ourselves from this mindless spending mania? We probably already have more than we need or can use. If some of us are too dense to pick up on what's going on here—perhaps that First House transit didn't do its magic—then the Cosmos has a nasty but revelatory way of pulling the rug from under our feet. All that it takes is for a fast-moving Hurricane Zaza to slam the coast, and there goes our fancy summer retreat! Freak floods sweep our new luxury sedan a mile away from home, rendering it permanently unusable. Heck, bad times could just as easily befall that old,

beat-up jalopy we've hung on to for so long because it unconsciously symbolizes our wounded feelings of self-worthlessness.
Disasters can strike in a flash as Poseidon harpoons us with his
trident. Much of what we own can be sacrificed to the angry gods
in one quick gulp. Who needs *that?*

Let's not panic, because this won't happen to most of us. Still,
we could be victims of financial fraud, shady deals, burglary, and
pretty much anything that feels like a big rip-off. The more we
thoughtlessly attach ourselves to what we own, the greater our
vulnerability. Sometimes Neptune's message is most clearly
heard when we are in deep pain. Neptune doesn't cause the pain,
but uses such suffering as an opportunity to make its presence
felt. Financial losses or damage to things we own can cause us to
reflect deeply on our material addictions. Should our total identity be wrapped up in these possessions, when we know that they
may not last forever? Neptune thinks not.

GONNA TAKE A MIRACLE

A lot of the above sounds as if I am addressing only those pampered folks you see luxuriating on "Lifestyles of the Rich and
Famous"—Palm Beach resorts, Armani suits, Porsches, and similar symbols of material wealth. They'd really have it tough if
they ever found themselves entangled in Neptune's killer undertow. But what about those of us who already are barely making it
financially? Does Neptune suggest that a total melt-down is waiting for us around the corner? Maybe, but typically it doesn't.
Neptune loves the underdog, the person down on his or her
luck—in fact, people who've had their hopes unfairly dashed in
the past. These are the ones who need (financial) redemption the
most. Such individuals have somehow lost their way, materially,
and need a miracle or two to get them back on the track toward
self-sufficiency.

The ability to preserve ourselves and survive in the material
world is important to our Second-House growth process. Neptune
helps us to let go of a disorganized, chaotic past that otherwise
would continue to make our current conditions stagnant and

bleak. We have to have faith that things will turn around. Besides, how much worse can they get? A measure of trust in ourselves as resourcefully talented—along with equal trust in a Cosmos that is all-forgiving of our past mistakes—now becomes critical. Our self-value may not be doing all that well at this time, and our inclination may be to further degrade ourselves by inviting even more financial disaster. However, this is where Neptune's healing energies can come to the rescue. We'll need to have our sense of worth restored before we can see any comforting light at the end of the tunnel.

SOUL APPRECIATION

We cannot take a passive attitude about our material struggles if we wish to make the most of this transit. Neptune will not condone escapist solutions or lame excuses during this period. Our predicament is not "karmic backlash" from a previous life as an evil, greedy money mogul! We are probably in a financial jam because, unconsciously, we don't appreciate ourselves. In order to survive in this world and comfortably support ourselves in physical terms, we must have a sense of self-worth. Some of us can't imagine prospering in the world, no matter how much outer encouragement we receive. We'll need to work consciously with Neptune, sincerely allowing for deeper insights regarding our blocked capacity to receive wealth and abundance from the world. We need to stop thwarting the material power that can be ours.

After a while, as our material attitudes take on an even greater spiritual tone, money may still come and go in our life, but we worry less about it. The tide rolls in, the tide rolls out—but the ocean never dries up. We can feel the bounty of the Universe in many ways, and not strictly in the sense of cash flow. For example, we may attract those who want to exchange valued goods and services: we give them our old floral print sofa and receive four reflexology sessions plus a few loaves of their home-baked banana-nut bread—a transaction that seems so right. This is how Neptune likes to cut a deal. With this planet, things always have to "feel" good, especially when bartering about Second House items.

CHEATING HEART

Feeling good is all right as long as it's legal. It's nice to have ready cash in hand, but not if we embezzle to get it—or lie, cheat, swindle, bamboozle, trick others in devious ways, or behave parasitically. A few of us may resort to such behavior, usually out of desperation or due to an unexplained lapse in morals. Maybe we just take on jobs that we loathe, even do work that shames us, because we need to eke out a marginal living. We may convince ourselves that there is no other choice—it's this way or no way. Neptune transits can be periods when self-deception must be addressed; therefore, we'll have to make sure we are not bypassing ethical standards in order to satisfy immediate financial temptations. These temptations can become especially highlighted during transiting Neptune's square or quincunx to a natal planet.

Some of us merely want quick, easy riches. However, if winning a cool million or so will ultimately do nothing to advance our spiritual development—if we become more hooked on fulfilling our insatiable, material appetites—then Neptune makes sure that we end up losers. The most common problems that we'll have to deal with during this transit revolve around sloppy financial habits. We can misplace valued possessions, lose money through carelessness, or mess up our credit due to unrealistic spending. We are to learn to be good to ourselves, financially, and to reward our efforts to earn a living without becoming nonsensically indulgent or wasteful of our resources. Let's also be charitable without going overboard.

ETERNAL APPRECIATION

Neptune transiting this house suggests that whatever it is we own and cherish here on Earth, we won't be able to take any of it with us. Once we die, our soul suddenly finds itself on the Other Side without suitcases. Hey, where did all of our precious stuff disappear to? Naturally, those of us with heavy past lives in ancient Egypt may still try to take it all with us! While Neptune needs to learn about wisely handling possessions in the material world, it ultimately knows that physical matter doesn't last beyond the grave. Let's love, but not worship, the beautiful things we own while we're alive. We realize that the person we can become after we've learned to deepen our self-appreciation during this Neptune transit is even more beautiful. Now that's something special we *can* take with us.

NEPTUNE/EARTH VENUS TRANSITS

INTOXICATING

Surprisingly, Neptune supports basic earth Venus needs, such as the desire to experience physicality through beautiful form and sense-pleasing color, texture, and sound. A greater artistic sensitivity can develop for us at this time, as a result of inhaling the essence of Neptune. Also emphasized is a shared awareness that the world of Nature provides us with maternal comforts. Neptune doesn't rule mothering *per se* (neither does Venus), but it is a planet associated with things that protectively envelope us and shield us in a womblike manner from life's harmful elements (which is why it's associated with our immune system and our lymph glands). Nature's benevolent, enjoyable, and sensual qualities, which evoke a ready response from the earthy side of Venus, also have Neptunian components. This transit can be a good time to cultivate a garden for its blossom and aroma, when the season allows. It will prove therapeutically restful for us to lovingly tend something that fills us with inner contentment. In addition, flowers are a visual delight.

Neptune transiting earth Venus can also sensitize our feelings of deep communion with the primal forces and wonders of the physical plane. An inner part of us is able to slow down and take in more of the natural beauty of our environment, and we'll want to savor the experience. Our appreciation of unspoiled, scenic places can reach inspirational levels. We may find ourselves magnetically drawn to areas that are secluded and untouched by modern, commercial development. Hidden lagoons, jungles, mountain hideaways, deep forests, hard-to-get-to places off the beaten path, and other areas where the life force is amazingly powerful, and made manifest by lush and abundant plant growth, may hold a seductive charm for us. They may also have a restorative effect, especially if we've been cooped up too much in sterile, urban environments (those concrete and steel jungles). Neptune helps us to discover unearthly places on our planet that can tremendously uplift our spirit and fill us with awe. Our travels far and wide can rouse strong emotions at times. We may even get misty-eyed while gazing at the enchanting color photos in the pages of *National Geographic!*

Some of us may find ourselves glorifying natural products of the earth, perhaps using many of these things to make us feel good. Our urge may be to decorate our home environment using nature-related items: rocks, shells, gemstones, feathers, pottery, wood, living and dried plants. Our place can start to look and even smell intoxicatingly exotic as we bring more of the outdoors inside. With the earthy side of Venus stimulated, we tend to desire whatever pleases our senses and helps us to feel calm, serene, and body-centered. Having visual symbols of Neptune-inspired energy around us can be restful and meditative.

WELL SOUL-FED

Of course, let's not forget the heavenly realms—Neptune also loves what is otherworldly and mystical. We may, therefore, adorn our body and our surroundings with symbols of the Cosmos, regarding both its universal mysteries and its divine, eternal connection to us. Mandalas, crystals, ceremonial gongs and bells, incense, candles, wind chimes, a futuristic artwork—they all help us to merge with our spiritual, inner core. Maybe we should even frame a decorative copy of our natal chart, done in pastel colors, and hang it on our bathroom wall where it can mystify our guests—just leave out those annoying aspect lines that usually end up looking like somebody's angry doodles! Earth Venus only likes things that easily please the eye.

Organic foods, in their original, unadulterated form, may also be very appealing to us at this time. Non-violent Neptune, who faints at the sight of blood, would probably push for vegetarianism and for beauty products that are chemical or additive free. Some of us could idealize growing from scratch what we eat on our plates—a nice thought, but a task only for the most dedicated. Maybe we will seek to learn about the spiritual side of food—the metaphysics of eating. We could develop little rituals as a result, such as praying or chanting over our food before we consume it, or eating outdoors under sunlight whenever we can, or chewing our food exactly forty times if that's what we believe to be the best way to release our meal's divine energy. The thought of going on cleansing fasts may cross our mind. They represent a mix of Neptune's self-denial urges as well as its need to purify gross matter.

Whatever we choose, food and faith often go hand in hand with Neptune and earth Venus aspects. Neptune/Moon contacts can adopt similar views, except that the Moon is into nourishing themes, while earth Venus revolves around self-gratifying, "feel-good" issues. The only caution here is to be careful not to succumb to food faddism or fanaticism. That's when food turns into too holy of an issue, as we strive to become elevated and saintly through the mere act of eating only the "right" things. A point could come when no one dares to ask us out to lunch anymore. At some later date, when we can evaluate our misguided Neptunian beliefs more clearly, we may have to eat our unrecognized, inflated ego as well. Our ego is always suspect when we authoritatively assume that we, and not others, know "the right way" to do anything.

Of course, on a less inspirational level, some of us could gravitate toward escapist junk food that's low in both nutrition and in the vital life-force. This is our signal that we have an emotional need that is not being met. Binge eating, sometimes as a way to sidetrack conscious recognition of pain or shame, can reach near-addictive levels for a few of us. The pleasure principle becomes distorted, as Neptunian masochism is directed toward what we take into our bodies. Sometimes the issue is one of neglect: we just don't eat enough, or we choose foods that hardly fulfill our body's requirements. Under Neptune's seductive trance, alcoholics and drug-addicts do this to themselves all of the time. They avoid wholesome food and probably don't take in three meals a day, but they make sure that they get the unhealthy substances that they're abusing. Physically, at some point, such self-abuse and deprivation starts to show. However, choosing such a self-defeating Neptunian path is not what this book's theme of alive and well is all about!

SPEND-O-MANIA

Earth Venus, like the Second House and Taurus, deals with money issues—usually those involving saving more than spending. When we see something that we like, we want to hold it, own it, and not let go of it. With transiting Neptune evoking this side of Venus, we often find ourselves yearning for things that we either don't need or will find impossible to possess. We should pay more attention to the yearning itself than to the actual, glorified objects of our desires.

With the right visual enhancements, Neptune can make anything look better and more valuable than it really is. Advertisers have long known the power of alluring packaging. Neptune does not prompt us to examine things closely or to objectively analyze our motivations for purchasing what we do. This could be a time when we buy items based on how they make us feel at the moment. Practical considerations are ignored and, even with the trine and the sextile, we may find ourselves spending freely on things that capture our imagination or that help us to feel a rush of elation mixed with nostalgia. Such expensive temptations could include a vintage Barbie Doll or rare Mickey Mantle baseball card.

The real problem with our compulsion to spend is that what we might actually hunger for is the human affection and physical closeness that we may not be getting from people. Unconsciously, we try to compensate for this lack by buying whatever momentarily attracts us, in true shopaholic style. It's a way to emotionally reward ourselves and pump up feelings of self-worth. While air Venus is looking for ideal companionship due to its major focus on developing relationships, earth Venus is satisfied with merely fulfilling self-gratifying appetites. In this case, they tend to be unrealistic. Still, because people are really not as compartmentalized as astrology sometimes leads us to believe, Venus probably operates from both its earthy and its airy perspectives simultaneously. After all, we love a partner's body and physical appearance as well as his or her inner beauty and appealing disposition.

Why are we so hungry for possessions? For one thing, Neptune touches us in ways that leave us vaguely discontented with our dull, mundane routines. Our expectations of life fall short of our inner ideals and unconscious dreams. Venus, feeling this inner lack and encouraged by Neptune's belief in magical results, assumes that accumulating more beautiful objects will somehow ease our discomfort. We figure that having sense-pleasing things around us will fill an emptiness inside, and that we'll instantly become secure and at peace with ourselves as a result. However, with Neptune, what we expect is typically not what we get. Sometimes we find that what we want is really *not* what we need, once it's ours to own.

GONE WITH THE WIND?

Neptune is a planet that gradually forces a development of deeper values through sacrifices and a sense of loss. Hanging on to physical possessions and amassing more earthly goods for the wrong reasons is not supported by this transit. We can literally lose what we own. With the square, quincunx, or opposition, there is a greater chance that our things may be stolen, or just disappear due to our carelessness or forgetfulness. Neptune deals with objects that mysteriously vanish. We may misplace our possessions or lend them to others, who then never bring them back. Perhaps they are returned, but damaged beyond repair.

Sometimes what we own is taken from us by forces beyond our control, such as hurricanes, floods, tornadoes, or fires. It's probably a good idea to look into property insurance options before Neptune aspects our Venus. It might be too late to do so when the aspect is operating. By then, we are not feeling as uptight about losing anything, because loss may be the last thing that's on our mind. We are swept up in Neptune's whirlpool of wishful thinking. We could be suffering the delusion that "somehow" we're financially protected, no matter how undisciplined and immature we have been with our money habits.

I don't wish to imply that this transit places our possessions in definite jeopardy. Suggesting that would be a form of the scary "old-school" astrology we can all do without. However, Neptune does not allow anything to remain in its fixed form for too long. This is why ice-cream melts, if not quickly enjoyed in the moment. The more emotionally attached we are to our "stuff," the more our focus becomes worldly and ego-driven. The more we tend to shut out any recognition of our inner spiritual assets, the more we become concerned with protecting all that we physically possess as exclusively ours. It's hard to feel lovingly at one with everybody else when we get like this. We feel on guard and stingy, instead.

Therefore, Neptune works at dissolving our finite awareness of materiality—and having the Cosmos mess with what we own is one surefire way to get our attention! We could throw in a karmic statement or two about why we are suffering the loss or the damage of something precious that we've owned and loved for years, such as the string of pearls we inherited from our dear great-grandmother. However, Neptune is only concerned that we not get too emotionally hooked on things that trap our energy and limit our view of the boundless and abundant Universe. Why latch onto anything so tightly? Let it go, and discover how something else, maybe something more rewarding, will take its place. We have to trust that life will not leave us empty-handed.

CASH FLOW

Another issue that we may grapple with is that of money management. The Second House typically says much about this, and so does the earthy side of Venus. When we spend money on things that please us, comfort us, and make our life more relaxing or enjoyable, that's an example of our earth-Venus urges in action. Neptune triggering this side of Venus does not sound like a time when we always use our funds sensibly. We may not feel encouraged to save money. Neptune lures us to dream big dreams; therefore, some of us may try to invest in whatever feels good or inspired at the moment. Usually, our approach to making business-oriented financial decisions is emotional, backed by total faith in someone or something. We often don't do our homework ahead of time or check out the details. Such faith-driven decisions could be our ticket to a better tomorrow, we hope. However, if we are already in trouble, quickie money deals become our desperate attempt to get out of the mess we have created—that is, as long as we are lucky and things fall into place.

However, unless transiting Saturn is also active at this time in our life, introducing a necessary element of caution, we could find ourselves making stupid, hand-shake agreements that fail to protect us legally. Neptune going through our Eighth also warns us to beware of this tendency. With stress aspects at work, our business instincts are not very sound and, frankly, we may not be attracting the most grounded people during this unstable period. We may expect others to save us from our predicament on some level. Instead, they help to create financial entanglements that we did not anticipate. Part of our difficulty is due to our desire for a quick fix to cure a long-term problem with the unrealistic way we handle our finances. We unwisely seek an escape hatch.

The scenario becomes less problematic with the sextile and the trine, suggesting that we're more intuitively attuned to our financial needs. As long as we're not wildly optimistic, life leads us to those who sympathetically try to fulfill our wishes. Neptune can be very protective at times. Much will depend on how open and giving we are in our hearts regarding material things. Are we charitable or conniving when it comes to money and possessions? Charitable folks seem to get rewarded for their good deeds in the past, which can feel like a gift from the heavens.

However, even sextiles and trines don't seem to work out as well for those who are greedy and rotten to the core. Neptune may initially grant the wishes of such types, knowing that this will lead them even more quickly down the road of self-undoing. By then, a crisis requiring self-redemption awaits. This is to be welcomed from the soul's perspective, although not from the ego's point of view. For those of us in a reasonable state of material stability, Neptune aspecting earth Venus usually means that we are a bit looser with our cash flow and impractical at times, but we're also prone to purchase things that inspire and uplift us—either because of their beauty, their mystery, or the wisdom they impart.

CHAPTER EIGHT

NEPTUNE TRANSITING THE THIRD HOUSE

MIND OVER MATTER

Before Neptune can do its finest work in our Third House, we first needed to divest ourselves of whatever had transfixed us on the limited material plane for much too long. That's what our sometimes security-challenging Neptune transit through our Second was all about. If this was a successful transit for us, we now realize that we don't have to grab at everything we see and want. We can enjoy whatever attracts us thoughtfully but with detachment, without undue acquisitiveness getting in the way. We can appreciate things without being possessed by them. We've learned to value intangible rewards, not just monetary ones. Our desire-nature has undergone a process of refinement that permits us to become more selective regarding ownership.

Hopefully, we no longer buy things just because we can afford them or because they create the right social impression. We have become more discerning regarding our earthly appetites and spending habits. Now, we may want to own only that which speaks to our soul, that which puts us in touch with something deeper about ourselves, or about the unlimited Universe of which we are a part. Now, we may not be so willing to attach ourselves to anything possessively. Once we psychologically release our instinctive hold on what we own and safeguard in our Second House, Neptune is ready to help clear our mind of narrow perspectives and false concepts. Paradoxically, it first does this by creating confusion and uncertainty, which force us to rethink every aspect of our lives. This time, the heart, as well as the brain, gets to help us in furthering our education about life and how it works.

OUR UNLEARNING PROCESS

The Third House is an area where duality thrives. We are encouraged to separate ourselves, with a measure of intellectual detachment and objectivity, from whatever it is we are observing. We are not motivated to fully identify and merge with the things in our immediate environment at this point in our development. Such unifying experiences may come later on our journey, specifically in our Twelfth House. In the Third, differences and contradictions are to be seen as stimulating. Oppositional viewpoints can prove energizing. Variety, in general, becomes mentally refreshing. It is "sameness" that becomes a tedious bore.

We benefit from experiences that allow us to develop flexibility and the capacity to juggle many concepts at once. This can become great fun for us in our "eager to understand things" Third House. We learn to deal with life's inconsistencies by developing a sense of humor and wit. We begin to enjoy the stimulation that adaptability affords us. As we become more alert to our surroundings, we quickly can scan for any changes that signal either opportunities or occasional threats to our established territory.

This is an orientation essential to our development, which explains why it is offered to us fairly soon after our budding self-image emerges on the scene in the First House. Here, we start to become more conscious regarding the life that we and those close to us live, and that alone can stir our sense of curiosity and our enthusiasm to know more. A Third-House mentality questions everything, wants to specifically define things, and even bestows identifying names on them.

However, when transiting Neptune begins to enter this house, we may discover that a process of unlearning previously relied-on information is required. What used to work for us, logically, when determining our life's direction, may no longer provide clear answers. Often, the smarter and more educated we are at this time, the more difficult this transit is on us. Why? It's often because we may have become ego-identified with our mind's clever ability—through its exclusive dependency on the powers of reason—to suppress unconscious and hard-to-define material that is natural to Neptune's realm.

We wouldn't get far in life if we couldn't reason. Logic helps us to better understand how things connect and interrelate. How anything links to anything else is always fascinating to the Third House. Ignorance may be bliss, but not when trying to cross a busy intersection. We have to use our smarts to survive in a fast-paced, ever-changing world. The Third urges us to be as bright, verbal, versatile, coherent, and clear-headed as possible. The left-brain approach taken by the Third House to get us to that point typically shuts out the wiser ways of Neptune, a planet that sometimes best conveys ideas non-verbally and with great subtlety. "A mime is a terrible thing to waste," quips Neptune! However, don't expect Neptunian consciousness to take over this house the minute this planet crosses its cusp. This will be a long, slow process, and only a gradual reorientation in consciousness is to occur.

NOT SO CONFUSED

It is common for us to now attract new information that will make us question what we formerly thought to be the indisputable truth. We are less prone to accept things at face value, especially from those "expert" authorities that we used to believe in without question. As facts unfold, we realize that different viewpoints are not only possible, but necessary for a broader understanding of our current situation. Maybe we have relied on erroneous or biased information. Maybe we have not been told everything we need to now know. Neptune here suggests that previously unknown data—missing links—can float to the surface and cast doubt on former assumptions. We may find that we were misinformed about how things really are.

Transiting Neptune should not automatically be expected to invite mental confusion. It can, instead, deepen our awareness by gently melting away the faulty thinking that has supported our distortions and illusions. This can help our mind's cobwebs to disappear. Neptune will never resort to the stun-gun techniques of Uranus in order to uncover underlying truths. Things that were previously hidden can magically unfold before our eyes under Neptune's influence. However, none of this happens without a commitment to keeping our mind open and receptive. We must also deal with the issue of faith versus reason. The Third House easily validates objective facts, but it's skeptical about vaguely generalized beliefs and wishful thinking, even though the idea of believing in divine guidance from "higher" planes of thought appeals to Neptune.

Putting faith to the test is what Neptune does best. Shooting holes in any faith that ignores obvious reality is what the Third House does pretty well. Thus, this planet and this house can be at odds. We may struggle to sustain our faith and trust in our future—especially when contradictory, outside indicators suggest that only the furthering of our earthly education can save us from our confusion. Even if this is true, it's not the whole story. We are also to be educated in ways that go beyond applied brain power and conventional linear thought. We need to learn to be more open to the flow of inspiration and the wonder of intuition.

Our "inner voice" begins to speak to us more often, but only if we are willing to be still and listen, which is not an easy task for anyone with Third-House emphasis. Even being alone for a while can be a big challenge, because the Third is a very busy place of comings and goings. Non-stop activity, both mental and physical, is normal for the development of this house. Exchanging energy with others also becomes a basic preoccupation.

However, Neptune periodically urges us to turn attention away from the external world and go within to dwell in the quieter depths of our being. This requires moments of solitude and also, these days, an answering machine that can intercept incoming calls. During this transit, we may learn about the value of meditation or of being contemplative. Somehow, our nervous system needs to become less wired for action and movement. Neptune brings with it a tranquil vibration, counteracting any "go-go-go" lifestyle. We'll need to clear out thoughts that make us feel fragmented and scattered. Otherwise, we can run around in a state of unrecognized mental exhaustion and thereby accomplish very little.

SIBLING TRUST

Another Third House topic is sibling relationships. Neptune, depending on the aspects it makes, can suggest unfinished business that needs to surface and be healed or transformed on some level. Issues involving past misunderstandings may now arise, calling for sensitive and heartfelt solutions. Neptune enables empathetic bonding, especially in areas where long-term separation has caused pain and emptiness. Learning how to again trust a brother or sister who has wounded us may be paramount. Maybe they've had good reason to be distrustful of us in the past. Whatever the case, now is a time of reconciliation and the dissolving of resentful feelings. Neptune can help thaw the ice—after all, it loves to make puddles!

One reason that we attract changes in sibling relationships that carry Neptunian themes is that this planet is hard for us to exclusively claim for self-seeking purposes. The same is true for Uranus and Pluto. We are compelled to unconsciously project some of Neptune's traits onto those people we magnetically draw to us—in this case, a brother or a sister.

By the way, siblings are the only relatives I associate with the Third House. Step-siblings could be symbolized in our Third if the union is very close, but more typically they are shown in our Ninth, because the Seventh from the Third becomes our brothers and sisters by law, not by blood. Maternal aunts and uncles are to be found in our Sixth, while the paternal side comes from our Twelfth. Cousins can be found in either our Tenth (our mother's sibling) or our Fourth (our father's sibling). Nephews and nieces, our sibling's children, belong to our Seventh. Of course, our neighbors and the neighborhoods we live in are also found in our Third.

Perhaps siblings are found here because they become our early communication partners. We can converse and play with them, spontaneously and freely, in ways that would be less appropriate with our parents or other adults. Besides, moms and dads don't go for much of that sassy Third-House name-calling banter that comes naturally to brothers and sisters!

THE SHADOW SIDE

If we project darker Neptunian traits onto a sibling or a neighbor, we tend to interpret him or her (not ourselves) as sneaky, deceptive, hard to read, irresponsible, delusional, aimless, or looking for escape hatches to avoid reality. Perhaps they're alcoholics or are hermit-like. We probably have a few of these unwanted qualities ourselves, but are refusing to acknowledge them. It's a brother, a sister, or the "weirdo" neighbor two houses down from us who plays out our projections, showing us a side of Neptune for which we have little tolerance, even though intolerance goes against this planet's non-judgmental disposition.

Sometimes, certain siblings or neighbors can take on victims' roles that bring emotional pain and hopelessness into their lives. They are down-and-out on some level, and have not approached their life challenges with the measure of self-assertion needed to ensure successful outcomes. Maybe they allowed themselves to be drained by addictions or have succumbed to emotionally crippling psychological complexes that keep them trapped in a self-defeatist state. Passivity and self-pity insidiously get the upper hand. Remember, all of the above could just as easily apply to us if we're the ones in a shaky mental state.

We may feel both empathetic and exasperated about a sibling's or a neighbor's chronic dilemma. On one level, we'd like to play a godlike role and miraculously find a way to cure them once and for all. On another level, we secretly loathe their situation, feeling powerless to change it. Frustrated, we want to get as far away from these pathetic people as possible. It's their sorry mess, not ours. They could have gotten help or taken positive action long ago but, typically, have kept their problems a big mystery, or else have irrationally turned away from loved ones.

We may say that we're not going to waste another minute feeling guilty about this miserable predicament but, subjectively, we still do, especially with our siblings. A vague sense of obligation to remedy the situation can haunt us. This kind of Neptunian ambivalence is common when we have to deal with people close to us who, nevertheless, have let us down at some point. Oddly enough, we'd be more accepting and understanding of total strangers in this pickle than we are of a family member.

In some cases, a sibling's Neptunian manifestation is physical. Fatal diseases, terminal illnesses, a slow but progressive body deterioration—all of these fall under Neptune. Genetic defects are partly Neptune and partly Pluto, because the damage they create, taking a long time to surface, originates from a hidden (biological) past. Therefore, during this transit, we may comfort a brother or sister in a health crisis. This would be a case of using Neptune to take the high road. You know you're doing your Neptune correctly when you start to feel as if you're channeling Mother Teresa! We can try to assist the psychological healing process that our siblings need, even if their physical condition is beyond hope. They need us and, in truth, we need to serve them.

BEAUTIFUL SOUL

What if our transiting aspect is a sextile or trine? Siblings can more easily present us with the beautiful side of Neptune. They can show a selfless social concern for bettering others in need. They could be involved in creating artistic imagery that captures people's imagination and lifts their spirits. They could even be on a dedicated path to soul awareness and unity consciousness. All of these would be examples of how we can also project this planet onto others in constructive, redemptive ways. The transiting square and the opposition can also present us with Neptune's beautiful side, but it's more apt to come with complications. The bottom line is that, for better or worse, a brother or sister may demonstrate traits that we, too, are capable of experiencing along similar Neptunian avenues of expression.

THOSE LITTLE LEAKS

How we're doing with our Neptune transit can be shown in minor but symbolic ways. Is our car leaking oil or other fluids more than usual? Are there any problems with our auto's water pump? Do we seem to forget where we have parked more often? Do we misplace our car keys more than usual? Maybe we are fantasizing about getting our old Chevy repainted. None of these things qualify as major events in the context of the larger scheme of our life, but Neptune is quite able to make its presence known in such small, everyday ways. Telltale oil spots under our car, especially, may be warning us that we have sprung a few Neptunian leaks in those typically unattended emotional areas of our psyche. They now need to be recognized and sensitively addressed. It may sound crazy to make such a cryptic correlation, but not to most astrologers. Our experience with cars during this period can give us clues about how we're dealing with Neptune's energy. At least, it might be good to always put the top back up on our convertible during an increasingly cloudy day. You never know when a sudden rain may fall. Neptune likes things on the wet side.

A SPECIAL LENS

Overall, this transit can make us feel like complete dummies from time to time, especially when we struggle to use logic and reason to handle every issue that rolls our way. If we are mental perfectionists, Neptune will work to undermine the inflexible part of us that cannot handle chaos, disorganization, and vagueness. Neptune wants us to try out an altered consciousness, explaining why we cannot always be as sharp and alert about decision-making as we have been in the past. Instead, we are to view life through a special lens that softens and blurs what and whom we are observing. Things become less cut-and-dried, less precisely defined. We may find ourselves more often reading between the lines, rather than accepting literal explanations. Again, it becomes a rethinking process. Maybe it's a case of think less, feel more, say less, listen more—something quite alien to the Third House, but also something that is an evolutionary necessity for us during this time.

Of Myths and Legends

Neptune transiting the Third signals a period during which we can devote more time to reading, because that's a peaceful, quiet activity that we can enjoy in privacy. The nature of our reading material can be very Neptunian: writings about spiritual journeys, depth psychology, legends and myths, ancient worlds, futuristic worlds, or fantasy themes in general. Anything that transports us to a limitless, inner dimension and makes us ask, "what if" smacks of Neptune. We sense that so much more is involved in life than meets the eye. Other realms, invisible as they may be, exist and interpenetrate this physical plane on which we operate from day to day. Neptune brings the reality of these levels of consciousness into our awareness. Our inner experiences are almost always too subjective to be convincing to anyone who comes at us from a typical Third-House perspective, such as skeptics who demand hard proof. We'll just have to be content knowing that *we* had our special vision or glimpse of a higher reality—and that's good enough for us. It's the rest of the world that will one day have to play catch-up!

Neptune/Air Mercury Transits
Soul-Minded

Neptune really needs the airy side of Mercury in order to translate to the world the energy of this water planet. Mercury can set up an advertising campaign, using hype, if necessary, to spread the word. However, Mercury first needs to get a better fix on just what Neptune has to offer. This is a problem, because Neptune doesn't articulate well, and air Mercury isn't a mind reader. Still, Mercury is one of the better planets through which Neptune can channel its energies. The Moon's another good one. If we think of having a pipeline to God and the heavenly realms, air Mercury provides the conductive piping. During this transit, something of a Neptunian nature is trying to emerge from the unconscious and travel along the mental circuitry that Mercury provides, until it reaches our waking self and enables us to contemplate the wondrous images that appear. Lofty, sublime concepts begin to take shape, thanks to the clarifying focus of air Mercury.

Much depends on how open we can allow our minds to be. Do strange and exotic ideas spook us, or delight us? Neptune will always seem a bit unreal to Mercury, even a little unglued and flaky. However, air Mercury is also curious about *everything* and, therefore, can find itself charmed by Neptune's fanciful presentation. "All right, sell me on you!" says Mercury, with the tape recorder going just in case something truly fantastic comes out. Neptune can be very persuasive, enchanting Mercury with the idealistic spin it puts on even ordinary things. We may find that, during this transit, our mind can become restless when handling anything too humdrum and conventional. We begin to dream about better tomorrows, where we can escape from whatever is currently hampering us. Neptune whispers to us, "Consider the limitless possibilities."

HALF-BAKED?

This "limitless possibility" stuff can be very tempting. Neptune has tantalizing tales to tell, stories of how we can devise remarkable plans that might help end humanity's mental suffering and pain. We may even be looking for miraculous solutions to our long-standing problems. This transit encourages us to solve inner conflict by putting more faith in our dreams and longings. However, our solutions may be too impractical at times, too half-baked, too much like pie-in-the-sky to work. Still, Mercury can be quite suggestible under certain conditions, so that some of us may be swept up by thoughts that nearly possess our waking self. In addition, we can fully rationalize what we believe at this time, no matter how implausible or outlandish.

We entertain ideas that can be inspirational and emotionally moving, but that doesn't mean that they are also workable. We may not be blessed with much common sense or sound judgment during this transit, and if that typically describes us anyway, then we're really in trouble! The tendency to exaggerate the potential of any "creative" idea is strong. Projects undertaken—sometimes fueled by a timely, universal vision—can become larger-than-life to us. Neptune is an expansive planet that doesn't recognize boundaries or limitations.

This situation is good for some of us who have been too constrictive in thought, too fearful to try out new concepts, or too narrowly driven by ambition to allow for less worldly-oriented activity. Staunch realists will have a harder time embracing the dreaminess that Neptune brings to any transit, especially one that interferes with efficient mental functioning. It could be that a few of us have become crystallized intellectually—we interpret everything too literally and are unable to handle ambiguities common to the human experience. Maybe we've become all head and no heart, smart with facts-and-figures but going nowhere when it comes to feelings or sensing our inner connection to others.

If any of this is so, then Neptune helps to soothe a keyed-up, overworked Mercurian mind that has become overly fragmented. Neptune tries to bring forth unity awareness by dissolving that which creates the illusion of separation. In contrast, air Mercury is a master at keeping things separate, distinct, and classifiable. This Mercury urges us to give everything a name, rank, and serial number. Neptune may only gets to deeply work on altering our Mercurian parts when we're asleep and dreaming.

A Bit Fuzzy

The square, quincunx, and opposition obviously pose more challenges for us. Neptune energy may seem intrusive whenever it catches normally alert air Mercury off guard and pulls the rug out from under it. Facts begin to blend with theoretical assumptions, and our dream material starts taking on a reality of its own. Most of us would say that our mind is playing tricks on us or that we are becoming strangely absent-minded. Maybe we are even recalling buried and forgotten childhood issues. They pop up out of nowhere, but in time-warping ways that temporarily disorient us. This can be a period of great sensitivity and reflection. However, we may talk as if we have marbles in our mouth, or as if not enough oxygen is reaching our brain. Some people claim to not understand us—maybe because we're not making sense. Logic flies out the window at times and we may express ourselves in ways that reveal strong contradictions. Sometimes the words we wish to utter mysteriously elude us. It's as if we are suddenly empty-headed.

It could be that our mentality is undergoing a spiritualizing process that affects our concentration and focus. Neptune is a planet that cannot remain just in one place. It drifts, diffuses, and spreads out in no particular pattern. Air Mercury receptively picks up on this. Suddenly we feel unusually distractible—especially at the beginning of this transit, during our transitional stage. It's wise to just go with the flow. Our mental wanderings are serving a purpose. A leap of faith may be required to make sense of all this. Trusting in a Universe that can guide us in our mind's unfoldment becomes important. The sextile and the trine suggest that we can absorb Neptunian energy with less fuss, but maybe that's because it's not coming at us or through us in such an overwhelming fashion. In that case, we are like plants being misted by universal energies rather than doused.

Do You Read Me?

Regardless of transiting Neptune's aspect to Mercury, we will begin to interpret the world around us differently. Many people have yet to sufficiently develop their airy Mercury potential. Ignorance abounds, superstitions still prevail, and lazy minds are more common than we'd like to admit. It's easy to blame the media and the "boob tube" for the dumbing down of our culture and its increasingly tabloid-like mentality. However, the best defense against mistranslating Neptunian images is to cultivate a discerning and a more fully developed intellect. In other words, a well-managed air Mercury knows how to handle Neptune advantageously.

Folks with lesser Mercurial abilities can evoke a side of Neptune that renders them credulous, unstable, capable of distorted thinking, and even liable to go loony-tunes. Neptune/Mercury communication is not always easy to follow, with its potential to ramble and lose its track of thought. We may add colorful details that never happened to our stories, although some of us could channel such story-telling skills into writing romance and mystery novels, and get paid for telling such whoppers! In contrast, a disciplined intellect knows how to take in information more effectively than one that cannot pay attention or organize thoughts. Structured thinking is important to balance out poorly integrated Neptune/Mercury expression.

This transit does have its uplifting features, so we shouldn't worry too much about becoming mentally lost in space. This could be a marvelously insightful time, as our ability to read people can be stronger. Still, we are very impressionable during this period, so we'll need to be discriminating in our thoughts and in our decision-making. It doesn't help to be suspicious about how and what others are *not* communicating to us, especially because, at times, we inaccurately read too much into things. Unfortunately, our Neptunian-derived thoughts, no matter how odd, are not easy to dismiss once we've absorbed them deeply—particularly when they trigger a sore spot or an area of great vulnerability within our psyche, especially an inner fear or a self-doubt that we may harbor. Our imagination plays into all of this in a way that blows things out of proportion in our heads. The results are not pretty when we eventually hit the panic button.

TRUTH TWISTER

We can bypass much of the above if someone we trust and respect will listen to and analyze our thoughts and feelings as we express them. We need to know when our "logic" is faulty, when we are jumping to wild conclusions based on incomplete data, or when there is more anxiety or sadness in our voice than we realize. We particularly need to know when we are trying to twist things around so that we come off as the blameless one in any complex life situation. A tone of self-pity can be apparent when we claim ourselves to be the unwitting victim of someone else's miscommunication. We may think that we are perfectly clear and direct, and that it's the other person who simply can't talk straight or who doesn't want to hear things. But maybe that isn't the case. Even our body language could be conveying something entirely the opposite of what we are saying.

Good friends and professional facilitators have a way of helping us to examine such issues without making us feel devalued or crazy. Besides, we can't keep all of this moody stuff trapped within, where it slowly eats away at us and erodes our spirit. Nevertheless, it is very important to know who we can and cannot talk to—an exercise, again, in selectivity.

VISION BLESSED

For those of us with an artistic bent, Neptune contacting air Mercury allows for visions that free up the creative process. All of the Outer Planets allow us to see things as "wholes." We flash on the overview. This is what helps inspire artists who envision what will be on the canvas or the page before they lift a brush or a pen. Our vision springs forth in its complete form, and the rest of the process deals with working to bring that vision into concrete expression, piece by piece. Neptune will allow beautiful and soul-lifting images to surface, but we'll need a sturdy fish net with which to capture them before they escape once again under the vast sea of our unconscious. Air Mercury urges us to sensibly plan out how we are going to communicate our creative dreams.

Anybody in the art or entertainment field can benefit from this transit—especially photographers and film makers—as long as the prime focus is on one's dedication to one's craft, rather than grandiose fantasies.

WINGS OF THOUGHT

The airy side of Mercury likes the stimulation of studying a variety of subjects. Neptune tends to steer us away from technical and dryly intellectual reading material. Books, articles, classes, and workshops about soul growth can be appealing. Techniques on meditating may capture our interest. Past lives may start to make sense; therefore, information about reincarnation or past life regression—even soul mates—may absorb us. Religious and spiritually uplifting pursuits in general help us to ponder the mysteries of the Godhead, the Universe, and the unearthly realms that we may visit after death or even before death, by means of mystical or out-of-body experiences. Even reading far-out science fiction and futuristic fantasy or horror novels can take us to another dimension. Some of us will simply get lost in gothic romances for our great escape. Whatever we read, we will enjoy it all the more if it removes us from the pattern of our daily life and puts us in a world beyond our wildest dreams, or else makes us profoundly ponder life matters. We feel as if our mind has left the ground and taken flight.

Neptune going through this house can also mean that we gradually learn to still our often overactive intellect. We'll need to periodically retreat from too much cerebral stimulation in favor of the inner stillness enabled by meditation or contemplation. Perhaps we at least learn not to talk constantly, especially if that's merely our habitual way of releasing nervous energy. Listening allows us to connect more deeply to others. We may find ourselves sympathetic to people's situations. They could even gravitate toward us to hear our words of wisdom. Transited planets natally in this house get lessons on how to expansively express their needs in less ego-driven ways. Alternative forms of non-verbal communication may feel less limiting than mere words.

THAT QUIET SPACE

Increasingly reflective and introspective as the years go by, some of us will find ourselves less able to handle certain social superficialities. Behavior that probably never bothered us too much before Neptune entered this house now can seem uncomfortably shallow. Neptune is no party animal, yet the Third is not the house of the cloistered life. We may have an internal conflict to deal with: we want human association, but not if it means participating in time-wasting, aimless activity. Saturn going through this house can generate similar feelings, except that Saturn probably could use some silly, goof-off time for its own well-being. Neptune, being so susceptible to mass influence, suggests that we need to choose our social contacts wisely. It might be better to delve within and uncover the many parts of ourselves during this transit, rather than to look outside ourselves for stimulation. Moodiness alone may prevent us from constantly socializing. It is sometimes wiser to be alone in our own head than to seek contact with those whose company can prove to be draining, depressing, or uninspiring.

CHAPTER NINE

NEPTUNE TRANSITING THE FOURTH HOUSE

AN INSIDE JOB

Neptune crossing the Nadir means that this planet is also entering the second quadrant of our chart, an area where we're less preoccupied with fulfilling the immediate, exclusive needs of our emerging selfhood. Instead, this sector begins by focusing on the family bond, especially regarding our tie with our mother. The Fourth is also the first "water" house in which Neptune gets to swim since it began its new cycle transiting our Ascendant. This house is ready to take us deeply within ourselves to learn how to be nourished by our subjective roots and our internal foundations.

If our natal houses were likened to rooms in an actual home, the Fourth House would start off as an unfinished basement or cellar—dark, quiet, and seldom visited. Later on, when further developed, it transforms into a warm and inviting kitchen filled with delicious, appetizing aromas—the place where folks want to hang out and intimately connect. But first, rather than opening up and moving into the external world, the Fourth redirects our attention toward an interior realm where emotional safety becomes a prime issue. Neptune itself has no problem with interior levels of being, because that's where it likes to dwell the most. This house provides Neptune a suitable atmosphere.

Both Neptune and the Fourth are keys to our level of sensitivity to our surroundings. Each can sponge in the environment and take in the vibes. When Neptune transits this angle, it probably first heads right to our less-visited, inner basement and begins its process of silent erosion. We probably have cluttered this interior space of our psyche throughout the years with all sorts of hurts and injuries based on our reactions to the alleged rejection or abandonment of others. Most of us would probably claim that we harbor no bad feelings about all of the emotional stuff that happened to us in childhood. We assure others that the past is far behind us. Therapists know otherwise.

SILENT MESSAGE

How we unconsciously revert to childlike behavior, with all of the vulnerabilities implied, can be shown by our Fourth House and our natal Moon. This is an area where we psychologically grow up less quickly. A part of us may still cling to the early, formative experiences that helped to develop our initial security patterns and defense tactics. Thus, the Fourth can describe how we regress to former emotional patterns when we're under stress; this is where our memory of ourselves as helpless babies still lives. However, this memory is buried under our many symbolic security blankets. Layer upon layer of family conditioning, symbolized here, often diverts us from knowing who we really are at the base of our inner nature.

Our family—especially our mother—plays a protective role here, shielding us from the cold winds of the "real" and sometimes threatening outer world. The slow physical development of a child ensures, theoretically, that there will be plenty of time for caring and nurturing by the parents. The Fourth House describes our development during our tender years. In the process, particularly as we start getting older and ready to separate from the parental bond, we find that such family conditioning blocks our need to be self-reliant. By then, unspoken parental messages have been deeply internalized, for better or worse. The sign on the Fourth-House cusp can give clues as to what those messages were.

With Neptune now ready to dissolve whatever has turned out to be faulty programming, we need to confront the hidden emotional baggage that we still may carry. Any distorted feelings that we have about our early unconscious conditioning, and the parent or parents who got a lot of it going, need to be exposed. We eventually may have to forgive that parent for the unwise ways he or she raised us, rather than hold in bitter feelings that will continue to undermine us.

HOME SICK

Neptune normally won't shake us at our foundation as vigorously as Uranus would or as violently as Pluto could. We don't immediately sense that our inner world is shattering or erupting in fury. However, it could slowly and quietly lose its original form. The signs of this can be exceedingly subtle in the beginning, although in some cases, they may be dramatic. We know that the Fourth rules our actual home. A flash flood, sweeping our house away with a rushing torrent of uncontrollable water, qualifies as dramatic, along with the emotional collapse that we would feel as a result of such a tragedy in our lives. It has already happened to some. Many memories of our past can be preserved in our homes, through antiques, photos, keepsakes, inherited items, and so on. A disaster such as this can wipe out all of that in minutes, leaving us homeless and without an emotional anchor.

Such a personal catastrophe is not going to be our fate, in most cases. However, even before Neptune crosses our Nadir, we should review our home insurance options realistically. We need to address the possible weak structures of our residence and its surroundings. Are we living in a flood zone, or maybe in a place where wildfires are possible? In the back of our minds, we should never forget that Neptune represents non-attachment themes; therefore, it will not allow us to keep the status quo of our lives unaltered. Something has to give way to change. Other home problems could be termite invasion, hidden water damage that weakens the foundation, or even the gradual shifting of the land beneath the building. All of these predicaments have great symbolic meaning for us, whether we know it or not.

Our outer home becomes a metaphor for our inner home. What goes on in our house parallels what is happening, psychologically, within us. I have often told clients with transiting Neptune in or aspecting planets in their Fourth about the need to observe the water phenomena where they live, especially involving water where water should not be. Leaky roofs are fairly common, as well as plumbing troubles or water pipes doing slow drips inside walls. In one case, a client's waterbed leaked unexpectedly and made a big, costly mess; new carpeting was the main expense.

Once the connection is made—that Neptune symbolizes leaks and water spillage—we'll need to ask ourselves what could be going on inside us, emotionally, that is getting ready to figuratively spring a leak or burst a pipe. Usually, we've been sitting on some deep sorrow or unarticulated disappointment for a long time. Our insecurities have kept us from dealing with it, so the home absorbs our sadness and "cries" for us. We have not aired out our emotions properly; therefore, they rot inside until we bring this hidden matter to light. Do we currently have a mildew problem or notice constantly damp sections of concrete in our home's basement? It's good to look around our place for clues that Neptune's energy is actively but is slowly undermining the structure of things. Then we need to get busy and open up our feelings to those who live with us.

HEAVENLY ABODE

In some instances, transiting Neptune can mean that we want a little bit of heaven to be brought down into our home. We seek to build the ideal, cozy nest. Neptune-related furnishings and accessories may become increasingly appealing, but forget that waterbed and go instead for a goose down comforter for a delicious experience of Neptunian warmth and insulation—unless you live in Florida. An obvious way to easily work with Neptune is to repaint the place. This could be a time to bring in more color and different textures. The make-over alone could help us to feel more alive and well. It can also help us to get in touch with the closeted artist or interior designer dwelling inside us who longs to be released.

Give that room-to-room off-white look a break. Some of us could get an inspired idea that a mural would be great on the wall of one of our rooms. We need to let our imagination soar, but let's not get too wild. It's harder to sell a place that has a bathroom painted the color of eggplant, a kitchen with wallpaper displaying porpoises or unicorns, or even wooden floors covered over with a few coats of a pastel-colored enamel! Neptune's not a sensible planet, so we need to consciously work at taking a practical approach to home improvements. Maybe we should get a little advice from a real pro if we're going to transform the whole house.

Not only will we want to create a look that invites domestic serenity, we will also need peaceful interchanges in our home during much of this transit. We can be touchy about loud mouths with "bad vibes" who visit us and pollute the air with their negativism and sourpuss criticisms of life (and of us)! However, it's tricky to keep such folks at bay when they are also members of our family. Still, with dedicated Neptune at our side, we should stick to our inner principles. That means defending the very "soul" of our home against invading barbarians at the gate! We will be wary of anyone who attempts to disturb the sea of tranquillity that we've grown to depend on daily.

Our home is now our protective retreat and quiet sanctuary, the perfect antidote for a toxic world that has little time for spiritual nourishment. Let us have our beautiful music, our blooming flowers, and our inspirational artwork. Leave us in peace to read our devotional books and tend the aromatic plants in our enchanted, backyard garden. For Neptune, a home is a very special place, indeed, to feed a soul.

MATERNAL SPIRIT

Our living quarters are an outer expression of our internal affairs. Therefore, decorating or beautifying our home means that we are beginning to celebrate our inner identity—seeing it in a more attractive, luminous light. It's a step in the right direction, because Neptune is signaling a need for much healing and self-nurturance in this private life sector. We are learning to spiritualize the maternal function, taking it to a level where we can better comfort ourselves, whether or not we have an actual mom in our lives. We discover how to ideally parent ourselves, this time without any of those limiting conditions imposed on us while growing up.

Speaking of mothers—another big Fourth-House theme—Neptune making tensional aspects here can have a tone of sacrifice and loss. This could mean that we can no longer attach ourselves to a parent in the way to which we have always been accustomed. Our mom (or dad, if he's the only surviving parent) somehow becomes less accessible to us. Emotional misunderstandings are common, because we may feel that we are not on the same wave-length as our hard-to-fathom parent. A once-tight bond may now be unraveling and dissolving. This can unsettle us, arousing all of the sticky, unfinished business that surrounds our unprocessed fears of abandonment and rejection.

Our mom can appear to be the insecure, childlike, needy one at this time, but our reaction may be that she's suffocating us. We know we cannot afford to drown in her identity, as we may have done in the past. Still, we may feel that, psychologically, we cannot afford to lose her support. In some cases, we may have suffered alienation from our mother and removed ourselves from her, and from the family in general, for a long stretch. Neptune is asking us to consider a reunion based on forgiveness. Both sides have to lay down their defenses, because the blame-game has no place in Neptune's compassionate heart.

One of the hardest situations to undergo with this transit is to stubbornly refuse to make up with a difficult parent, even if they've nearly driven us crazy in the past, and then to have that parent die before we were able to reconcile matters. A possible Neptunian scenario is a mom or a dad (when Neptune opposes our Tenth House cusp) who slowly dies due to a terminal condition. This is heavy on our heart, *if* that's what it takes to enforce a true soul-healing between child and parent. Movies have shown us a lot of such teary deathbed scenes. A variation on this parent-child theme was portrayed in the movie, *Terms of Endearment,* with actress Deborah Winger as the dying daughter who had to finally patch everything up and make peace with her uptight, dominating mom, played by Shirley Maclaine.

However, in most cases, this transit doesn't have to be gut-wrenching. Neptune is telling us to surrender to our own innate goodness—our Higher Self—if that will finally end this unnatural state of separation from others to whom we are so karmically linked. We need to soften a hard heart at this time in order to allow ourselves to merge, once again, with the one who first brought us into the world. Yet this is not always possible. A parent lost to the insidiously Neptunian Alzheimer's disease will not be able to partake in this exchange with the awareness needed, although we can hope that, on the soul level, this parent knows exactly what's going on. Maybe our parent is so overtaken by the physical and psychological ravages of alcoholism or drug addiction that they are totally unrecognizable to us. Again, we've lost them.

Whatever the situation, we need to let go of this Fourth-House parent and hope that he or she makes it back to God, or at least enjoys some inner peace in the future. We can't become miracle-workers, tapping our parent with our magic wand and making all of their pain vanish, even if we pray for it. However, a deep transformation can occur inside of us as we allow ourselves to be released from this complex relationship.

INNER REWARDS

This seems like a good time for some upbeat information about this transit. What's so great about having Neptune passing through our Fourth? For one thing, we can become more aware of our own depths. We are less able to be sucked into mindless social patterns that would otherwise keep us functioning on the surface. All of the Outer Planets moving through this house seem to want us to find security strictly from within. Once we can effectively do that, we are less prone to feel unsafe in the outer world. However, we have to be willing to take a chance and let go of our past conditioning. Such programming has had a powerful grip on us and is not easy to turn off. Neptune allows us to make our changes gently, prodding us to continue along our evolutionary path by inspiring us to believe in our inner strengths. We need to be aware of the solidity of the bedrock of our internal foundation.

Neptune and the Fourth both encourage the development of receptivity. We can become more psychically attuned to what's happening around us. If we are still trapped in a web of our own troubling insecurities, becoming more receptive to our surroundings can render us too fragile to cope with life matters, or too sensitive to know how to detach properly from people when necessary. We could also "smother-mother" others too powerfully to do them any real good. However, let's not push for psychic unfoldment at this time. Let it emerge as a natural consequence of doing effective inner growth. This advice also goes for Uranus and Pluto in the Fourth. There is little about this transit that is demanding or forceful, so we need to simply follow our instincts one step at a time and always at our own measured, emotional pace.

AMBIVALENT AMBITION?

There can be a time during this transit, when it conjuncts the Nadir within a reasonable 1–2° orb, when Neptune also opposes our Midheaven—a key to our professional unfoldment. This can be when we have second thoughts about how much ambition and drive we are willing to apply to reach certain career goals. Perhaps we thought we knew where we were going, but now feel some inner ambivalence regarding these objectives. Things may not seem as clear to us. If our job is going well, this transit may mean that we want our private life to feel equally successful and fulfilling—and it doesn't. Maybe we have neglected to develop our Fourth-House needs while continuously chasing after our Tenth-House dreams. This becomes a time to determine how to better juggle these life areas. Hopefully, we can have the best of both worlds. Feeling more secure from within will, in the long run, improves the way we present ourselves to society and do our part to contribute what is collectively needed for its growth and development.

NEPTUNE/MOON TRANSITS
TORN FEELINGS

When Neptune aspects the Moon, our security will have to come from inner, self-affirming sources, because Neptune will not support the limiting ways in which we've sought outward safety and shelter in the past. This may not be apparent in the beginning, which is typical of Neptune's subtle influence. Nothing that we've long depended on is necessarily going to be abruptly yanked away from us. We can cling, for a while, to our accustomed attachments. At some point during this transit, however, we begin to feel uncertain and insecure about our emotional ties—whether they are to people, things, or ideals. Inner doubts may enter the picture, reinforced by external situations that discomfort us and make us yearn for an ideal change. The question that confuses us is, "When?"

When our Moon is triggered by an Outer Planet, implied, upcoming changes can seem threatening to our internal status quo. Something very personal about us is ready to undergo a deeper alteration, although we may feel that we're not ready for this unstabilizing experience, even if, subconsciously, we are. We may try to stall for time rather than commit to action. Perhaps Moon in Aries or natal Moon conjunct Uranus is always ready to drop an attachment and try something new. In most cases, however, our lunar instincts prompt us to fear and resist the invasion of the unknown, at least until we can better grasp what's happening.

With Neptune involved, a planet notorious for creating visibility-limiting fogs, we sense that we cannot see what's waiting for us or what our next step should be. When the square, quincunx, or opposition is involved, we can't even put our finger on what's happening at the moment that's making us feel unsteady. Confused feelings sidetrack us. At times, it may seem as if we have no clear directional signals to guide us, and that alone can be unsettling. It's as if our normal inner-tracking system is malfunctioning, and we cannot find our way back home. Things may begin to look and feel less familiar or less trustworthy. We may be in a state of greater vulnerability regarding our current life situations, especially if we are having trouble sorting through psychological issues. What are we to do with our emerging insecurities?

When in doubt, Neptune is a believer in doing nothing. Why take action while the blindfold is still on? Where is the energy needed to dynamically make new moves when we are feeling this out of sorts? Our emotions are in a state of conflict, making us feel torn by indecision. Perhaps, instead, we are to learn a thing or two about inner stillness, even as storm clouds gather around us. Unless we are in a psychologically or physically dangerous predicament, we'll need time to clarify the issues that disturb us. What's really eating us?

If we are undergoing a sextile or a trine, then the best way to absorb much of the finest energy that Neptune has to offer is to be quietly receptive. Getting emotionally worked up only invites this planet to stir up chaos. By remaining calm, we allow Neptune to seep gently into us and delicately infuse our soul with a deeper understanding of our situation. We also allow any troubling outer circumstance to take its natural course, which often works out for us in less obvious ways. A degree of passivity can be expected with all Neptune/Moon aspects, and this is sometimes necessary, because struggling to either push for drastic changes or to run away from them is never a good idea. We need to realize that we are ripe for an uplift of our feelings, especially with harmonious aspects activated. Our emotions need a shot of inspiration. We may also want to feel more connected to others, spiritually, for the betterment of the social collective.

Peace Within

Self-absorption becomes increasingly unsatisfying. Neptune helps to wean the Moon from its normal preoccupation with self-protection. We are less defensive and more open to attending to the needs of others, especially those who qualify for underdog status. Then again, this could simply be a time of greater self-reflection. Our security comes from withdrawing a bit from the outside busyness of the day-to-day world. It becomes important to have quiet times to nourish our emotions. That means we need to feel good about and deserving of being alone—and not catering to others as much—so that we can relax and get to know more inner peace.

With the tensional transits, we could absorb too much Neptune, too soon. Our feelings become flooded with urges and images that can be anxiety-producing. The more unattainable the urges and images are, the more anxious we become. We sense that we cannot hang onto what we have always depended on in the past. Either someone is detaching and becoming harder to reach, or we may be becoming less involved in a relationship that is losing its structure. Somebody's feelings in this partnership are drifting elsewhere. That makes at least one of us unavailable for intimacy, or even honest confrontation. A close bond may be about to dissolve. We can even feel out-of-tune with our surroundings—for some, that means feeling trapped or suffocated.

It's critical at this time that we don't panic or cave in on ourselves. We need to realize that Neptune sometimes magnifies problems—facts are exaggerated and distorted, in the same way that our appearance changes when reflected in fun house mirrors, warped and strange. This simply draws more attention to these bothersome issues. It's safe to say that anything that feels emotionally queasy during this period needs to be explored, although without the needless fears that are aroused when we assume that our world is falling apart. There are things about our life thus far that can be salvageable and redeemable. We just need the candor required to deal with what's wrong with any relationship or dependency. Have we been latching on to either for all of the wrong reasons? Neptune makes it clear that any union in which we've lost ourselves was never based on solid footing. This also goes for transiting Neptune in the Seventh or aspecting air Venus. Here's a case where Neptune tries to dissolve old emotional patterns that no longer work for us.

ENTANGLED

Sometimes the main issue is that we have outgrown something or someone, but have allowed ourselves to be stuck in a situation that is unhealthy. Neptune erodes this self-defeating structure that we have set up for ourselves. Although we sense that we now feel imprisoned, some of us may try to fix the damage by pacifying another and end up going against our inner voice. This "solution" only lasts a short time before we realize that we've accomplished nothing. It could be that the entire framework of a relationship, riddled with elements of deception and illusion, needs to collapse so that we will be free. Until then, we may suffer ups and downs, as if caught in choppy waves.

If this sounds a little too dramatic, talk to anyone undergoing a transiting or even a natal Neptune/Moon square or opposition. They may feel as if they cannot break loose from an almost addictive entanglement, and yet, inwardly, they know that they must. Remember, Neptune only seeks to break down and dissolve that which has become toxic and soul-deadening. In some cases, we could be heading in that direction because we just met someone who has aroused our feelings to new heights. Things feel sublime, heavenly. We feel comforted in ways that we have never known before, yet this "ideal" person is still a stranger to us. Much of what Neptune/air Venus has to say sounds a lot like Neptune/Moon when it comes to our emotional attraction to others—except that when it comes to the Moon, unresolved neediness is the issue, rather than romanticized love.

WELL ATTUNED

On the other hand, let's say that we don't have much psychological baggage to weigh us down during this period. Maybe we just survived a series of "brutal" Plutonian transits, or so they seemed at the time. Pluto will not tolerate the spaced-out "nonsense" that sometimes captures Neptune. Instead, it strips away illusions using strong-arm tactics. Thus, at this point, few emotional blind spots from our past are likely to remain. With Pluto, we've hard-ened up a bit, but in a healthy way, having rebuilt a sturdier and more powerful sense of self, perhaps from the ground up (Saturn's transits can have similar results). In that case, Neptune will prob-ably put all of its energies into nourishing creative rehabilitation.

This means that we are able to explore Neptune's fuller poten-tial with an open acceptance of our strength and focus. It's good to truly feel drawn to some sort of impersonal social vision that moves us. Impersonal doesn't have to mean detached; it can imply something group-oriented that helps us to go beyond ourselves and toward a collective need. The trine and the sextile, while not always trouble-free, can steer us in directions where our emo-tional attunement to Neptunian principles can be very satisfying. We effortlessly attract people and situations that help us to feel secure with our Neptunian experience. Even the challenging aspects serve to muster up a stronger need to manifest Neptune dynamically in our lives. We work harder to activate this planet's promise so that we feel that we are a part of all that's around us.

SACRIFICE?

It is typical for Outer Planets in hard aspect formation to not ful-fill solely self-centered desires, at least not without extracting a price later. With conflictive Neptune/Moon patterns, putting our emotional energy into working with the masses on a nurturing level becomes more viable than trying to create reliable, pre-dictable structure in intimate one-on-one relationships. At times, even our attempts to mother loved ones, particularly children, seem to fail. We may feel that we are sacrificing a lot, without the emotional payoff expected. Neptune suggests that we could, instead, receive their moodiness and their alienating behavior. Even when they do reciprocate, we may feel it isn't enough. This leads to disappointment and disillusionment. Our lesson here is to not demand such personal fulfillment. People can and do fail us when we expect too much of them. This realization is brought home very clearly when Neptune challenges our vulnerable Moon, especially if the natal Moon is in a water sign.

Dream Home

On a more mundane level, Neptune contacting our Moon can be a great time to create new styles in the home and to feel like an instant interior designer, which is also what we're trying to do spiritually—redesign parts of ourselves to better manifest our inner beauty. Home-improvement urges merely reflect this internal process. Beautifying our living space is a fantastic way to use up some of the available energy of transiting Neptune trine or sextile our Moon. We may have an urge to paint walls, experiment with richer fabrics, reupholster furniture, get artsy, add a lot of color to our surroundings, buy a better sound system, and maybe experiment with growing exotic house plants, such as orchids. We are slowly turning our residence into an enchanting place in which to retreat and relax. That alone could put us into a more spiritually centered mood.

We may have the same urge to change the look of our place with the conjunction, square, quincunx, or opposition. However, our choices tend toward impracticalities based on emotional impulsivity and poor planning. "I want rainbow-patterned wallpaper in the bathroom. That would be incredible!" we say. Once the wallpaper's up, however, the look may not be as captivating as it was in our mind. What *is* incredible is how duped we feel. Even when it comes to painting the walls, we have to be careful of our color choices. Someday we may wish to sell our home without a hitch and make a decent profit. Therefore, it's best to forgo that heavenly "blue sky and puffy clouds" paint job we're contemplating for the ceiling of the family room. It's also best not to come up with future design-plans while sipping margaritas!

In some cases, all of our creative impulses may be on target, and yet our home's physical structure is in need of repairs. Hidden problems now become exposed, as well as those we put off, praying that they would just disappear. We discover things wrong about our home that we never knew existed. Let's attend to these before we plunk money down on those lovely, decorative touches that we crave. Fix the leaky dishwasher first, *then,* maybe, buy the salt-water fish aquarium of our dreams—after carefully considering the cost of keeping such fancy Neptunian critters alive and well!

LOST AND FOUND

It's also a good time to get rid of useless, space-robbing junk that's just gathering dust. Repair what's broken, or get rid of it! Go from closet to closet and from nook to cranny. Confront anything we have managed to hide that we no longer need. Check under the beds, too. The good news is that we may find items that have been missing for ages—maybe ever since some forgotten Mercury retrograde phase many, many moons ago! Attention is to be put on less glamorous—although not necessarily less expensive—projects that must be done to avoid further clutter and disrepair. This evokes the sacrificial principle of Neptune. It's time to draw on any Virgo or Saturnian inner resources we have (orderliness, common sense) in order to cope with such domestic realities.

In general, Neptune/Moon puts us in touch with deeper layers of our emotions. It will be less easy to be detached or aloof. That alone may sensitize us to feelings that we never knew existed, but perhaps this is one of the benefits of this introspective transit. We can no longer afford to be phony with ourselves and others. The blinders must come off. Whatever hurts us needs to be looked into with greater self-compassion. We need be victimized no more. Dissolving self-ignorance heals old wounds and establishes needed closure.

CHAPTER TEN

NEPTUNE TRANSITING THE FIFTH HOUSE

JOY RIDE

Neptune entering the Fifth House can be a time of "cosmic" realizations about fun and play. Although ponderous Neptune has often been associated with things holy and sacred, we will discover that spiritual enlightenment doesn't necessarily require heavy-hearted lessons in pain and loss. Of course, some of us may already cringe when we hear about Neptunian self-sacrifice and the letting go of our desires and attachments. There's probably a time and place for such ego-surrendering and renunciation, but it's not now and it's not here. In the Fifth House, we are to let our hair down and party with the Universe!

In the Fifth, some of us get to admit—finally—that we are ego-driven to the core, which confirms our thriving thirst for self-validating experiences. In this house, we are to learn the pros and cons of being "full of ourselves" by showing off aspects of self-made individualism. We then witness the audience's response. Transiting Neptune's purpose is not to dissolve ongoing self-interest promoted by this attention-seeking house. We are persuaded instead to direct our egocentric energy toward the upliftment of an even broader "audience"—humanity at large.

There's no need to panic at hearing that our challenge may be to raise the spirit of the masses. Those of us who have stage fright or are not gregarious won't be forced to audition for any major, starring roles during this period. Neptune is itself uneasy about being in the limelight. Still, Neptune allows us to quietly "do our thing" behind the scenes, where we can be masterfully effective without high visibility. However, grabbing for both the spotlight and the microphone are natural Fifth-House preoccupations. Feeling alive and well, *and* at the top of our form become really big objectives here! Deadbeats and dullards need not apply. Both Neptune and the Fifth seek to do wonders on those who aren't afraid to sparkle and shine.

Neptune has other things in common with the Fifth. It believes in boundless expression, just as the Fifth loves to pour its energies into the world without imposed restrictions. Neptune also agrees with the Fifth that the sky's the limit, so let's shoot for the stars! Neptune has a whimsical side filled with enchanting fantasies and vivid imagery—what strongly creative Fifth-House psyche doesn't need the services of a good costume designer and make-up artist once in a while? The Fifth likes to put on a colorful show and will use theatrical gimmicks and high drama to fully capture the audience's attention, while Neptune captivates our imagination with its own glittering bag of magic tricks. Both planet and house enable us to experience life—at least *our* life—from our radiant heart center, helping us to better understand the illuminating power of love and the childlike joyousness of sharing that love fearlessly.

A KID AGAIN

It's unlikely that most of us will have the urge to take to the stage or screen when Neptune passes through our Fifth House. In some manner, however, we can immerse ourselves in our life story with greater emotional investment and a fuller yearning for the chance to throw ourselves into something enjoyable. My professional experience has shown that many clients don't allow themselves to explore their Fifth House potential to the fullest. They say that they feel supremely untalented, or else there's too little time and energy to devote to interests as seemingly "minor" as one's hobbies and other recreational play. They consider such activities secondary to doing what it takes to merely survive economically in today's world—work, work, work—and they seldom see their job as a source of fun or play.

Members of the Pluto-in-Leo generation, however, tend to defy this notion. They'll work hard to reach high ambitions, but they're also compelled to play hard. Merely getting older won't stop them from having fun while getting noticed. Still, much Fifth-House attention is typically put on raising our children and watching *them* happily discover their self-affirming talents. Neptune now signals a readiness to change this pattern. Instead of living vicariously through our kids, we need to reclaim our inner child—the key to youthful vitality at any age.

Transiting Neptune takes the Saturnian starch out of our disposition, allowing us to kick back and loosen up. We aren't able to remain fuddy-duddies for long. Those who are having this transit should take a short break after reading this paragraph. In the name of Fifth-House spontaneity, let's stand up and do our best version of the hula, while humming "Blue Hawaii." Even a slow, wicked "Macarena" will do, because dance crazes are very Neptunian. If your first reaction to this impromptu request is, "That's ridiculous!" then you need Neptune's help more than you realize!

Play-acting comes naturally to very young kids, who still have a foot in Neptune's realm. We all were once that young and innocent. Neptune transiting our Fifth becomes a time to reacquaint ourselves with the forgotten part of our being that, at one time, wasn't self-conscious about seeking playful fun. Silliness or "make-believe" is never a problem for highly imaginative children. When did it become our problem? Neptune is trying to help us to clear away traces of "old-fogey build-up" before it suffocatingly clogs our pipes and drains our life of all color.

If we tend to be too rigid and uptight as adults, and try to live up to some fixed image of maturity, we may unwisely shut down our childlike instincts. Of course, they really haven't gone anywhere, but simply have been shoved into the underground of our unconscious. We'd better watch out when that happens—the psyche's underground is too close to Pluto's hangout. Pluto will try to annihilate whatever's not being effectively used—and Pluto is a notorious *kid*napper.

Neptune, therefore, is on a quest to aid us in saving our child-spirit from death through starvation and neglect. The fact that it's going to be in this house for years on end tells us not to pressure ourselves to quickly come up with joy-releasing activities. We can take our time. It might be wise to first look within and visualize what went on in our lives when we were children. Did we know how to entertain ourselves then? Were we willing to try a bit of risk-taking in the name of a good time? Did our parents encourage us to show off in healthy ways? Did we get sufficient attention when we wanted to shine?

If we can answer "yes" to most or all of these questions, then we shouldn't worry about this Neptune transit. If anything, it means that we may have to tone down that kid-energy inside us. Apparently, it never went underground,which explains our youthful behavior as adults. Neptune will simply open up new creative territory to explore. As a member of the Cosmic Gang of Three— or Four, if you include that new inductee, Chiron—Neptune will prompt us to experiment freely with its inspirational energies.

If there's a downside, it has to do with over-extending ourselves with hobbies that are too expensive or that lure us away from life's practical demands. For example, be careful of "chat room" enthrallment—in cyberspace, we can become fluid in playing out colorful, fantasy roles, but we may lose our true sense of center in the process, if those roles start to become critical to our well-being. That's when returning to our less glamorous, "ordinary" self becomes a big letdown. It's hard to go from being the flaming "Czarina of Antares" by night to just plain old "Gertrude J. Smith," nondescript local librarian, by day!

Those who haven't had a decent childhood will have to watch it with Neptune here. What starts off as fun stuff to do in the Fifth can turn into a nasty vice or two that will take its toll on us by the time Neptune exits this house. Some of us who've been struggling all of our lives with the scars of a repressed childhood may use this period to lose ourselves in questionable pursuits. However, our inner hunger goes on when we indulge in escapist activities that seldom satisfy us.

HOOKED

If our self-esteem is already on wobbly ground, we tend to overdo the Neptunian temptation to drop inhibitions. We can overcompensate and get too loose, putting few sensible limits (if any) on our pleasure-seeking appetites. Addiction can be a problem, whether it's the usual drugs-and-booze route, sexual exploits, or even gambling away our bucks at the dog races and slot machines. We may not know it at the moment, but we are playing out the role of a lost soul, using the "let the good times roll" excuse to, ultimately, treat ourselves badly. Self-punishment is not what the Fifth House supports, but "happy" does not really describe us at this juncture. Neptune is warning us to get a grip the minute we feel we are being seduced into a hypnotic world of unreality. No short cuts to ecstasy will be allowed during this transit. The results of any self-damage done become apparent by the time exhausted Neptune enters the Sixth on its shaky crutches.

STONED LOVE

In the love and romance department, we can be very vulnerable. We may long for an enveloping, emotional relationship to make the rest of our monotonous life bearable. We hope that it will transport us to a place where we can be at peace. If we are single, we may have hopeful feelings about finding "the real thing." With idealistic Neptune, no other kind of union will do! However, it may be impossible for others to fulfill our expectations. Neptune tempts us to think in terms of soul mates, powerful karmic ties, destined encounters, and other forms of spiritual romanticism. We can get high on a vision of idealistic love that leaves no room for mere physical lust. We have an unconscious desire for the perfect experience of two hearts beating as one in a flawless, unfettered relationship. It all sounds pretty unreal, however.

This shouldn't imply that we can never develop a very special love connection. However, any strong attraction that we feel is probably going to be more hyped-up in our head and heart than is reasonable. In addition, the Fifth tends to make ordinary events seem more important than they are. We run the risk of entertaining impossible dreams. An Olympian god or goddess might be able to fulfill them, but not the mere mortals we meet at crowded, smoky singles bars.

However, if we have been without warm, loving companionship for too long, this transit is all that it takes to make us believe that the time has arrived to get deeply and totally involved. It's as if we want to surrender, unconditionally, to whatever the mysteries of love will offer, even if we haven't a clue as to what kind of lover we need! Neptune can be a sacred vow-maker—unlike Uranus, the notorious vow-breaker. We vow to have faith in an understanding Universe by taking a chance to give love and be loved in return. Hope springs eternal.

Our emotions regarding love can be mixed. Neptune is always ambivalent about its feelings, especially the more earthy desires. We could feel that nobody is beautiful and noble enough to satisfy our ideals, and fear that searching for love and failing in this quest will only bring unnecessary sorrow. For example, what if transiting Neptune in our Fifth is also squaring our natal Saturn in our Seventh or our Eighth? It's unlikely that we'll be in the radiant mood needed to attract a partner, much less be willing to confidently pour out our love and trust to anyone.

In some cases, this particular Neptune/Saturn transit could suggest a dry spell regarding romance, leaving us feeling empty, isolated, inadequate, or unattractive. We may compensate by throwing ourselves wholeheartedly into other, less touchy Fifth House pursuits—safer activities that won't end up hurting us, such as learning to paint watercolor landscapes, or swimming laps at the our health spa every day after work.

Whatever our situation, Neptune is telling us to be more reflective about love. Ideally, haven't we learned by now to love without fear, due to all of the inner work we had to undertake when Neptune was passing through our Fourth? Haven't we learned that true security comes from within, at the soul level? If so, then we can become more willing to attract the love that we so richly deserve, without becoming unraveled by any rejection that may come along. We could find our heart's desire, or we could be unfairly dumped after what we thought were two glorious dates. What we can't do is manipulate people to love us back. We'll need to let go of unrequited love experiences, rather than allow them to cripple us emotionally.

DREAM LOVER

If we are married, let's hope it's a solid and contented marriage. Neptune begins to erode any structures that have imprisoned our spirit. The Fifth House is where we seek attention and respect—rave reviews, even. If, instead, we are continually ignored or dishonored in our marital relationship, Neptune lures us to look elsewhere. Perhaps we simply withdraw our warmth and our vitality from our alienating spouse and think about celibacy. This may not be obvious to us in the beginning. We may merely feel disenchanted or bored. Our marriage makes us want to sigh, and we remind ourselves of all those karmic dues we're supposedly paying.

If we opt to stray, we are susceptible to the charms of "fantasy" lovers who are too good to be true. In the beginning of our affair, we may feel that a powerful fate has brought the two of us together. This describes the seductive bliss period that Neptune often brings to the initial stages of a love relationship. However, there's often a lot of hidden baggage that comes with these people who magically appear for us. We eventually wonder if we are playing the role of shrink as well as secret lover.

These folks may see us as enticing, forbidden fruit, probably because we—and perhaps they—are still married. The fact that our marriage is miserable may attract such suitors even more—they, too, are motivated by Neptunian urges, and Neptune often describes situations where victim/savior roles are played out. When stress aspects are involved, it's very unlikely that we're in real love. Instead, we're enraptured by the warm, emotional attention that our lover gives to us. The sack of cold potatoes waiting at home is no competition! There will be more about this soap opera when we explore Neptune's Seventh-House transit.

HARD TO REACH

Back to the theme of children: if we have kids, we may find that they are going through a transitional phase that's mighty hard for us to fathom. They could appear listless and aimless, melodramatic and unstable, or just plain hard to connect with on some level. Complications could subtly creep into their lives, although our kids may be good at masking their pain or anxiety. They're keenly aware and wary of how we tend to overreact to their life issues, so they may choose to clam up.

All of the above may not describe our continuous experience with our children; such behavior may come and go like the tides. However, we may sense that they are doing things—perhaps abusive or addictive—that they shouldn't be doing to themselves. This assumes that we can tune in to them at all. Neptune going through this house can make some of us feel almost psychically connected to our kids, for better or worse. Our hopes and fears regarding them could be exaggerated. We could blow things out of proportion. Then again, some of us haven't a clue. The kids most likely to be candidates for Neptune's hook are either experts at being tightlipped or at lying when cross-examined. They know that we probably couldn't handle what's really going on behind our back.

We struggle with the choice of not prying into their personal affairs at all, versus hiring a private eye—ha! In today's world, that's not as far-fetched as it sounds. As with Pluto, there's a Neptunian temptation to spy on them or to covertly acquire information. Well, maybe we're not that desperate to know everything.

What we really need to do at some point is to have a good, heart-to-heart talk with our children, honestly and nonjudgmentally letting them know how we feel about them without the shrill of our Neptunian hysteria tuning them off. (Imagine the dramatics of Neptune crossing over a Fifth-House Mars.)

Now more than ever, our children are sensitive to sharp criticisms and thoughtless words. If we are too direct or irrationally angry, they're likely to withdraw and become unreachable. We also need to be open to their goals and ideals about their future. They may have a visionary sense of themselves that needs our emotional support in order to develop. We shouldn't be too quick to steer them only in the safe life-directions that we might prefer. This could be a wondrous time of unfoldment for them. Their budding dreams do not deserve to be crushed prematurely by our skepticism or lack of imagination. Maybe we're the ones who are vision-starved, and our kids are unconsciously coming to our rescue!

Of course, if we just had a child and are new to parenting, the honeymoon is still on. We can develop a touchingly beautiful feeling of being totally bonded with our baby. Such a transcendent glow can last for a few years. Realize, however, that Neptune can remain in this house until our precious little one is in his or her mid-teens, or older! Things can change quite a bit by then. We should note that our accumulated experience of this kid has been colored by the sometimes distorting lens of Neptune. We'll have to be careful about how we project our unfulfilled needs and hidden, unwanted traits onto all children during this time.

A Fast Buck?

How are investments and speculation affected? Neptune is not into money-accumulating *per se;* hoarding wealth goes against its nonmaterialistic nature. Still, older texts suggest that we'd do well to invest in oil stocks, pharmaceuticals, and anything dealing with the fishing industry! This may be true, but first we'll need to examine our motives regarding why we'd want to invest in anything at all at this time. The more selfish and greedy our motives, the less successful we'll probably be in the stock market or with other financial gambles. There is a side to Neptune that makes us fantasize about getting rich overnight and waking up the next day to find all of our mundane problems solved. That kind of miracle-seeking mentality can interfere with the patience needed to ride the ups and downs of the world of financial risk-taking. It's better to do our homework first and weigh all sides before making any radical financial moves. We can't simply follow our feelings here. We need expert advice from those who are trustworthy and non-intimidating.

NEPTUNE/SUN TRANSITS

TRUER COLORS

Any Outer Planet contacting our natal Sun can signal a major phase for us, involving milestone events or critical turning points, often with new people entering our lives to help us reorient our consciousness. A sextile or a trine may not be as momentous or memorable as a conjunction, square, or opposition, but it still can stimulate an expanded development of our core self—the seat of our ego and our individuality. The square and the opposition leave us little choice but to willingly make quantum leaps in inner growth, or else be forced to change because of uncompromising life experiences. All of these transpersonal planets detest stagnation—procrastinators and escape artists, beware!

Transiting Uranus aspects to our Sun can provide us a wild and crazy time, when more of "the real me" freely bursts forth, whether the world is ready for us or not. We get to come out of many closets, finally, looking and acting quite different than anyone ever suspected. Out come our true colors. Uranus/Sun transits can be highly daring, invigorating, and exciting for us. Such energy feels urgent in its thrust as we push out toward life with greater self-clarity. In contrast, with Neptune/Sun transits, energy apparently wants to go in the opposite direction—back toward a primal, undifferentiated state, where ego and selfhood were never issues. They weren't needed in that unknowable condition before the "Big Bang." Neptune is now trying to give us another taste of that awesomely inconceivable state of Oneness.

Neptune reminds us that ego-awareness is now alive and well only because of the illusionary nature of all manifest existence—blame it on maya imposing a universal deception of duality. A big problem with these transits is that anti-duality Neptune doesn't recognize the ego's right to be and operate in its state of separate existence; therefore, it tries to minimizes our ego's power. Neptune perceives the human ego as too puny and limited in its perspective to be of any long-lasting value. From its rarefied vantage point, Neptune is right—our ego is like an annoying gnat, buzzing around Nirvana.

I'M MELTING

When we identify only with our ego, especially an over-inflated one, we can lose sight of vaster, underlying realities beyond our waking consciousness. We block out a otherworldly phenomena that nevertheless operate—even if invisible—in a continuous, multileveled manner. Of course, we are better able to stay focused in our body precisely because our ego takes over, sets up boundaries, and runs the show during our lives. This helps to keep our solar consciousness centered and contained. (The Sun as a fixed star, relatively stationary compared to the "wandering" planets, is an apt symbol of our ego-center.)

With this in mind, a Neptune transit to our Sun challenges us to break down and dissolve ego-structures that have kept some of us feeling too separate and individualized from everyone else. Neptune will poke holes in our ego, making its structure more collapsible. The result is that we start to feel on less solid footing with ourselves. Imagine if we already felt insecure and uncertain about our life's direction, even before this Neptune transit kicks in.

The Outer Planets present us with inner rumbles in the beginning. With Neptune, however, we usually don't feel them coming—life can seem promising one day, and then we are inexplicably plunged into those infamous, murky depths the next. We can be driven with ambition and are eager to fulfill worldly goals—that is, until Neptune hits us with a strange wave of discontent. Things central to our life begin to seem unclear, even purposeless. Uncertainties usually come from internal sources first, rather than as a result of situational shifts, especially with the square. Eventually, however, we will see signs of Neptune's influence in our circumstantial affairs, especially if that will get us to pay attention to what's happening inside us. We may start to crumble for a darn good reason.

"I'm melting...melting!" wailed the Wicked Witch of the West in *The Wizard of Oz*. She obviously had a heavy Neptune/Sun transit on top of some mismanaged Pluto/Saturn upheaval! She vanished in a smoky puddle in a truly Neptunian ending. We, too, may feel as if we're disappearing into a dark puddle, because much of what our ego has fed us is beginning to do its own meltdown—even if we haven't turned green and ugly with wickedness.

CORE CONFUSION

Our solar-identified ego in today's competitive society is susceptible to adopting masks and roles that make us appear important and highly valuable to the world. The Sun seeks potency and can prompt us to feel superior to others, although this is more emphasized in Leo's makeup. We are urged to develop a commanding presence and an air of utter self-confidence—meaning zero tolerance for personal weakness and vulnerability. Looking good on the surface, especially when living in a society that endorses this, is sometimes more desirable and easier for the Sun than being gut-real with oneself, and perhaps risk ending up humble but unnoticed. Neptune during this transit has a different agenda, which involves remodeling our sense of essential identity.

Although Uranus/Sun transits provoke us to release our true self, they do so more dynamically and impatiently than Neptune/Sun will. Neptunian transits are subtle and gradual in their unfoldment, even though the Sun doesn't care to deal with life's subtleties. This is why knowing astrology helps. We can see an upcoming Neptune square or opposition to our natal Sun long before we actually have to deal with it. Why not pretend it's already happening now and start to "rehearse" the inner adjustments symbolized by the aspect in question? After all, pretending that certain things are going on when they really aren't is, in itself, a Neptunian exercise. We could start by running a number of "what if" scenarios in our head, then try to imagine how'd we'd deal with them in our present state of consciousness. This exercise requires much self-honesty if it is to prove effective.

Neptune's transiting touch can be gentle and understated. Breakdowns occur ever so slowly, giving us time to reflectively go within while we are *just* beginning to feel uneasy with our life patterns. The trick is to pay attention to that uneasiness without being too quick to blow it off as solely due to temporary, external frustrations. Some of us are better than others at knowing when we are at odds with our basic self. Neptune seeks to target folks who are the most out-of-touch with their core level of being.

With the Sun as the aspected planet, conditions fundamental to our core identity are the prime focus. Who do we think we really are, at this point? How have we chosen to validate the real person inside? Do we act in ways that show healthy self-respect and true integrity? Do we honor ourselves—which is not the same as being self-adoring? If so, Neptune will further enhance such qualities. It helps if we direct such positivism toward broader, collective objectives, since Outer Planet energy cannot comfortably remain self-contained within the limits of an isolated ego. This can be a time when we'll have to lose ineffective parts of ourselves in order to find the hidden treasure buried within. Again, Neptune attempts to weed it out whatever is unhealthy before the entire system is hopelessly damaged. Pluto does this too—but the intense, drastic way it often does so can leave us speechless!

PEDESTALS AND PITFALLS

With Neptune, our nobler qualities can be elevated to new heights due to this planet's expansive nature. In fact, many things about us become magnified during this transit—that includes our less attractive traits, which can result in distorted self-expression. People might misread us, maybe because we are not coming across the way that we think we are. Of course, we could seem more captivating to people than is truly warranted. Some could try to idolize us, lionize us, even megastar us—all of which can be very tempting to an ego used to overcompensating. We could be worshiped by adoring "fans" or manic "followers" if we are in a powerful position to impart Neptunian dreams of hope, faith, redemption, or inspiration. Charismatic leadership can come from all Neptune/Sun exchanges; we can be put on a pedestal for being an all-knowing "big cheese." There's also a tendency to project Neptune/Sun energies onto spellbinding leaders, and then become an unquestioning follower.

In terms of serious pitfalls, a few of us might unconsciously attempt to further damage an already weakly-structured ego during this transit. A weak ego usually implies a poorly-integrated Saturn—guardian of the ego's locked gates—which leaves a hidden back door open for all sorts of unconscious influences and collective forces to invade our rather defenseless core-self. This can take some of us down the road to insidious self-destruction. Should our sense of self dissolve rapidly, we can find ourselves too disoriented to relate to others as an independent, self-sufficient individual. We can be overtaken by people and situations that rob us of our autonomy. Our power to live *our* lives, *our* way, is wiped out by escapist responses that undo all that we've struggled to build for ourselves.

Neptune invites melodrama. There's no need to list the possible scary things that can befall us. Let's just say that Neptune will take us as low as we are able and willing to go. The horrors of alcoholic psychosis or of advanced stages of heroin addiction, and the attendant squalor involved, emphasize what it means to lose a sense of one's inner core while inviting demons to tear us apart. In a few instances, we may really feel that we are losing it, mentally and emotionally. With the Sun, such disintegration can have a dramatic effect on us. If we've been flirting with a nervous breakdown, this could be the time to give it a whirl and finally get all of our stored-up junk out of our psychic system. We may have to hit rock bottom with ourselves, on some level, before we re-emerge, cleansed and purified.

STORMS AT SEA

On the other hand, what about big-shot egos that run around and try to control the rest of us? Neptune, in the beginning, may swell our ego as we are lured by promises of greater power and recognition. A hungry Sun has a huge appetite for such glories. However, a trap is being set, even while we haven't a clue about what's really driving us. We can blindly continue to let our ego grow and grow, until it creates grave imbalances in our psyche's system. Anything under the firm grip of an out-of-control ego can become misused for exceedingly selfish, even *heartless,* purposes.

That's when the Universe calls on Neptune to puncture this ballooning, overgrown ego of ours, reducing it to a more workable size or letting out its hot air all together—just before things really get out of hand. Otherwise, we'd recognize no boundaries. We'd start to believe that nothing is going to limit us, as if we're magically protected by the strength of our narcissistic self-will. This is when we can really get reckless, egging Neptune on to begin its unraveling process by creating internal storms at sea. Poseidon is unleashed, and things get messy as we lose our focus. In the end, when everything is falling apart and we feel *powerless* to stop it, Neptune gives us an option to "repent and sin no more" or otherwise abandon whatever we were doing to get so out-of-kilter with our lives and relationships. It can be a humbling experience, but one that can turn us around for the better.

POOPED OUT?

Transiting Neptune/Sun aspects correlate with feeling devitalized. Maybe that's one way to get us to slow down and rest. Naps may be required more than usual. We also may sleep longer and harder. Getting up in the morning might be more of a chore. The more we sleep, the more we visit the soul's theme park—

Dreamland—where we give our overworked ego-consciousness a break from concrete reality. It's important that we don't try to go full blast while we're up and about, because we'll risk needlessly depleting ourselves. It's more difficult to do high-quality spiritual, inner work when we're drained and exhausted. We will need to pay attention to our body's limits and not push things here. Let's get off our tired feet and relax!

ILLUMINATI

Whether we are cracking up emotionally or we're trying to mani-acally overpower the galaxy, or doing a bit of both, Neptune's healing powers offer us a way out of chaos and into a reborn world of peacefulness and true inner contentment. We can learn to feel universally connected in all of the right ways. In this new world, we don't have to struggle or force ourselves to do anything or change anybody. We just have to reclaim our spiritual center and operate from now on according to a "do no harm" policy. We'll also need to wisely accept life's terms, even when we don't understand them. Then we can freely follow our heart, with the hope that things will unfold and benefit us when the time is right. At all times, we should continuously help to co-create the beautiful inner and outer experiences we need. A lovingly cooperative Universe is now on our side, whispering to us to never again lose our faith in our essential goodness or give away our power while in a state of self-ignorance.

It may be that we get to define a spiritual path for ourselves at this time, one that is attuned to our heart and soul. Our urge is to integrate spiritual vision into a personal life pattern to which we can authentically adhere. The Sun can turn whatever it openly embraces into an important, strength-producing facet of living. If we work with this transit with the conscious intention of growing wiser from it, greater self-illumination is ours.

CHAPTER ELEVEN

NEPTUNE TRANSITING THE SIXTH HOUSE

THE DIRTY WORK

In our Sixth House, we meet with many situations that can make physical living a real chore for an ethereal planet like Neptune. Here can be found issues revolving around the drudge work often demanded by earthbound existence. This is our "It's a dirty job, but someone's got to do it!" house. To help us feel better about undertaking the sometimes labor-intensive tasks that this sector demands, astrologers emphasize the self-rewarding values of orderliness, punctuality, and productivity. We are training ourselves to do things correctly in this house—and if mistakes are made, let's at least learn from those mistakes and not repeat them! This is a basic Sixth House attitude.

Life may be full of pitfalls and dead-end roads, but we can work around them using our intelligence, common sense, and ability to educate ourselves regarding the nuts and bolts of how anything works—how the various parts involved are made to effectively and reliably interact. This sounds like a preparatory stage for Seventh-House dynamics. In the Sixth, we also learn to micromanage energy and time, which involves becoming selective in what we do and how we do it. There's always a smart way and a stupid way to do just about anything. With Neptune, we'll need to pay better attention if we want to do things the smart way, rather than waste time. Efficiency is not Neptune's middle name.

Many minor and relatively insignificant Sixth-House activities must be routinely maintained so that we can more fully enjoy life's greater pleasures. These trivial tasks may seem like small nuisances at times, but they are the daily rituals that help us to operate competently. Through the repetition of these experiences, we enable ourselves to develop practical organizational skills. Thus, in the Sixth, we can learn precise methods and techniques that enhance our proficiency in handling necessary details. Here's where alertness, concentration, and patience pay off. In general, the Sixth House teaches us to cope with life's day-to-day functional requirements. When done well, we become intelligently adaptable to situational changes.

WAKE-UP CALL

If you think about where Neptune just came from, it's easier to understand how this planet's entrance into the Sixth can be a sobering experience—a wake-up call. In the self-promotional Fifth, our heart's desires, backed by focused will power, made creative things spring to life. Now the party's over. We've made a mess of the place, and had fun in the process, but now it's time to clean up the joint by first taking out bags of trash, vacuuming the carpet, and then running the dishwasher. Such activities sound wearisome to otherworldly Neptune, who would urge us to sleep off our hang-over instead! Unfortunately, life becomes more difficult when we habitually fail to pick up after ourselves or refuse to tie up our loose ends—a chronic problem for some unfocused natal Neptunians.

When Neptune crosses the Sixth-House cusp, it's time for us to clean up our act, especially if we've craved pleasure and indulged too much when Neptune was escaping from certain practical realities in the Fifth. Few of us are in near-perfect condition regarding Sixth-House matters. It seems that there's always room for improvement—just ask Virgo, a task-oriented sign attuned to

Sixth-House approaches to the job of living. At least in the beginning of this transit, Neptune might feel like a fish out of water. The structured manner in which this house neatly compartmentalizes life is alien to Neptune, who would rather scatter sundry items in unusual combinations here and there. This planet might have cluttered closets, but everything in them touches everything else, creating the sense of unity that Neptune worships. This is not a tidy planet. Neptune finds much of the Sixth House too regimented, while the Sixth is afraid that Neptune too easily ignores instructions and established procedures.

HEALTH SECRETS

Certain Sixth-House themes may appeal to Neptune. The Sixth deals with purification and healing, usually on physical levels. The goal here is to have our body and mind interworking as well as possible. This ideal alone attracts this planet's attention, because Neptune also seeks to rid us of whatever poisons our spiritual system or keeps us sick on psychological levels. Wise Neptune knows that such "dis-ease" eventually works its way down into our body, where it gets trapped on a cellular level. Neptune is a great planet for advocating fasts, cleansing diets, and other techniques that purge or flush out toxins. Even sweating them out in steam baths and saunas is appealing to Neptune. Pluto is also associated with this, but Neptune's techniques are usually less drastic or extreme. This is a house of health matters, so we'll probably need to pay close attention to how our inner attitudes and beliefs directly influence our physical functioning. These are not separate realities.

A typical interpretation is that, while we may be alive, we may not be so well at this point. We may have suffered years of body wear and tear due to bad habits, especially during Neptune's Fifth-House transit. However, Neptune does not easily disclose physical symptoms, which may mysteriously come and go. We could be fooled into thinking we are in relatively good shape when, in truth, something inside of us may be beginning to malfunction. Neptune can be maddeningly slow when it comes to revealing what's wrong, so it could take years before a serious problem surfaces. That could give us plenty of time, however, to correctively deal with conflictive, inner issues related to such body problems. Once symptoms finally surface, they typically send doctors and other healers on a wild goose chase, thanks to their vague or contradictory nature. Misdiagnosis and ineffective treatment are likely.

Rather than becoming paranoid from reading this, we would do better to take an honest and object look at ourselves and confront a few hard questions. Have we knowingly done unhealthy things to our body? What are our specific vices in this area? Do we abuse not only the usual culprits—alcohol, tobacco, narcotics, and stimulants—but even food? The Sixth has a connection with eating—specifically, the taking in of proper nutrition to fire up our bodies. This house is not into eating for the sake of sensual enjoyment (Taurus/Second House) or emotional need (Cancer/Fourth House). The Sixth House urges us to carefully prepare and consume only the purest foods in their most unprocessed, uncontaminated forms. It values things "natural and organic," free of chemical additives and empty calories. Why try to run the body-mind machine by using only low-grade fuel?

OUT OF SHAPE

Neptune may love to fantasize about fresh, lovingly prepared food that has come from beautiful, sun-kissed vegetable gardens. The reality is that, under Neptune's spell, we can forget that we even have bodies that need care. Bodies require constant upkeep, but during this transit we can shirk our responsibility to maintain physical well-being. We are less inclined to do what we know we must to ensure good health and vitality. Some of us may forget to eat or put off doing so for much too long, thus playing havoc with blood sugar levels. We may not be getting proper rest, due to sleeping too much or not enough. On top of that, the only thing we seem to exercise these days is our wild imagination, leading to hypochondria. We could be on ridiculous fad diets that don't work wonders for us but do undermine our health. Some of us may look out of shape as a result of Neptunian water retention posing as excess fat, possibly as the result of long-term mineral imbalances.

We may even slack off in our grooming habits. We can start looking sloppy, frumpy, unkempt—now where *did* we misplace that iron? Such an appearance may be linked with low self-worth. Also, any former dedication to meticulous housekeeping may be abandoned for now. We have a hard time mustering up sufficient energy, concentration, or motivation to slave away at uninspiring chores. If this is how this transit is manifesting, it's a case of mismanaging its dynamics. Neptune is going a bit *too* much with the flow, weakening self-discipline.

The purpose of this planet passing through our Sixth House is not to make our lives more messy than ever, turning us into secret slobs moping around in ratty bathrobes (with or without a beer in our hands)! Instead, we are to find outlets for Neptune that can encourage us to be constructively health-conscious, although not fanatically so. This is harder to do than it sounds. Neptune can turn mere beliefs into religious awakenings. We may expect overnight miracles once we have "seen the light" and gotten back "on the right path," as we "solemnly vow" never to stray again. Such an approach typically doesn't last very long, and we may find ourselves regressing to old, nasty habits. Nevertheless, the Sixth House itself pushes for sensible, less emotionally based decisions about changes in diet and exercise that we can incorporate into our new way of visualizing ourselves. It's a house that always supports moderate solutions, not the dramatic, faith-driven ones that tempt Neptune.

DAMAGE CONTROL

In this house, a lot of us grapple with inner inadequacies that cause us to feel inferior and never quite up to par with others. Self-criticism can be a stumbling block for people strongly oriented to the Sixth House. Both Neptune and the Sixth, when working in harmony, teach us how to take curative measures to heal inner wounds. The Sixth works on the tangible self (the physical and biological) while Neptune tries to fix the damaged parts of the intangible self (our psyche and our spirit). Both planet and house have our self-betterment in mind as a shared goal. Each tries to restore us to higher and more satisfying levels of functioning. Before this transit is finished, we may have gained some insights about the complex and delicate body-mind-heart-soul connection. The rewards are good health on all levels of our being, thanks to an effortless flow of vitality.

OF SPECIAL SERVICE

What about work? This is another issue that absorbs us in this house—our job. The Sixth represents not our career *per se,* but all of those necessary, daily tasks that we have to do to keep busy and get things done. Sweaty, hard labor is not appealing to delicate Neptune, but uplifting service to society is. In the Sixth House, we are first exposed to the idea of going beyond self-interest and into the world of others who need to be served and bettered on some level. What an adjustment in thinking this is from the overall consciousness of the Fifth House, where everything has to revolve around self-absorbed ego-demands in one way or another. The Fifth expects big personal pay-offs, but our Sixth House knows that self-centeredness is followed by payback time.

Neptune intuitively understands that willingly serving others in society becomes a way to link up with people from all backgrounds, thereby encouraging unity-consciousness. It's a first step on the path to collective awareness and spiritual understanding. Neptune urges us to put our personal desires aside and open our hearts for the sake of others who need our help. The Sixth House teaches us, however, to serve and assist wisely and selectively. That involves using good judgment, which Neptune must learn regarding all worldly matters.

Of course, not all of us will easily embrace this more enlightened view. What if we have a feisty natal Mars in the Sixth square our cardinal Sun, and have already shown a great amount of aggressive self-interest at our workplace? We have made a few enemies, but have also gotten ahead because of our headstrong determination and gumption. Neptune's arrival may cause much inner confusion and resistance. Hustling to get things done quickly comes naturally to Mars, even if a few toes are stepped on in the process. However, with Neptune in this house, our pushy tactics may no longer serve as well. We may not realize it, but Neptune will work quietly during the next few years to soften our approach to our job or the tasks at hand.

Usually this means that we'll need to listen more than we speak, reflect on issues first before impulsively doing things, and find better ways to get along with co-workers. What can we do create an atmosphere of greater unity and caring? How can we allow our emerging intuitions to improve the flow of business? Can we learn to be gently assertive on the job, incorporating more of Neptune's humane values, while still making sure that we are not being taken advantage of as a result?

OFFICE DRAMA

Actually, Neptune means that we may not see the situation at work clearly; certain realities are veiled to us. We may assume things, due to our idealism or our suspicions, that are not actually going on. As we project the less-attractive parts of this Neptune transit, others in our workplace could appear inattentive, unreliable, hard to understand, underhanded, or disorganized when it comes to handling assignments. Co-workers could rely on us to fix their problems, bail them out so that they don't get in trouble with the boss, and even play their shrink. We may also begin to confide in them. This is not the kind of Neptunian experience we should welcome. Yes, we are showing that we can be kindhearted and compassionate, but we could also slip into a co-dependent relationship without knowing it.

The real kicker is that, once we withdraw our support from such an incompetent co-worker, that person may turn on us and try to make us look bad. Our image can be smeared by such a backstabber. Who needs this? Well, maybe we do. This is how we learn the hard way about establishing boundaries in our Sixth

House and about being less innocently open to doing other people's jobs. Being serviceable has its limits, something we must realize. Also, trying to "cover" for anyone is a form of deception—which is why it backfires on us in the long run.

The above describes a less-than-ideal work environment. Fortunately, Neptune can also put us in touch with very giving, supportive, highly creative people on the job—folks who look out for one another and try to work warmly together, showing some real teamwork spirit in action. It all depends on how dedicated everyone is. Each person has to believe in what he or she is doing. We are probably attracting a mix of the inspired and the disgruntled; therefore, the pragmatic Sixth House is teaching us to detach a bit and throw ourselves into our own work, without having to feel that we must harmonize with everyone. There will be no perfect office setup, but we can make the best of things by having faith in our own work performance.

In some cases, Neptune here means that we are discontent and unable to find satisfying employment. Sometimes this transit suggests no work, under-employment, or a string of part-time odd jobs that pay our bills but keep us feeling unfocused and lacking in direction. With Neptune, it's always good to gravitate toward doing something that we strongly believe in, something that emotionally moves us. The material rewards of work—salary and prestigious title—are less important. We unconsciously seek soul enrichment and may be drawn to jobs that pay less but nonetheless fulfill a humanitarian need in society.

This unstructured Neptune transit may be easier to cope with if we're self-employed and are used to a lack of steady work and a predictable weekly income. However, even here, we may have doubts about our future regarding what we have chosen for ourselves. We'll need to do some soul searching to make sure that we aren't stuck in a line of work because of unrecognized insecurities and fears—the fear of success as well as the dread of failure. We may not be tapping into our greater talents and are stagnating more than we realize. Perhaps we do realize it, and are secretly depressed. We'll need to trust in our dreams and visions of a better tomorrow while remaining willing to let go of things that no longer work for us. Realistic self-appraisal is a must to counteract the Neptunian tendency to sweep a few harsh truths about our employment under the rug, in hopes of making them vanish.

NEPTUNE/EARTH MERCURY TRANSITS
VISIONARY WORK

Neptune is a planet that needs to find suitable channels for the expression of its subtle and highly refined nature. If it cannot, the blockage of its energies can give rise to discomforting inner yearnings, a strange sadness, or a hard-to-appease melancholy. The inability to ground our strongly felt Neptunian urges can be a cause of much unspoken suffering and a disquieting sense of being "not of this earth." We feel as if we came from another solar system and are being punished by "doing time" on this dense, hard-to-comprehend planet. Luckily, artists, musicians, actors, photographers, and poets all have found how to evoke Neptune in ways that appeal to our senses and emotions. However, this doesn't just happen with the tap of a magic wand or a few "abracadabras." Creative individuals must work at perfecting their vision with dedicated devotion. It takes effort to bring Neptune's most exquisite sounds and images into tangible form.

The earthy side of Mercury is the part of our mind that wants practical results and seeks simple solutions. It devises and revises sensible plans of action before making the first move, suggesting an economical usage of time and energy. Efforts are not to be wasted or scattered ineffectively. Earth Mercury is also an excellent analyst and problem-solver. If our mind was purely a product of air Mercury, we would talk a lot about our stimulating ideas, then constantly change them. Seldom would we flesh out the details or fine-tune the practical strategies needed to make such ideas work in the real world. In contrast, earth Mercury naturally surveys the details and trouble-shoots when needed. Versatility may not be its gift, but resourcefulness and practical "know-how" are its strengths. Common sense is another important feature of this facet of our Mercury experience, a useful asset for dreamy Neptune.

DOWN FROM HEAVEN

Neptune transiting our natal Mercury and triggering its earthy side means that we are challenged to find avenues that will allow us to pull lofty Neptunian images down into our everyday consciousness in order to make them more concrete and seemingly permanent. This may not always be satisfying in the end, because anything that's too concrete can feel like a prison to Neptune and to those devotees who try to channel its transcendent power. Neptune, in response, gradually attempts to undermine structures that have become too fixed, even if it takes a long time. This suggests that we are seldom completely satisfied with what we've created out of our Neptunian inspirations. Once they are trapped in three-dimensional form, they can't quite capture the glorious image initially revealed to us by our imagination.

All of this ties in with earth Mercury. Our dreams and visions during this transit can be worked on to create—with an additional application of Saturnian patience—physical representations of that which is otherwise intangible. We learn to craft our Neptunian vision carefully, turning it into something solid and enduring. The problem is that we may seek to achieve a state of creative perfection that is just not possible on the physical plane. Still, it helps if we are artistic visionaries who are unafraid to use our imagination, or at least if we are the idealistic, philosophical kind who regards the mind's potential as limitless.

People who invent computer programs that are heavy on complex, mind-bending 3-D graphics may be channeling such a Neptune/Mercury transit very well indeed. Writing the requisite lines of computer code takes all of the stamina and persistence of earth Mercury (and Saturn) that one can muster. Otherwise, there would be no fantastic images for us to behold on our computer screen. Earth Mercury is telling us that the manifestation of an awesome level of Neptune is possible, but it will take diligence and skill—unless we're God, and then it's apparently pretty easy, as shown by the magnificent panorama of nature.

PONDERING THE POSSIBILITIES

We will likely find ourselves learning to unclutter our life. We should dismiss what is uninspiring, and let go of what no longer benefits our inner growth. This can include concepts and attitudes, as well as job situations. We may entertain new thoughts about the kind of work we'd really like to do and the things that authentically speak to our soul. We may be a darn good bookkeeper, but what about that fantasy we once had about being a landscape designer? Why are we thinking about it again after so many years? Is this pure daydreaming, or is Neptune trying to inspire us to revamp our life's direction?

If we are experiencing the conjunction, square, quincunx, or opposition, we'd better take our time pondering the possibilities and not act rashly or passionately to enforce changes. We are not analyzing all of the details, the way earth Mercury normally would in its need to be well informed. An inner yearning to break free of monotonous patterns may also cloud our judgment. We could be more confused about our life than we realize. We have no real game plan and are prone to make moves based on blind faith or crazy hunches, which is not good enough to satisfy earth Mercury, although our restless, free-wheeling air Mercury side might want to give it a go. At this time, we could gamble with our security and end up a loser.

Have we always wanted to open a little vegetarian café close to our home, instead of teaching fourth grade seven miles away? "Fine," says the Cosmos, "but not now." We're probably getting conflicting advice about this from people we know, which should be a sign telling us to wait. Still, it doesn't hurt to dream while we start to research things and do our homework to see if such an enterprise is feasible. Our dream may come true, but probably only because we take time to let things unfold in typical earth-Mercury style—that old, Virgo-endorsed "look before you leap" approach. This is especially important if Neptune is forming a square, quincunx, or opposition to our natal Mercury, suggesting a greater urge to dissolve currently unsatisfying structures.

Neptune making a sextile or a trine may have an easier time persuading earth Mercury to break a few patterns, change some routines, and loosen its grip on managing the details of living. We could even be hit with weird attacks of what appears to us as laziness. Actually we are trying to relax and just don't know it. Maybe we are more tired and unfocused than usual when on the job. Once at home, we revive, as long as we are taking time to delve into creative projects that pique our imagination and curiosity.

Such transits could also suggest an encouraging time to consider how to make our job experience more ideal. Practical application is always big on earth Mercury's list. How can we improve things in small ways? What needs to be gradually weeded out in order to help everything else run more smoothly? Uranus is not the only brainstormer in town. Neptune can also come up with fantastic concepts, although they don't zap us like lightning—instead, they gently float up from our conscious depths. Such wondrous ideas enter our awareness effortlessly, almost magically. We may wake up and realize that we just dreamed about them. We can solve a problem by literally "sleeping on it."

Our Neptunian insights can improve work-related efficiency, because we can now utilize our intuitive understanding of how things fit together to form a greater, functional whole. All of the Outer Planets help us to look at the overview, or the bigger, unified picture. Our Neptune/earth Mercury transits use subtle strategies and maneuverings to help us to arrive at savvy solutions—the kind that make others scratch their heads in amazement and ask, "How in the world did you *do* that?"

MIRACLES IN HEALING?

Another manifestation of this transit is an awakening interest in alternative medicine and health. Neptune is decidedly vegetarian, in my opinion, because that is the least violent way for us to take in nourishment. However, in *The Secret Life of Plants*,[1] Peter

Tompkins mentions studies suggesting that plants can sense danger and feel pain—think of *that* the next time you toss your salad a little too vigorously. With its ability to inspire us to cleanse ourselves of toxic substances, Neptune stirs an interest in anything that promises to be pure and unpolluted. This desire smacks of a yearning to return to the pristine Garden of Eden—that original vegetable patch. Therefore, it's a desire that has much emotional and spiritual appeal for us.

Neptune often encourages strong, unwavering beliefs. We put great faith into what we do to stay fit and healthy. We can swallow our vitamins and our herbal supplements religiously, or face east to do our *tai chi* and deep-breathing exercises every morning. We're even willing to drink our wheat-grass-and-chlorophyll "cocktail" until our teeth turn green. Whatever we choose, it's done with a certain reverence and with much hope that we will physically rejuvenate and transcend our old, tired self. Such rituals and expectations are pure Neptune at work. However, earth Mercury doesn't want us to get too manic about anything. It urges us to be moderate and objective about the actual results gained or not gained. This is the cautious part of Mercury that acts like a research scientist, just like Virgo at work in its Sixth-House lab.

The earthy side of Mercury says that we need to take our Neptunian idealism and blend it with a sensible health regime. We'll be able to endure whatever realistically fits in with who we are, not with what some health or fitness guru tells us we should do. Why force ourselves to jog off a few pounds when we know that we'd much rather walk than run? Hiking down a nature trail with the birdies singing could do wonders for us. Why shop around for exotic, imported, hard-to-pronounce items to add to our diet when, in many cases, true health benefits can come from merely eating less? Smaller meals with fewer combinations of food types alone could do the trick. Earth Mercury will always opt for simpler remedies first—unlike Neptunian solutions which can get pretty elaborate, impractical, or much too far-out for some folks.

In general, this could be an excellent time to listen to our body's signals, especially the ones that trouble us and that we've tried to avoid hearing in the past. Do we have breathing disturbances? There may be a specific reason for them, and not just stress. Perhaps we are afraid that it's an early sign of lung cancer. Neptune/Mercury sometimes gets us to think the worst. Instead, it may turn out to be an allergic reaction to some new "floral-scented" bug spray that we've been using in the kitchen. Our inner voice is pressing for us to find out what's really going on.

The practical side of Mercury reasons that it's better to know the facts and make necessary adjustments than to remain in the dark and suffer needless anxiety. Even if we do take orthodox routes to pinpoint what's bothering us, both air and earth Mercurys will want more than one expert opinion if the diagnosis is serious. This helps to counter-balance Neptune's tendency to play the passive patient who goes along with procedures uncomplainingly.

All in all, this can be a good Neptune transit for getting our bodies and psyches back in order. We can't expect Saturn to do all the hard work! "Back in order" doesn't just mean back to how we once were—it means a new level of operating whereby we expand our capacity to function in life-affirming ways. We can learn to visualize ourselves performing at our optimum, but it will also take discipline and persistence to get to that point. Rather than waste time wallowing in futile self-delusion, we can aspire to do our best to make our life click, to feel that we are on the road to recovery if needed, and to share all of the wisdom we've learned in successfully getting there without becoming evangelistic.

NOTE

1 Peter Tompkins and Christopher Bird, *The Secret Life of Plants*, HarperCollins Publishers, Inc., New York, 1989.

CHAPTER TWELVE

NEPTUNE TRANSITING THE SEVENTH HOUSE

PREPARATORY WORK

If we have successfully made the inner adjustments required by our Sixth-House Neptunian experiences, we've learned to let go of an exclusively egocentric mindset, which should have peaked in the Fifth. Our Sixth is a transitional sector, in that it prepares us for social exchange on a larger scale. Giving to others becomes just as important as allowing ourselves to take from them. Just the fact that we are willing to accommodate another in less self-serving ways is a clue that our consciousness has been altered. Emphasis in our Sixth House is put on being more a helper than a hinderer—although, with Neptune, sometimes we serve others too much in terms of sacrificing time and effort. Perhaps we have difficulty allowing others to give generously to us, as if we are undeserving. We apparently haven't arrived at a state of inner balance yet. However, the opportunity is soon to come.

Whatever the case, we discover in the Sixth that we can get beyond our self-absorption and begin to observe and study others more carefully, learning about their needs. This, however, is not done with real intimacy in mind, basically because most Sixth-

House relationships do not warrant that kind of deep inter-change. Our concern with people's welfare is mostly practical: we feel that we can't do our job or otherwise function correctly if *they're* having problems, so we try to fix things for them, or in them, that are not working well. The Sixth is also a house that doesn't establish equality between people. Somebody plays a sub-servient role and follows orders or instructions. Another gives out the instructions and upholds pre-determined rules of expected behavior. This is common to most company/employee relation-ships. Varying levels of inequality in rank and service typically exist among co-workers as well.

With Neptune transiting the Sixth, perhaps we have learned to have caring, empathetic connections with people, transcending any social barriers that separate us. We may not feel unequal. We can take our new awareness with us into the Seventh House and learn to apply it in this life department, where give-and-take becomes critical. Here, we ideally can attract someone who could be our match, someone who's on our level, as in a peer relation-ship. This requires constant effort on our part, because the need to adjust and readjust to another is even more pressing here than in the Sixth. We are challenged to accept someone else on his or her own terms, without trying to "fix" them. Who says they're in need of repair, anyway? Why do we assume that *we* are the only ones responsible for and capable of doing this high-maintenance job?

FALLING APART

The Seventh House demands clear-headed interactions and much objectivity, something we hopefully begin to develop in our Sixth. We are learning to see more than one side of any issue, both human and theoretical. This is a radical departure from our First-House perspective. Our point of view is still important, but now, so is another's. Equal consideration is to be given. In this house, we learn to take turns and deal fairly with the contrasting needs of a partner. Our own needs will not always be met, or left unmet. It's an alternating situation, which is *so* very Seventh House in theme.

The first thing that Neptune does when crossing this angle is to oppose our Ascendant. How we typically emerge into the day-to-day world is ready to undergo a breakdown and reassembling of self-expression. Neptune reshapes things for the better whenever possible, even though the process involved can be unstabilizing. Things have to fall apart before Neptune can do its special make-over. Our accustomed ways of presenting ourselves to the environment, and to any "significant other," have grown stale to the degree that we have remained uninspired by fresh alternatives. Fixed rising signs can have a problem with the Neptune opposition, because they typically block change that comes from the outside. Still, given enough time, Neptune can break down such factors of resistance. Nothing is to remain forever self-contained and impenetrable in Neptune's realm.

We are in a vulnerable stage throughout Neptune's transit of our Seventh, but most so when it opposes our Ascendant. This period can last about eighteen months. Things may look the same in our lives but, for some obscure reason, won't *feel* the same. There is a vague discomfort in realizing that our actions don't make sense at the time. Give it a few years more, and it still may not make sense! We can wake up one day to discover that we're out of touch with our normal emotional patterns, especially in close relationships. Some of us may deny that our current, committed partnership has problems. However, we may not feel secure with perceived changes in our partner, and we take these changes too personally. Little do we recognize that *we* are going through internal changes, too.

NOBODY'S TALKING

Usually, a planet passing through our Seventh implies that we unconsciously allow our partner to play out that planet's role first. We witness it at a safe, arm's length before eventually trying it on ourselves and identifying with it. This may not even happen at all, because we may never allow ourselves to own our projections. Instead, they get dumped onto someone else, who then must forever live out all of them for us—the good, the bad, and the ugly. As an Outer Planet, Neptune is impossible to "own" completely. Many of its themes will have to be transferred to another, who then repackages and displays them back to us during the course of our relationship.

What a partner might currently be showing us is disinterest and indifference, which are ways to express Neptunian non-attachment. This can also be a defense that masks unaddressed hostility and resentment. Rather than confront us by unleashing Poseidon's turbulent emotions, our mate psychologically removes himself or herself from feeling anything uncomfortable. He or she can tune out. There's a hard-to-define strangeness in the air, but nobody's talking about it. We could feel that our partner is not really "there" when in our presence. He or she has withdrawn, but it is hard to prove. It's a subtle but ever-present feeling for us.

We may wonder if we are just being too sensitive. Well, we *are* unusually sensitive, for good reason. Truths about our union must come out from hiding. Our internal radar system is picking up on something, all right, but our conscious self may scramble the incoming data if it doesn't match up with our long-held assumptions about our spouse. Our urge is to not want to see things as they really are. It's less painful for us that way, as we'll realize later.

FAKING IT

We should also remember that Neptune can play the chameleon, suggesting that a partner at this time can fake whatever emotion we desire just to avoid addressing our marriage's problems. If we can't handle sadness and despair, our "other half" might attempt to appear bubbly and sociable, although that's not how he or she feels inside. We can better attune ourselves to this transit by realizing early on that cover-ups on anyone's part are destructive to the health of this marriage and to our other intimate relationships. This is not the way to become alive and well with Neptune. We will have to allow for some therapeutic self-analysis if we wish to get to the bottom of our reluctance to handle the less-than-perfect elements of our partnership. It doesn't get any easier by the time Neptune enters the Eighth, if we fail to confront this issue now. Why does our partner prefer to masquerade or bury feelings rather than come clean with us? Was it always like this, or just lately? This transit demands that we pay more attention to the overall emotional tone of our union than ever before.

Neptune is teaching us about true compassion, and along with that goes non-judgmentalism. Perhaps we have shown ourselves in the past to be more critical of our mate than we realize, putting him or her down in ways that are not obvious to us. Maybe we appear to never be satisfied with what our spouse does, yet even our silent disappointment can be felt by our partner. Do we lose our temper and blow things out of proportion when something goes wrong in the marriage? Do we point the finger of blame? If any of this is so, our partner has probably learned to go underground as a way to cope with marital discord. We need to realize how we have helped to co-create the situation in which we find ourselves, as well as why we have unwittingly enabled it to continue. Neptune is ready to dissolve our bond if we don't wake up to what's really going on.

TWIN SOULS

What if we are not married? If we are currently interested in having a relationship, which in itself is sometimes not so easy to figure out with ambivalent Neptune, we have to be alert to the down side of this transit. Because of emotionally crushing experiences in the past (Saturn or Pluto to Venus transits), some of us have vowed to stay celibate and unattached as long as we can. In that case, we'll have to find other, creative outlets to use up our Neptune energy. However, many of us who are single will find that we are feeling a hopeful yearning to meet someone out of the ordinary, someone operating on a different dimension from anyone we've known. We dream of a hassle-free relationship with another sympathetic soul who's not afraid of deep intimacy, someone who'll share everything without reservation. We cannot bear for our beloved to be selfish or to hold back emotions out of distrust. There's also an innocent anticipation that our deep love will allow us to telepathically tune in and simply know what the other person needs, without words being spoken.

With Neptune in this house, the suggestion is that we are looking for unconditional love, a total merging, a sense of twin souls intertwined as one. If we are still relatively young, perhaps in our impressionable twenties, this is a poetic, misty-eyed subject for us, if we were born with Neptune in our Fifth. We just know in our hearts (where else?) that *our* love will be a true love, uncorrupted by the cynicism of the times or the skepticism of close friends and family. In fact, the less others accept our lover, the more we may put him or her on a pedestal, because our partner has now obtained the "underdog" status to which we are unconsciously drawn. At issue here is our naiveté and a potential for gullibility. The dream that Neptune weaves for us is very powerful, especially if we have not better integrated this planet within ourselves thus far—either natally or by transit.

FASCINATING RHYTHM

In a crowded room of strangers, the one who stands out above the rest and captures our interest will be a Neptunian. The person is Neptunian either because of potent natal patterns, or because he or she is also undergoing a major Neptune transit. We are magnetized to and fascinated by this type. Contact with more stable Saturnians does nothing for us. Our emotional and physical chemistry is ready for nothing else but a Neptunian experience regarding Seventh-House relationships. The problem is that, although any initial connection with a new partner can feel very inviting, we may not get the person we think we are. We color this relationship with great hope and idealism, raising it to a sublime level. Our chosen partner holds a special charm for us, but people who know us well may not understand or appreciate it. If they advise us to think twice before getting any further into this union, our urge is to ignore the warning and to continue swimming in deep waters. We could even feel hurt by the very suggestion that there is something wrong with our wonderful companion.

This response alone—that we are not recognizing the less-attractive qualities of our new partner that others quickly pick up on—is a clue that our subjectivity will blind us at some future point in this encounter. If we have a lot of earth or even air in our natal chart, then we are not so readily fooled. Earth is reality-grounded and air can detach and objectively analyze. Perhaps we take our time letting this Neptunian situation unfold and are more alert to anything irrational. However, if we have lots of water and/or fire instead (more passionate elements), we could get caught up in much romanticism and unrealistic expectation. This suggests that we are not interested in hearing about the potential limitations of our partnership. Why believe the naysayers when our spirit is soaring with a rising energy that is opening our heart so fully? The rhythm shared feels so right. Since this transit will last for several years, what we feel now is probably not what we'll be feeling once we've had time to become further immersed in Neptune's mist.

INTO THE MYSTIQUE

Much has been made of Neptune's association with victims and saviors. The passive role to be played out here is that of victim, although sometimes it can be a passive-aggressive victim. Our partner may come to us with hidden baggage that involves a personal history of failure or weakness. Life has given this person reason to feel unwanted, unworthy, dejected, rejected, or socially insignificant. We are put into the more active and potentially empowering role of savior, like it or not. Usually we do like it a lot at first, because part of the mystique of this union for us is the feeling that we can give and share like never before. We also feel truly needed like never before, even though we are not sensing just how needy our partner actually is. If we did, we'd think twice about this union...maybe. To some extent, we feel okay about this unspoken contract because we see ourselves in a redeeming spiritual light. There has also been a rosy glow surrounding our relationship from day one.

There can come a stage in our partnership when we may be feeling victimized, perhaps not even directly, which makes it all the more confusing. Perhaps our loved one is sweet and supportive of us, but has one hard-luck situation occurring after another. It appears as a string of rotten events that are beyond our partner's control, or so it seems. We feel torn about it after a while, but are quite certain that we won't abandon someone who's in such a shaky state. Uranus transiting the Seventh would have urged us to bail out long ago. Neptune does appear to have this crazy staying power, hanging on to dreams that may never ultimately fulfill us, while we attempt to do whatever it takes to keep the magic alive and potent. In the Seventh House, Neptune is an energy that comes to us through the attitudes and behavior of someone else. That other person needs to make a tremendous effort to evoke the beautiful, uplifting side of Neptune to keep our dream from becoming a nightmare.

There is something addictive going on both sides. Maybe our partner goes to Alcoholics Anonymous meetings or has just come out of a detox clinic and is dedicated to recovery, and we're glad of that. Then we watch him or her still abuse his or her body or become a "junkie" of another substance because of a need for escapism that we don't share. Even we can become our partner's daily "fix." We may be too intoxicated by what we think is a true soul connection to understand how we have become dangerously hooked on this potentially draining union. Isn't it clear by now why astrologers are not too keen about quickie marriages with this transit? We may not know everything that we're going to really need to know later about our potential spouse. Once we are wed, we'll find out such things the hard way, and we'll probably feel trapped. That's when we feel ourselves the victim instead, asking, "How did the Universe ever let this happen to us!"

BEAUTIFUL UNION

All right, now it's time for some good news. Most of us are really looking for a true, lifelong mate, not a psychiatric patient in need of a miracle worker! Assuming that we are clear about the futility of clinging to any illusions that we have about others, and knowing how astrology can help us here, we can attract a union in which two sensitive people understand what a struggle real spiritual growth can be, and how difficult and frustrating reaching higher stages of perfection really is. By having a lot of heart-to-heart talks with our partner (beware of the *weak,* silent types), we can deeply share the best that each of us has to offer while still retaining our individuality. Any total-merging-into-another fantasy has to go, because that's when we can lose our identity in someone who becomes our Universe—someone whose importance to our very existence has been inflated to dangerous levels.

We might find the enchantment that we yearn for by attracting someone who is very dedicated to collective goals that help to bring more peace, beauty, and unity into this world—especially if their approach is humane, gentle, and unassuming rather than overly dramatic and messianic. They can help the world to make needed social changes in quiet ways. We will have to watch out for our tendency to project larger-than-life qualities onto one another, although there's nothing wrong with honest, mutual admiration for each other's special talents. Neptunian unions tend to be very private. We will need to make sure that we are dealing with someone who is comfortable with introspection and reflection, because we will be wanting to exchange a lot of personal information in our quest to get as close as is healthy for any couple. An element of trust is critical.

The outside world sees little of what really goes on behind the scenes in our union or marriage. However, if we are in a poisonous relationship, we can't afford to keep everything secretive and internalized due to shame and fear. Neptune will try to dissolve what is corrosive to our spirit. We can trick ourselves and live a big lie wherever Neptune transits, but getting foggy and inarticulate about our marital issues leads us further down a path of self-undoing. We have attracted a mortal like ourselves whom we cannot afford to idolize, and *vice versa.* We'll need to stay firmly on the ground with our emotions, while believing that a little piece of paradise can still be ours. This is a union that basically thrives in an atmosphere of clarity, honesty, and lots of tender, loving care.

We are to bring our humanity into the picture, not an unreal aura of saintliness that can lead to martyrdom.

Neptune/Air Venus Transits
No Greater Love

Neptune transiting our Venus, when evoking its airy side, becomes a time to reflect about the nature of love. We see how it has worked so beautifully for some, and now we start to yearn for such an intimate experience ourselves—even if only in our dreams. However, unless we go out of our way to play the hermit and disappear from the social scene altogether, we are more magnetic to others than usual. We may not even be aware of this fact. Whom we actually draw to ourselves determines whether or not all of this magnetism is a good thing. With Neptune doing the fishing, you never know what will be reeled in—it could be an angel fish, or a slippery eel.

We probably are giving off unconscious signals, advertising to others that we are understanding, compassionate, tolerant individuals who have a lot to offer. This may not really be who we are but, with Neptune, this is how we appear to people, especially strangers. We give off an aura that some find irresistible at this time. Usually, we attract people who create their own glowing interpretations of us. If the transit is a square or an opposition, we'll have a harder time trying to convince another that we're not perfect. At this time, our love interest doesn't seem to see our flaws or weak points, or simply is not bothered by them.

If we feel ourselves to be kind and decent, yet for some reason are often lonely, then Neptunian energy more easily infiltrates our consciousness with feelings of how fabulous it would be to fall in love right now—with an extraordinary person who is on the same wavelength. We want an ultra-compatible relationship, above and beyond the ordinary experience that most people have. We want a miracle to walk into our lives and sweep us off our feet! Once we realize this, finding that kind of lover can become an all-consuming goal, as suggested by the energy that we feed to our continuous romantic fantasies.

HEAVENLY UNION?

Before we even begin to attract anyone, it's wise to do some honest self-reflection at this early stage of the Neptune process. Yes, we sincerely want a loving partner, but why must it be the *perfect* partner, one who is expected to melt away all of our emotional problems? Why must this partner always be supportive and caring, no matter what; a person who is never to leave us, no matter how difficult our behavior? Irrational fears of abandonment can plague us during pivotal Neptune transits, although we unconsciously are looking for someone who will never walk out on us. Ironically, should we choose the wrong partner due to our self-deceptive expectations, we'll be praying later that he or she *would* just walk out that door with that bottle of Prozac and leave for good! However, that might not be easily accomplished, because Neptunian relationships involve complex psychological attachments. They can be as sticky as spider webs. Some partners seem to want never to leave us, no matter how badly *they* are behaving!

Sometimes we depend on that other person to help us merge with the Divine. Unknowingly, we may be seeking a sense of oneness where we no longer feel separate from others or divided within ourselves. We blame such feelings of being separate and alone as a fundamental source of our long-term pain. Anyone who enters our life now is subconsciously expected to have godlike qualities, such as being able to heal our suffering and help us transcend who we are. We can submerge ourselves into that other person in hopes of losing ego-awareness of all that we loathe and reject about ourselves. Our lover is to make us feel beautiful and complete. Anticipating such perfection from someone else can result in even more pain, because our partner is human—not a god or goddess, or even a demigod. Disappointments are inevitable when we exalt others this way. We also could dissolve existing unions that disillusion us, then move on to someone new just to repeat the same psychological dynamics, with the same disheartening results.

SUFFOCATION

With Neptune, we'll need to establish healthy boundaries if this union is to offer true growth for us. Two healthy egos will have to remain intact. It's hard, but essential, to learn how to assert ourselves and say "no" to a partner, instead of giving in to the urge to always please and comfort another. We can be overly protective. We may also need some breathing space from a lover or mate who tries to be everything and do everything to make our world perfect, because we may then begin to feel suffocated with this fixated attention. After all, what if we were born with Venus in Aries, Sagittarius, or Aquarius? We wouldn't care for someone taking action for us all of the time, even out of the kindness of trying to spare us from making difficult decisions.

If we are inadvertently sending out signals of helplessness—perhaps a weird situation has temporarily put us in that role—it is important to nip things in the bud and be clear about who we are. This alone may trigger our Neptunian partner to drift away, because we refuse to be saved from whatever gloom-and-doom he or she has projected onto us. These lovers cannot satisfy a psychological function important to them; therefore, the energy that they offer to us must be withdrawn. We have to be willing to take that chance if we want to honor our individuality in any relationship at this time.

SECRET AFFAIR

If we are married during a Neptune/Venus transit, things can be very nice if the aspect is a sextile or a trine. This becomes a time when mutual understanding can be heightened, through a willingness to extend levels of marital cooperation. Unity is emphasized (air Venus loves harmony) and any rough edges in our union can be smoothed over. A certain romance is reintroduced into the relationship, but it's nothing that goes overboard. Emotional exchanges are more reasonable and less fantasy-oriented. Still, with Neptune, we'll have to watch out for wishful thinking when it comes to trying to change our partner "for the better." This is a time to be more accepting of what is, rather than regretting what could have been but isn't. We can enrich our marriage with small gestures of kindness and consideration that let each of us know that we are valued, appreciated, and very much loved. It can seem that the honeymoon is on again.

However, if the marriage has already been damaged, leaving at least one of us deeply wounded and mistrustful, a transiting Neptune/Venus conjunction, square, quincunx, or opposition can mark a time of further alienation. We may harbor fantasies of escaping from our dilemma into the arms of someone who can rescue us. Usually, at this point, there are very unpleasant things about our marriage that we've managed to keep secret from friends and family. We feel ashamed, perhaps, about the sorry state of our union. There may be periods of uneasy silence when feelings are suppressed, then moments of emotional chaos when stormy Poseidon lashes out. Our union is having more than its share of ups and downs—and the ups are not very "up" at all.

We are typically bewildered about what to do, and may stall for time. Divorce may be contemplated, but legal proceedings are seldom set into motion. In this stage of vulnerability, we could seek comfort in a stranger, or at least someone to whom we're not married who can dress our wounds, caress our soul, and make us feel that we are alive and well, and definitely worth a lot more than we realize. Neptune is not a sexual planet like Mars or Pluto, but it still can get us into situations where we can be seduced or set up to play out a seductive role. Sex is not the goal, but merging with another as intimately as possible usually is. We use our sexuality as a way, hopefully, to get to that deeper point. The big problem here is that we are not consciously thinking it all out at the time. Our unconscious is taking over, increasing our compulsion to act.

Transiting Neptune/Venus relationships are heavenly at first, convincing us that we have found a true soul mate who will help us to finally get away from "that beast at home" who torments us.

We can be oblivious to our unrealistic choice of partner. Still, we cherish any clandestine rendezvous, seeing it as our only chance to get out of jail for a while and breathe fresh air. We also can become more attached to our new lover than we ever thought we'd be, although we're not too sure if that was supposed to happen. It seems our lover professes to feel the same way about us. We just know, inside, that the special bond between us is strong and powerful. However, our capacity to wildly project all sorts of superhuman qualities onto our partner can backfire. Two people in a vaguely defined love relationship are not seeing one other in real terms, and the unreality involved cannot be sustained forever. The foundation, reeking of fantasy, collapses as Neptune's waters rush in and eventually drown us.

It's not so hard to imagine what can happen, the longer this affair continues. Much of it involves the horror of seeing our heartfelt idealism trampled in the mud or nailed to the cross, as our "inspired artist" lover turns out to be a paranoid alcoholic with a vicious streak and little true ambition to succeed. Or perhaps our very gentle, loving, spiritual partner—who helped to open up our inner universe—later is forced to admit that he or she is also married and wants to remain that way. Even if we, too, have a spouse, such news hurts us very much. When our new lover finally comes out of the closet, we don't like what we see very much. We don't even recognize it. We feel tricked and cheated. If our self-worth was shaky at the start of this extramarital affair, we're on even shakier ground now that the truth has surfaced. While caught up in this surreal scenario, some of us may think that we are going mad. How did we ever get to star in this badly written soap opera?

With Neptune, planet of entanglements, it is best to work on our existing relationships, to either heal or dissolve them, before attempting to bring any new individual into the picture. We have to be completely available for any relationship to get better results, rather than be stuck in a crazy limbo stage. We still may suffer disappointments, but at least we are honestly offering any new partnership a more realistic start. If we are single, let that other partner also be single. This isn't Saturn talking, with its moralistic rules of social behavior. This is coming from a wiser Neptune, who has seen people get burned too many times by bogus affairs that first send us to cloud nine, then plummet us down to the lonely pits of hell. The remorse and emptiness felt is sometimes too much to bear. We need to stay conscious and realize that we have choices. We can't afford to walk out of or plunge into relationships with blinders on. Escapism will not lead us down the path of emotional fulfillment that we seek during this transit.

CHAPTER THIRTEEN

NEPTUNE TRANSITING THE EIGHTH HOUSE

COVER UP

When it comes to intriguing psychological mysteries, Neptune and the Eighth House share a few things in common. Both deal with less-obvious aspects of our emotional life. The Eighth is where we can hide out and go underground with parts of our psyche. We are not comfortable exposing such qualities, except sometimes in controlled and calculated ways in an attempt to either "master" those parts or—failing that—to manipulate the environment, a tactic that sometimes backfires when done too forcefully. Drives and urges found in the Eighth are not qualities that others are easily permitted to discover. We can be guarded here, unwilling to freely offer what we have, which is a pity, because this house works best when mutual, inner resources are shared in close and committed relationships.

Secretive Neptune favors working behind the scenes, out-of-sight, where we are urged to go deeply within rather than operate superficially. To evade exposure, Neptune can adopt chameleon-like defenses, throwing others off track who try to gather information about us. Neptune, like the Eighth, has an association with invisibility and with things sometimes better left unseen. It doesn't wish to be found in the spotlight or be directly scrutinized by others. Instead, it seeks the shade. Hidden psychological disguises can be used by both planet and house to thwart detection and keep others at bay.

Together, Neptune and the Eighth suggest that we'll have to enjoy a good mystery while we play the intuitive detective if we are to ever find out what is actually going on below the surface. Neither planet nor house take simple, direct routes to get anywhere. There are always twists and turns in the road, adding to the complexities that already exist. Neptune and the Eighth also deal with fateful life-endings, where we feel our losses deeply. Neptune dissolves our earthly attachments, and relationships can permanently die in the Eighth. However, in learning to let go, we can transform ourselves and transcend the limitations of ego-driven emotions. Both planet and house push for our release from anything that keeps us too structured and inflexible.

REMOVING THE BLINDERS

Neptune's journey through our Seventh House introduced a few disturbing realities involving the underlying truth about our relationships. In many cases, we've had to free ourselves of illusions involving our marriage—perhaps, if necessary, even letting go of our partner. Our idealism regarding intimacy may have been tested by painful truths that life forced us to see in both ourselves and our mate. We've learned to remove our blinders during this period. In some cases, that made a difference in the quality of our current relationships. Now we may be interacting on an expanded level of understanding and cooperation with those who are close to us. There may be room for a spiritual connection and for more honest exchanges of the heart.

If we ended our Seventh House transit with a realistic sense of greater hope, then Neptune going through our regenerative Eighth can further solidify our union, making our bond stronger. Any marriage barely kept alive by weak and illusionary excuses will need to be dissolved before Neptune gets to our Eighth, where it would probably never withstand the rigorous methods of analysis typical of this probing house. This house is only for hearty survivors, who are in their relationship for the long haul.

Before we can potentially reach profound levels of marital fulfillment, our Eighth requires that we dive into deep pools of unexpressed feelings and buried desires. Not everything will be openly worked out in our Seventh. A relationship's more complicated issues are reserved for Neptune's Eighth-House assignment. In this house, our urge to merge becomes intensified and focused. Issues are put under the microscope, where hidden flaws and defects are more easily seen. The sexual dimension of our committed union is usually under serious review. Transiting Neptune can break down barriers that have formerly kept us from fully surrendering ourselves to shared sexual experience. This requires ultimate trust in one another. Neptune cannot endure restrictions for too long, and will seek to open the flood gates of passionate arousal—although for Neptune, the yearning to lose oneself, disappear into another, and momentarily transcend self-awareness is stronger than any hunger for mere erotic pleasure. During this transit, we can gain insight into hidden sexual hang-ups, learn to dissolve their grip on us and, in some cases, free ourselves of them.

FIGHTING DIRTY

Resolving power and control issues between marriage partners is an Eighth-House theme. If we have become enlightened by Neptunian insights in our Seventh, then we may now better realize how damaging it is to manipulate people just to satisfy our selfish and often conflicted needs. We may get our way for a while, but not the love and respect that we need, as we play out our unrealistic roles. Therefore, in the Eighth, we have an opportunity to further explore the inner treasures offered by our Neptune-inspired partnership, without power plays or silent resentments getting in the way. In this case, nobody controls anyone, and possessiveness or jealousy is less of a problem.

However, if we made a mess of our Seventh-House Neptunian challenge, we bring our distorted views of relationships to a battleground where people can be dirty fighters when threatened and provoked. We can try to control or punish others by using sabotaging strategies, or be similarly controlled or punished by them. With Neptune, things can get pretty sneaky and underhanded. This is not the road to take if being alive and well is the outcome we hope for.

If divorce is imminent, Neptune suggests that the waters are muddied when it comes to working out legal and monetary negotiations. Even in the best of conditions, we'll need to be clear and direct about divvying up joint resources. We'll have to do more than just what feels good or spiritually correct for the moment. We'll need to be practical about our future financial realities. When the air is thick with antagonism—and maybe a little vengeance—money and possessions can become the weapons of choice used to get back at one another. Even child custody struggles become part of the action. Mishandled Neptune and Eighth-House energies suggest that we or our spouse can suffer bouts of paranoia, and may plot and scheme to avoid being further injured by a failed marriage.

Neptune here *could* also mean that we take the high road and walk away with only our fair share and our integrity in tact. We want to cleanly dissolve this union, not look back with bitter regret. It can feel like a "no-fault" divorce—*c'est la vie* and *adios!* However, going down that bumpy low road means that we either take all that we can get away with (boundless greed), or try to take only what our partner wants the most (twisted revenge), or maybe sacrifice taking what is rightfully ours just to avoid the unpleasantness of divorce court (martyrdom)—we want to put it all behind us quickly by abandoning our responsibility to legally protect ourselves. We who opt for that last choice can be undermining ourselves in ways that do not become evident until later. By then, we may be feeling financially victimized enough to wear a "kick-me" sign on our back. The spiritualizing energy of Neptune gets in the way of common sense when it comes to such emotionally triggered money matters.

Healing Wounds

If we are single—and no special relationship magic has occurred during Neptune's transit through our Seventh—it's time for us to surrender to the healing inner work needed to face up to any unprocessed pain generated by years of rejection and feeling unwanted. This could apply to everyone undergoing this transit, not just those without partners. It would be typical of some of us to believe that we really don't need a mate or miss having one. We may view marriage as a complication and invariable disappointment that we can live without. Feeling that the Cosmos obviously agrees, we assume that we must be here for some purpose "higher" than marriage. We may convince ourselves that it's our karma to remain single. Wherever Neptune is, our need to give of ourselves and to serve others spills over into broader social realms. Neptune cannot be completely fulfilled by exclusively personal relationships, especially when we allow our expectations to run unrealistically high.

Cleansing ourselves of hidden grief—especially over the way that life has treated us emotionally during transiting Neptune's Seventh-House phase—becomes critical at this juncture. We can't afford to keep such heavy-hearted energy inside, because it becomes toxic. Both Neptune and the Eighth are good at flushing out poisonous things that could otherwise pollute us. Even psycho-therapy, associated with the Eighth House, becomes a way to purge emotions that could otherwise sicken us. It's better to be conscious of the Neptunian purging process now, rather than evade our unresolved issues and later need to undergo physical surgeries to symbolically cut out what may be increasingly harmful to us. An emphasis on internal house-cleaning may be an excellent way to heal our psychological wounds.

Neptune can make miracles happen. If we exorcise whatever has been haunting us all of these years about partnerships, perhaps we'll find ourselves emerging empowered and more able and ready to share deep intimacy with another. We don't have to do this, but we can be successful if the time feels right. The Eighth is very supportive of rebirths. Neptune can expand our potential to feel attuned to others, enhancing shared experiences. Transiting Neptune can help to heal feelings of isolation in our Eighth for those of us who have not opened up and revealed who we are, due to our basic distrust of the world.

JUGGLING FINANCES

Another side of the Eighth deals with the mundane realities of money management in business. Just as the Seventh rules our business associates, the Eighth deals with the money side of these relationships, which includes all types of legal financial affairs in which we can become embroiled. Neptune can be profitable for businesses that are imaginative, glamorous, or inspirational. Are we in a field that offers hope or makes big promises to the public? That would resonate well with the nature of Neptune. Business ventures that depend on hype and illusion also are tied in with this planet. It is important to realize that Neptune's influence is not as good for businesses where monetary profit *per se* is the main objective. Neptune goes instead for those less tangible "inner rewards" that can be gained through a dedicated effort to serve others in some way. That sounds sweet, but still, this is not a planet that cares to develop the competitive edge needed to be a winner in the no-nonsense world of business. Neptune's not aggressive enough to handle what it takes to make a "big killing" in any chosen field. Passivity sometimes becomes a problem.

The Eighth House, in contrast, is strong on critical survival themes and dramatic "do-or-die" confrontations. If pushed to the edge, where we feel forced to reach for our hidden arsenal of power tools, our Eighth can trigger hidden ruthlessness and a single-minded determination to succeed at any cost. Imagine what it could be like when Mars, Saturn, or Pluto feels threatened here. This can be a house of cutthroat tactics and shark-like strategies, given the right stimuli. However, that's certainly not Neptune's way to cut a deal. During this time, we could have a business partnership wherein an associate is not assertive enough to bring in the clientele needed to keep our business thriving. Perhaps *we* are the one who lacks the proper drive to succeed. With Neptune, money is not easily saved. It disappears due to unforeseen expenditures. Sometimes the problem is the unintentional waste of resources. Neptune rarely takes the cost-effective route.

This could undermine the stability of any business, slowly draining it in not-so-obvious ways at first. This is *our* personal Neptune transit (our co-partners are probably not having the same transit), so we could help remedy the situation by insisting on developing sensible and orderly fiscal habits from the start. Detailed records of all transactions are a must. Neptune hates paperwork and that can get us in trouble later, when we cannot find the vital records needed by the tax agencies to verify our business expenses. We'll need to fight the urge to be too casual (or sloppy) with our bookkeeping. A problem that sometimes occurs is the misappropriation of funds, whether accidental or otherwise. Sometimes it happens because someone with sticky fingers "borrows" (even steals) money that should be strictly earmarked for business expenses, period! Neptune is the planet of the embezzler. Unless we are the guilty ones, this activity is going on behind our backs and we haven't a clue. This is especially the case when we try to avoid directly handling finances by letting someone else, including paid financial managers, tend to all of the detail work regarding money transactions. During this transit, we'll need more hands-on involvement with this facet of business. This also applies to the shared financial responsibilities of our marriage, or other intimate relationships where money transactions are involved.

TAPPING IN

We should also pay attention to our hunches, which are not to be confused with ego-involved wishful thinking. Any Outer Planet moving through the Eighth suggests that we can have uncanny insights into hidden matters typically overlooked by others. Neptune, while not known for the laser clarity of Uranus or the keen, penetrating ability of Pluto, can still have a feel for the underlying reality of anything. It can innocently tap into what's going on from a quietly intuitive level. We don't experience the startling sense of being zapped that Uranus provides, for example, and therefore could minimize the significance of our hunches, even in business affairs. Although they don't feel intense or urgent, we will need to take such Neptunian impressions more seriously. They pop up from nowhere, it seems, but for a good reason. Pluto has little trouble playing the bloodhound and sniffing things out. With Neptune, we just get these hard-to-explain "vibes," and we don't always know what to do with them. In our Eighth, we are learning to get more deeply in contact with the source of our hunches. When we feel such vibrations, it's time to do some investigating and psychic snooping. Something probably needs to be uncovered for our own protection, so we cannot afford to ignore odd feelings when they mysteriously arise.

In general, Neptune passing through our Eighth House is an excellent time to throw away the emotional junk that we have accumulated for whatever reason—all of the inhibiting blockages that have left us feeling compulsive or obsessive about people and things. Neptune sometimes provides the necessary healing by helping us to reclaim the darker parts that we've rejected—and thus projected onto others—thereby enabling them to better fit into our sense of psycho-spiritual wholeness. Unification is always Neptune's ultimate goal. When done right, this transit can instill a sense of being reborn into a revitalizing dimension, where self-love can establish a transformative marriage within.

NEPTUNE/PLUTO TRANSITS
THE SHADOW KNOWS

Neptune and Pluto share some common denominators, besides the fact that both are transpersonal water planets. Each deals with what is concealed from view or hidden below the surface of life. Both like things dark and shadowy, and each planet can be secretive and subtle, as well as fascinated with the mysteries of

life and death. They also can give us the creeps when their sometimes compelling but disturbing images arise from our unconscious, as happens in our nightmares. Neptune entangles while
Pluto complicates; therefore, very little remains straightfor-
wardly simple and direct once these planets are activated.
Everything becomes multi-layered with meaning that creates
deep and vivid impressions in us. Both planets also work on our
emotions, especially those we have managed to conceal or repress.

Neptune and Pluto are also at home with utter silence. Non-
verbal expression feels natural to them. When they do speak, it
comes from an intuitive "gut" level rather than a rational "head"
perspective, even though Neptune would rather believe that it's
really only coming from one place: the "heart." There can be a
loner streak, because these are planets that often feel alienated
from the mainstream interests of society and its shallow emphasis on the value of material success. The intentions of Neptune
and Pluto to improve society are not readily understood, and may
even seem subversive or counter-establishment. Both deal with
breaking down things that have outlived their collective need,
which is something that the Mighty Saturnians who run the
world find endlessly unnerving and threatening. Don't forget,
mythological Neptune and Pluto were brothers who shared the
unfortunate experience of being swallowed by Saturn. Since then,
they've been enemies of rigid structure and form. They won't obey
the laws of Saturn in the physical world if that means that their
energies will be stifled.

THE LONGEST SEXTILE

Both planets can release eruptive power under certain conditions.
Neptune symbolizes a steamy, hot geyser, furiously shooting up
from an underground waterway, while Pluto becomes the vol-
cano's fury, belching fiery lava from its depths. Interestingly
enough, these two planets have been in sextile formation for about
fifty-two years during the twentieth century (from late 1942 to
1995). Even with the non-agitating sextile, conditions on our

planet have been pretty intense. Old social patterns have been dissolved and swept away, while powerful new structures have added layers of complexity to our societal experience and have demanded of us much psychological stamina—rush hour traffic alone is a good example! After a bit of a break during the closing years of the 1990s, this sextile gathers momentum once again as it continues into the twenty-first century—until around 2032.

Perhaps this sextile's biggest phenomenon, which affects societies throughout the world, is the birth of television with its steady stream of images that travel along invisible Neptune/Pluto air waves. We forget how wondrous and amazing this concept is, as anyone who's been dead for centuries would emphatically remind us, if he or she could. In many ways, what we know about our developing society mainly comes from watching TV, a more immediate experience than reading newspapers and magazines. Also, its visual impact can be mesmerizing in ways that the printed word cannot emulate. Another awesome Neptune/Pluto manifestation to emerge during these sextile years is space travel. The ability to finally defy gravity and leave the earth's orbit cannot help but alter the collective unconscious from now on regarding assumed human limitations. We now know that we are not doomed to be forever earthbound.

What about those of us back here on the ground? When Neptune transits our natal Pluto, it might trigger the natal sextile with which some of us were born. If so, we may have an opportunity to learn how to bring the principles of these planets into even sharper focus, so that they can be intelligently used. Sextiles arouse curiosity and enable us to try out and adapt to different ways of using the energies involved. The important tensional transit for this Neptune/Pluto sextile group will be Neptune's square to natal Pluto. Also significant is transiting Neptune's opposition to natal Pluto.

We need to look through our ephemeris to see when the square happened to us. My parents had the transiting Neptune/Pluto square during their early twenties (during the year I was born, in fact). For me, the transiting square began in the mid-1960s, at around age fifteen—when I was just starting to explore life-after-death theories, Edgar Cayce's trance material, and reincarnation. I remember idealistically wishing that I could see auras, like Cayce, and help people in need. I was hit by a wave of humanitarian inspiration. Being just a teen, I also began to devour all of Ian Fleming's "James Bond" paperback thrillers. Alternative health interests were developing for me, as well (my natal Neptune is in the Sixth) and, by the time I graduated from high school, astrology and theosophy entered my life. Not every teenager takes such a route, but it worked for me. Much of this I attribute to transiting Neptune, ruler of my Twelfth, squaring my Pluto.

RAGING WATERS

In theory, Neptune will entice Pluto to leave its dark cave and will try to help this planet feel more like an essential part of the whole of life rather than a shunned outcast, living on the edge of town. Pluto has been storing up multi-dimensional realizations of life on our unconscious levels throughout the years, and Neptune now signals this powerhouse planet to finally release its hidden knowledge for the good of the world. Ideally, Neptune would wish to make use of Pluto's power in order to rebuild a better collective future, but it doesn't seek to resort to the harsh and abrasive revolutionary tactics common to Uranus' transit to Pluto. Neptune reforms through a gentle persuasion that plays on our feelings and imagination. It effortlessly seduces us to accept Plutonian transformation of our reality by appealing to our aspirations for ultimate beauty and soul refinement. Artists and visionaries can draw on the potency of this planetary combo in action, especially when transiting Neptune trines Pluto.

Few people spend much quality time directly plugging into their natal Pluto parts; therefore, these drives and impulses often remain hidden and primitive in expression. If you think it takes guts to handle Uranus, you'll find that it's even more the case with Pluto! Neptune transiting Pluto can arouse many turbulent feelings that we've managed to suppress for a long time. They begin to erupt in raw ways that can frighten us and others. Sometimes such feelings deal with rage that we never knew we had. At other times, they intensely focus on insatiable sexual energy that seems to obsess and consume us. For a few of us, self-destruction becomes a dark theme, perhaps indirectly experienced through chaotic body symptoms. We may feel a stronger-than-usual need to withdraw from people, because we feel driven to explore our inner world.

Fixations can develop that make little sense to us, especially during the square and, later, during the quincunx phase that occurs past the mid-life crisis years (for the natal Neptune sextile Pluto group). Feelings of alienation from society, with all of its set rules and regulations, can lead to problematic behavior. When we see some of the horrific criminal acts of today's teens between the ages of thirteen and seventeen, we should realize that they are undergoing Neptune's square to their Pluto. Their actions may or may not be gang related. Pluto symbolizes an anti-social, lone-wolf temperament. Ages fourteen to fifteen can be particularly stressful, because transiting Saturn opposes natal Saturn as well. Our parents and grandparents had this Saturn cycle at the same age, but never while transiting Neptune was within orb of squaring their natal Pluto. The first generation to have the Saturn/Saturn opposition, to be followed shortly after by the Neptune/Pluto square, was also one that spawned those famous malcontents labeled by society as "juvenile delinquents" in the 1950s. A major cultural expression of their defiant energy was the birth of rock-and-roll—quite an apt description of the inner pressure and turmoil that they felt and expressed in that decade.

Many kids today, during their Neptune square Pluto period, simply want to defy social standards regarding appearance and behavior in ways that may seem bizarre to older generations, but this is relatively harmless Neptunian expression—yes, even the tattoos, shaved heads, and body-piercing (the Pluto part)—will all be understood later as fitting symbols of a chaotic phase of identity confusion. More seriously, Neptune squares are prone toward escaping from whatever feels overwhelming. In addition, a triggered Pluto could fear being overpowered by harsh, dictatorial authority figures. In this case, some impressionable youth may seek to psychologically run away from the brutal realities of a world that appears out-of-control with global aggression and hostility. The downbeat newspaper headlines only fuel the fires of teen discontent, fear, and hopelessness. Some escape by shutting down their emotions and becoming unreachable. (Both planets are good at being inaccessible and inscrutable.) Ironically, a few may even lose their sense of themselves and their unarticulated terror by playing an active role in perpetuating the violent climate of the times. Neptune here provides them with a distorted urge to become one with their own Plutonian projections through intensely surreal but dangerous actions and thoughts. This transit can describe a tough transition for many kids these days.

POWER UNLEASHED

Where is the promise of "alive and well" to be found? Things sounds pretty bleak so far. We'll need to realize that trying to consciously direct the energy of two Outer Planets is never an easy task, because they'll pretty much override our ego's impulse to take over. Also, the more self-centered we are, the less satisfying such transits turn out. With transiting Neptune, there is always the hope that those barriers which prevent us from realizing our spiritual essence will disappear as our self-understanding deepens. Neptune hates walls and can make them dematerialize. In contrast, Pluto loves fiendishly-protected fortresses—complete with barracudas swimming in the moat to thwart would-be invaders. However, even Pluto is not immune to Neptune's ability to seep through and saturate everything with its dissolving energies. Now it's Neptune's turn to have its way, and most constructively so during the trine phase.

Pluto should be grateful for Neptune's influence, because Pluto now can come out of its inner sanctum and fluidly snake its way up the path to our consciousness. As Neptune eventually allows things hidden in our shadowy depths to float to the top, Plutonian energy makes a rare appearance, surfacing to reveal our intensities and how they need our constructive channeling.

Pluto can vent its compressed, powerful energy in Neptunian ways, although it's our job alone to come up with suitable avenues of dynamic release.

Both planets have a lot of the dramatic in them, so whatever we do has to charge up our emotions and make us feel dedicatedly involved in some Big Social Objective. We can pour ourselves totally into any experience that enthralls us, and it could turn out to be a magnificent obsession. Is there anything in our life at the moment to which we could give our *all*—our 110 percent—in a creative way or for a humane cause? This would appease these planets, no matter what their actual aspect. Remember, besides the sextile and the square, we'll have the trine, quincunx, and even an eye-opening opposition to test.

SEX, DEATH, AND SHADY DEALS

Pluto does have several Scorpian associations—mainly sex, death, and legal finances or joint resources. Transiting Neptune helps to relax any tensions surrounding these issues so that we can permit ourselves to be guided by the inner voice that tells us to be less resistant to changes that may occur. Pluto alone would want to control everything and not risk the unexpected. Neptune works best when it can stay loose, elastic, and not all that focused. Pluto, therefore, has a chance to become less intense about wanting to dominate through power and control. Neptune also can provide Pluto with just enough charisma to enable this passionate planet to be highly persuasive and less intimidating. Both planets can be seductive and compelling, but Neptune reminds Pluto that there's a nicer way to be persuasive!

Sex at this time can be infused with much imagination and fantasy. However, once it's made real through actual physicality, it can lose much of its intoxication for us (a typical Neptunian let-down). Still, Neptune aims for ecstatic experiences. Pluto, known for sexual stamina, is used to tremendous energy surges that release themselves with the force of an atomic bomb. We're talking about a major orgasmic response. Pluto won't be satisfied until we ground our erotic energies so that the life-force becomes highly charged. Maybe Neptune is trying to refine what it deems to be an insatiable lust factor in Pluto, hoping that this will result in a more spiritualized form of sexuality. Some of us might be fascinated with tantric or kundalini yoga as a result. However, Pluto has little tolerance for illusions, even sexual ones; therefore, it won't be swayed by any "making love just with our astral bodies" kind of Neptunian fantasy. We could end up in a conflictive state of sexual ambivalence or confusion here, with Neptune wanting us to seek less physical expression.

Death is no stranger to Pluto, ruler of the Underworld, or Hades, the fabled home of the deceased. Pluto does not fear death because it knows that nothing remains truly "dead" forever. Everything is in a transitional state. It's Neptune that gets emotional about the subject, even heart-broken and grief-stricken. At least, that's how many of us evoke our Neptune when a loved one dies. The experience of death during this transit can stir up hidden or unspoken feelings that take us to Pluto's uncharted world. Our reactions to our loss can be stormy and even violent at times, with self-destructive attempts to annihilate more than just our pain. Neptune becomes numb with denial at some point, but Pluto is intent on feeling things vividly and with stark clarity. With the square, quincunx, or the opposition, we'll have to get to our inner Pluto fast to avoid the soul-wrenching phase in which Neptune can get stuck. At least with Pluto, we only feel agonizingly awful for a concentrated period, after which we fully let go and accept death's sobering reality. However, if we get too hung up with Neptune, we can feel endlessly haunted by the experience. It becomes a form of needless self-torture.

When it comes to legal financial affairs, both Neptune and Pluto may have something to hide—shady deals or secret monies, such as hidden Swiss bank accounts and other undisclosed stashes of loot. We might need a refresher course on the ethics of money, because there is a temptation to get away with financial transactions at someone else's expense. Actually, it could be others who slyly try to pull one over on us, or perhaps unfairly and unethically coerce us. This is a good combo for blackmail games on many levels. Neptune can draw in situations where deceit and manipulation complicate joint ownership arrangements, whether in our business life or in a marriage gone sour.

We may want to do some "reality testing" regarding money sharing during the sesqui-square phase (135°), which can occur during our forties for some of us in the natal Neptune sextile Pluto group. By then, we've had enough time to learn about our financial patterns with people so that we can recognize our weak spots, where others could take advantage of our vulnerabilities.

CHAPTER FOURTEEN

NEPTUNE TRANSITING THE NINTH HOUSE

MELTING POT

In our Ninth House, we are encouraged to dream big and to allow our spirit to soar as far and wide as the wings of consciousness will permit. This includes an innocent willingness to indulge in mind expansion and joyous intellectual journeys. The Ninth is more excited by the sweeping adventures to be had during our amazing voyage than by our ultimate arrival at any destination point. Our life can become a colorful tale of epic proportions, a personal odyssey in the name of self-discovery. Burning zeal and fervent conviction, accompanied by expansive vision, are welcome here, as long as they don't overheat and fuel the mania of fanaticism. In this house, we easily can go overboard regarding what we deem to be Right and True for Everybody.

Much about our Ninth springs forth from inclusive "big picture" concepts rolling around inside our head, such as our beliefs and theories about life's ultimate purpose. We want to know the meaning of existence: how is everything set up in the Universe and what, ultimately, are its guiding principles? In the Ninth, we become "higher path" conscious, eager to discover our greater purpose. We can feel inspired by the wisdom of the Cosmos and by the upward pull of our spirit. Perfection-seeking principles that guide how we are to optimally live—those dealing with morality, ethics, righteousness, and human decency—are formulated in this house. Big Questions here demand Big Answers. This is where we get to interpret life's "meaning" on a grand scale, in ways that can be collectively applied—at least in theory. Our consciousness becomes global, able to spread out and make connections in a multitude of social directions. We can feel like citizens of the world.

This is the first house that stimulates us to be philosophical and to consider our link to the human race, an extended concept of the family. Here, we realize that we are all in the same boat, trying to make sense out of our common experience of living. Our grasp of this is typically more cerebral than emotional or mystical. The mass mind begins to codify social rules of ideal conduct that are to ensure better living for all. During this Neptune transit, we can start to see a glimmer of a truth that this planet has always known first hand: we are all one, indivisibly united. In this house, the concept of a mass consciousness is born. Neptune takes on a protective role, inspiring cohesion through humane social interchange.

SKY OF ANGELS

Transiting Neptune warms up quickly to the Ninth's spiritual search for universal knowledge and understanding. This house is certainly intellectually and metaphysically open-ended enough for an expansive planet like Neptune. Compared to the Eighth, the Ninth House never wants to lock its doors—it keeps its windows wide open, willing to take a chance on whatever may enter. Ideally, everything here is wide-angled; the starry sky goes on forever. In fact, the theme of overcoming human limitation through mental exploration is strong in our Ninth House. This is the result of our tremendous efforts in our shadow-confronting Eighth to generate self-renewal by casting off soul-defeating fixations and inhibitions.

After all of that introspective plumbing of our depths, and after a few inner demons have been exorcised, we get to move out into life once again and optimistically pump up our consciousness with noble, high-minded concerns. Some of us even try to communicate with God and the angels, something that really turns Neptune on—as long as we don't get too crazy and try to define the Divine in fixed, absolute terms that we then expect everyone to adhere to. We have to allow room for understanding why people's spiritual paths can and should be highly individualized.

Mainstream religion may not satisfy our needs during this period. Even if it does, transiting Neptune's goal is to inspire us to slowly broaden our existing faith by considering less-orthodox pathways to knowing God. Besides our standard prayers, some of us might include a little yoga and meditation. Even visualization techniques and affirmations can uplift us. We may become intrigued by less-acknowledged mystical elements of our own chosen faith, perhaps developing a keener interest in miracles or similar otherworldly phenomena described in venerable, holy books. We may have a knack for interpreting certain scriptures in a whole different light, as we are moved by inspiration. This could be a good time to take a comparative religion course so that we can contemplate the similarities found among belief systems. We could develop greater tolerance as a result of our new understandings.

Whatever the case, with Neptune we tend to alter our viewpoints regarding the nature of the Cosmos gradually—that is, unless we have reached rock bottom with ourselves at some pivotal crisis point (a failed Eighth-House rebirth) where, after much chaos and suffering, we desperately turn to the God we once ignored or abandoned. It is then that our Neptunian changes become swift and dramatic—an overnight conversion from "lost soul" to "born again" becomes our own wondrous miracle.

EXALTED MISSION?

A few of us can feel filled with the waters of Spirit, as if anointed by God and chosen to be the ambassador who spreads words of revelation. Such a Neptunian religious conversion makes us feel like an exalted being on a special spiritual mission—perhaps we are self-consciously humble and giving, but we're also charged up emotionally, knowing that we are one of the truly "saved." This is bound to kick our ego-drives into full swing because, although we don't recognize this to be the case, it's our ego that likes to feel singled out for special honors. With Neptune, who knows no restrictions, we pour out our new revelations with much faith in the rightness of our actions. Some of us may evangelize with great fervor and a zealous commitment to our beliefs, even those of the political kind.

However, some of us may have a personal blind spot here. Neptune is inclusive in its beliefs, wanting to leave no one out in the cold and empty void. No matter what our spiritual message is to the world, we want everyone to trust and value our vision unconditionally. We also don't wish to be intellectually challenged regarding our beliefs. We are not open to debating our inspirations with hard-nosed skeptics—after all, what do they know? Despite this, we may try to teach or preach our faith indiscriminately, whether people want to hear it or not. Some of us are convinced that it is for the highest good of all to hear our beliefs. We would like to wander far and wide to broadcast our faith in the Ninth.

Obviously, Neptune in this house sometimes suffers from its own unrecognized religious or spiritual pushiness when fired up by godly matters, especially should it also be in aspect to preachy Jupiter. Neptune, a planet that envelopes whatever it touches, doesn't permit the proper breathing space necessary to human individuality. This conflicts with the personal freedom themes of the Ninth, a house which promotes any spiritual-seeking that is tied to an inner realization of who we really are, especially considering how intensively we worked in our Eighth not to be coerced by others or to force our values on them. This implies that we can each travel down individualized paths to higher awarenesses and still eventually wind up at the same ultimate destination at the end of the soul's journey.

TICKET TO TIBET?

A basic problem with this transit is that Neptune's vision of total Oneness—implying the dissolution of all "identity" labels—does not support our Ninth House's interest in exposing us to life's cultural diversity. Principle Nine, including Sagittarius and fiery Jupiter, does not want everything or everyone to be the same, blended together in a thick cosmic soup, without variation, difference, or sharp contrast. This is not where undifferentiated unity is to be sought—that's a goal of the boundary-disintegrating Twelfth. Although this is an impassioned house where we may march down streets in group formation with our signs or banners, shouting, "World Peace Now!" the Ninth certainly does not promote the dissolution of cultural and ethnic variety, because that could result in a totalitarian social vision, with dreadful consequences. Even phrases like "a new world order" can be scary to the Ninth, although it may be perfectly acceptable to a utopian like Neptune.

Perhaps by washing us with waves of wanderlust, Neptune is trying to help us to absorb more of our big, wide world, and how people are all interconnected. We may yearn to be elsewhere, faraway from our present drab locale, as we glamorize whatever is distant and not easily reachable—how about two fascinating weeks in Tibet or Tasmania? However, the Ninth House by itself would always be ready to buy a fast ticket to fly somewhere exciting, were it not for those stick-in-the-mud earth signs and old, insecure Saturn dampening our spirit of adventure.

During this transit, which is very *un*Saturnian, we may wish to be around people of foreign backgrounds whose personalities, nonetheless, feel familiar to us. We may have a hard time accounting for the strange kinship we feel, because it cannot be logically explained. Of course, Neptune would automatically lead us to assume that past-life connections are why we currently have strong attachments to Japanese culture, Native American rituals, or the unhurried way of life on Bora Bora. We can paint all of this in rosy hues, seeing only the more ideal elements of the

Ninth-House situations to which we are drawn. That's why a few of us could fantasize that living with the natives of the Amazon jungle would feel so right for us at the moment—but just wait until we faint away after seeing our first anaconda emerging from the river's edge!

Many of us might idealize traveling abroad to some exotic place. Taking a dream trip-of-a-lifetime may be one of our private fantasies, and that doesn't have to be somewhere out of the country. Maybe we live in Bangor, Maine, but yearn for a week's escape to the Grand Canyon or to Yellowstone National Park. Neptune beckons us to experience some place that's enchanting and almost unreal in its natural beauty. Of course, fantasy-minded Neptune may also opt for a wild weekend in Atlantic City playing the slot machines; or better yet, the roulette wheels in picture-postcard perfect Monte Carlo.

With Neptune here, a planet notoriously absent-minded and not very detail-conscious, we'll need to pay close attention to the laws and social customs of the place we visit. We should do our homework and learn what's what before even leaving for our trip. We may inadvertently break the rules and land in hot water with the locals and the authorities because of an offensive or illegal action that seemed perfectly innocent to us. We could be misunderstood in our behavior, and a simple mix-up in communications could make things complicated and expensive. It's also good to guard against being ripped-off (don't travel with the family jewels) or swindled by cool operators who know a sucker-tourist with "lotsa dough" when they see one.

We are subject to victimization on some level when traveling long-distance, so we'll need to be more mindful of who we are dealing with, especially if Neptune is making squares and oppositions to personal planets in our chart, such as our Moon, Mercury, or Venus—in fact, any planet. However, under the right aspects (perhaps a sextile or a trine to Jupiter or the Sun), we could visit places that are totally uplifting and soul-affirming for us. Who says we can't feel alive and well six thousand miles away from home? It would be typical of Neptune to turn our vacation into a pilgrimage, where we are drawn to holy sites and other sacred areas where spiritual energies are very high. Even fantastic museums like the Louvre can quench our thirst for exquisite beauty.

A HIGHER EDUCATION

With Neptune in the Ninth, there can be an ongoing fantasy for some of us to go back to school and get a degree. However, the process of doing so is very Saturnian in the long run, especially when we already have a full-time job and loads of other, pressing commitments. We may not realize this at the moment that we register for classes. The grass is usually greener elsewhere wherever Neptune is found, so the dream of being a student on campus again may be appealing. If we are in a dead-end job that offers little satisfaction or secure advancement, then improving our education sounds like an ideal solution, a way to change our boring or stagnant professional pattern. We must make sure that we have the mental energy needed to attend classes, do our assignments, and pass our exams. After all, we can't go to classes in a state of exhaustion because we're also trying to juggle too many worldly responsibilities at once.

Of course, a few of us could be going to college for the first time when Neptune is passing through our Ninth. We'll need to work on concentrating on our studies, because certain distractions can get us off to a wrong start. Neptune is not a studious planet, nor is it well-organized. We could get lost in our social life and forget that our first and foremost concern should be a solid education. Sloppy study habits can derail us while we are also sidetracked by escapist activities—and our parents didn't know that they were paying dearly for us to indulge in such fun.

Perhaps the biggest problem to face is not knowing what we want to do in life. We're confused about choosing our college major. Little seems to grab our attention for long. It can be very tempting to want to change schools when we can't cope with the rigors of our academic environment. Some of us even may drop out, disillusioned by the whole scene. This is not a smart option, considering that Neptune will next spend fourteen or so years in our Tenth House of career. (This can be an agonizing transit if we haven't developed a sufficient educational structure to help us to find our place in society.) It's also a perilous choice in today's world, where long-term unemployment can lead to homelessness. Let's not make rash decisions regarding our education, based on emotionality and an itch to wander.

Tuned in, Turned on

This Neptune transit allows us to feel that we are a part of humanity's rich historical heritage. With this imaginative planet, we can go back pretty far to unrecorded ancient times, to periods during which, we assume, people were more in direct contact with the spirit realm than they are now (i.e., times when tuned-in beings allegedly had magical powers that skeptics scoff at today). We could be fascinated to read about the "secrets" of Atlantis and the "mysteries" of Lemuria, or of other long-ago, forgotten lands that cannot be easily traced back in history. It is also Neptunian to feel a yearning for an ideal, eternal home beyond this Earth. We could imagine ourselves to be exiled space aliens—travelers from another planet in some faraway galaxy who have taken on the mission of incarnating for a while on this "less evolved" planet. It seems that we can speculate about *anything* that gives us a spiritual rush and can find others who'll reinforce our beliefs while Neptune is passing through our Ninth.

Neptune rivals Uranus in its ability to pick up on "vibes" in people and in the environment, except that Neptune doesn't experience Uranus' lightning-fast flashes of insight—it's no instant mind-reader. Neptune's intuitive awareness is less startling and interruptive. Still, we may feel strangely prophetic at moments, sensing and feeling how certain things may unfold over the course of time, often on a global scale. This is not an analytical process. Neptune works best when we don't try to logically break things down into detailed specifics. Images and thoughts inexplicably pour forth. They seem to rise up from somewhere deep inside of us, or from far outside of us. Our Ninth House can help foster a degree of cosmic consciousness. Therefore, Neptune's passage here helps us to remove barriers that prevent us from believing that we potentially possess spiritual gifts and from recognizing our true, eternal nature.

One benefit of such gifts is an inclination to dissolve boundaries between people. Neptune reminds us that we are more than just separate, ego-contained entities, living subjectively in our own private and sometimes lonely Universes. Psychic sensitivity allows us to realize how intertwined everything is, how fundamentally attached we all are to each other on invisible but interwoven planes of being. As part of our spiritual practices, it would be good to include a little meditation or contemplation each day, because both involve the discipline of silence and stillness. Being by ourselves, closing our eyes, and remaining quiet quickly puts us in touch with Neptune's realm. Daytime naps and nightly dreams may be more vivid and phenomenal during this transit. The same is true for Neptune transiting our Eighth, except, in that case, our dreams are prone to be disturbing, cathartic, and stress-releasing. Ninth-House dreaming, certainly an inner journey of sorts, taps into ethereal levels, where the spirits of the buffalos and the archetypes roam!

NEPTUNE/JUPITER TRANSITS
SOUL BROTHERS

Mythological Neptune (Poseidon) and Jupiter (Zeus) were brothers, suggesting a kinship between these planets. Astrologically, they have a lot in common. Both are planets that naturally expand and spread out, extending their contacts as broadly as possible. Each is faith-oriented, convinced of the power of belief. These planets want to feel uplifted by the ideals they glorify, and are willing to share their vision for the benefit of all. Both can be kind-hearted and philanthropic, genuinely concerned with solving society's ills and improving the world's future. Princess Diana and Mother Teresa both were born with Neptune/Jupiter aspects. However, fiery Jupiter is more able to drum up the will and the assertiveness needed to directly launch its do-good campaigns.

Neptune, a water planet and less pushy than Jupiter, nevertheless can seductively captivate an audience, inspiring them to pull
together for a worthy social cause. Both planets can be charismatic and spirit-lifting when filled with their visions of hope.
Having such a sense of hope is very important to each.

Although Neptune is motivated by unconscious forces, Jupiter
operates heartily within the realm of the ego. Jupiter is not as
boundless as Neptune. It seeks to expand within an existing
structure and cannot endure the chaos and formlessness that
Neptune tolerates. Jupiter may be religious, but it stops short of
being mystical. It's true that Jupiter co-rules Pisces, but water
Jupiter reminds me of a friendly friar rather than a true
Neptunian mystic-visionary. Neptune tries to obliterate the ego
and its false boundaries of separation. Jupiter, in contrast, doesn't
want to lose any sense of itself, but instead wants to enlarge what
it is in order to fully promote its big-shot goals. There can be an
innocent sense of opportunism in Jupiter, mixed with a generous
heart that wants everyone to profit and be happy. It would be a
mistake to only look at this planet's high-minded, soaring idealism and forget that it's also very worldly and indulgent in orientation. After all, that's how Jupiter got so darn fat!

FUTURE PROMISE

What might happen when Neptune contacts our natal Jupiter is
not easy to guess, but it is likely that our feelings of luck and our
sense of protection from danger make us assume that we can do
anything our heart desires and still end up a winner, with no limits to stop us. We may anticipate that something especially good
will happen to us. It's just around the corner, and we may already
feel that we'll really deserve it when it comes, whatever it is.
While there may not be any actual indicators of such benefits to
enjoy at present, we may feel that these will surely appear if we
stay positive about things and not lose faith in ourselves.

Neptune may glorify all things Jupiterian at this time.
However, both planets are not always reliable when it comes to

delivering what they promise. Jupiterian enthusiasms, while strong and convincing for the moment, do not always endure. Meanwhile, Neptune in transit cannot readily manifest our dreams in concrete, workable terms. There is a greater chance that we could overextend our faith in less practical areas, with disappointing results. We can overreach and assume that our inner goodness and spirituality will ensure success in the outer world. Sometimes it's our timing that's off—we prematurely take the plunge while keeping our fingers crossed, only to find out that the tide is low and no big fish are nibbling at the bait.

Both planets are subject to naiveté and gullibility. Both want things to turn out perfectly, without hassles. Of course, Jupiter in an earth sign, or in shrewd Scorpio, is usually less prone toward such grand expectations. However, we can often fault Neptune for putting a gauzy veil over certain realities, and even Jupiter alone is not very keen on noting life's finer details. Things can slip us up due to our carelessness or our misjudgment. Blind spots at this time can be big ones, as Jupiter doesn't do anything on a small scale! We are probably less willing to weigh the pros and cons of any action we want to take. Instead, we wish to envision only satisfying outcomes that reinforce our current, upbeat emotions. Jupiter will reach for the stars and move into the future with great trust, so it believes that things only get better, not worse. We figure that the Universe would certainly not try to treat us badly at this time.

This Neptune transit allows us to see how our optimism can remove barriers to our happiness and open up doors of opportunity. Some of us have been sitting on our potential for too long, and now may be a time to let loose and take a few chances with life—perhaps less exuberantly if the aspect is a square, a quincunx, or opposition. A well-managed conjunction, sextile, or trine could help us to become less inhibited and more willing to fly high with our ideals. Expanded vision is a strong theme for both planets. Do we have a vision at this time that fires our imagination? Is this vision backed by a realistic capacity on our part? Are we willing to work hard to turn a dream into something solid and tangible? By the way, that last question was asked by a somewhat doubtful Saturn, who has heard a lot of Neptune/Jupiter's hype and "hot-air" in the past. For Saturn, seeing is believing!

It would be a good idea to check out our transiting Saturn. (*Twelve Faces of Saturn*[1] offers tips on how to use this planet's supportive energy.) Saturn is an excellent reality-testing planet, and its concurrent transit in our chart can let us make worthy visions come true, if we have the staying power needed for success. Of course, Jupiter can be quite lucky regarding the resources it's able to magnetically draw to itself from the world. Neptune, meanwhile, can bring in people and situations that show us selflessness and kindness in action. Together, these planets imply that we may have well-wishers and guardian angels— even the human kind—ready to protect us from harm. Much success here depends on our integrity, the degree of our spiritual centeredness, and how blessed we are with common sense.

THE PERFECT SUCKER?

Rip-off and con-artists with these transits might get away with some fraudulent activity for a while, making them even more cocky and over-confident than ever. Eventually, however, Neptune will conspire to create self-defeating scenarios where everything suddenly collapses and dumb "luck" finally runs out. These planets together are not too smart when it comes to covering their tracks—after all, this isn't devious Pluto/Saturn masterminding at work! Instead, the Neptune/Jupiter transit can be a bumbling, inept combination in the hands of amateurs looking for a fast way out of a jam.

Any transiting combination involving Neptune and Jupiter can be very damaging to those who are already deficient in their ethical make-up. Laziness and wanting the easy way out become the less mature ways such individuals express their Neptune/Jupiter energies. They can unrealistically assume that they're untouchable, above the law, and immune to certain consequences that beset the rest of us. Their moral structure starts to deteriorate fast, once they believe that they have an unquestioned right to take whatever they want from life without earning it.

Some of us who may become the perfect sucker, making any con artist's job easier, can also be undergoing a Neptune transit to our Jupiter. Neptune is a planet that at times requires sacrifices, but why should we unconsciously set ourselves up to be robbed blind just to show the Universe that we can quickly let go of material possessions? There has got to be a better, more conscious way to demonstrate such non-attachment, like going from closet to closet to see what we can donate to charity—a much more sensible Neptune/Jupiter route to take. That way, we become willing participants, freely giving to others in need, and not the victims of slippery characters looking for a quick buck!

GENEROSITY

Jupiter traditionally is a money planet, but not one that likes its money to stay safe and settled for too long (that's more common with Venus in its earthy, Taurean facet). Jupiter sees money as a chance to engage in risk-taking investments that could pay off handsomely. Having more of a spirit of wheeling-and-dealing than Venus, Jupiter envisions its money making money. It loves the concept of compound interest. Profits that can be reinvested are very important to this confident and self-assured planet. However, money-making becomes a game played for fun at times, because Jupiter loves to gamble and try to beat the odds whenever possible. It loves feeling that it's on a roll. Financial speculation of all types becomes appealing to this adventure-hungry planet. Of course, big risks can invite big losses, but pure Jupiter energy doesn't care. It expects to win; and when it hits the jackpot, everyone is nicely rewarded, which is how generous Jupiter deals with its wealth.

Neptune is not much of a financial planet, especially when greed and power become the driving motivations to make money. Neptune's not all that self-protective in this realm. It certainly doesn't understand why people would want to hoard their wealth or their valued goods when there's so much to go around for all to share. This doesn't sound very capitalistic and, indeed, Neptune has strong socialistic leanings. However, under certain conditions, Neptune can miraculously provide money, because it realizes that most collective dreams will not get off the ground without an impressive flow of financial funding.

When people pledge big bucks for research to fight against certain diseases, that's Neptune using money compassionately. The same goes for funding humanitarian causes that provide material assistance to those countries suffering economically worldwide. Astronomical sums of money can be generated almost magically by Neptune when it pulls on our heartstrings and arouses our empathy for fellow human beings going through difficult times.

Neptune transiting our natal Jupiter can make us feel like Santa Claus, J. D. Rockefeller, and the Fairy Godmother all rolled into one. We want to help people who don't have much to sustain themselves, for whatever reason. We can become quite charitable and willing to use our money to support humane programs that help the underdogs of society, or communities in need of disaster relief, or those who are absolutely destitute and at the mercy of others. Neptune/Jupiter can be filled with mercy. Our concern may be not just for people, but for animals, or for Mother Earth herself. Perhaps we feel the urge to send donations to groups trying to save wildlife habitats. Some of us will want to generously give to a needy world while under this transit's influence. However, we'll have to look at our own financial reality before we go hog wild with our philanthropy. We'll have to learn to give within our means. Also, is money the only way that we can satisfy our impulse to give? What about offering our time to do needed volunteer work? In some ways, that's even more giving than just quickly mailing off a fat check.

If truth be known, some of us are not feeling all that noble and high-minded when it comes to money matters at this time. Instead, we pray for that bulging pot of gold at the end of the rainbow. Whether it comes as a result of lottery fever, a lucky streak in Vegas, or a business enterprise that becomes an overnight sensation with the buying public, we dream of enjoying instant wealth and big-time material comforts.

We are likely to be totally ego-attached to such dreams, so Neptune is probably not going to cooperate with us. It's wise enough to know that becoming an overnight millionaire could lead some of us down the road to ruin—a major hard lesson in dissipation and foolish wastefulness when, suddenly, we can afford the most expensive vices and addictions. It's probably a blessing in disguise when we only win twenty bucks at the local bingo parlor, not the cool $15 million we were unrealistically yearning for.

FEELING GOOD

In general, these transits can make us feel very good about life, almost euphoric at times. Our intuition is active and strong, so we should take advantage of any reasonable hunches when exploring any opportunity at hand. However, if we're feeling positively manic about anything or anyone, beware! Both of these planets underscore the need to trust that our quiet, inner voice will guide us by the light of wisdom and a touch of divine protection. Prosperity may be in the air, but it requires that we remain alert and grounded when things eventually open up for us. We can't afford to be blinded by illusionary glamour or deceptive forms of invincibility. The limitations that we don't see at the moment are still there, waiting to be confronted with Saturnian restraint later. We can't make such limitations vanish by using a few credit cards. Life can be full of wonder for us when we think big and refuse to cave in to self-abnegation. With Neptune, though, we'll need to take time to reflect on our deeper values before jumping off the diving board into a pool of endless material or spiritual possibilities.

NOTE

1 Bil Tierney, *Twelve Faces of Saturn*, Llewellyn Publications, St. Paul, MN, 1997.

CHAPTER FIFTEEN

NEPTUNE TRANSITING THE TENTH HOUSE

INSPIRED MISSION

Considering Neptune's notorious lethargy, it's amazing that this planet was able to make the long, uphill climb to our Tenth-House summit. It should have pooped out long before now, held down by the weight of earthbound living—maybe it levitated to our Midheaven! Apparently, transiting Neptune's on some kind of uplifting mission to save the world from spiritual short-sighted-ness, which explains why this planet seeks the broader public exposure provided by the Tenth. That could be exactly what's going on for some of us. Realize that not everyone has Neptune passing through his or her Tenth during a lifetime. This transit's inspiring energy supports those whose special destinies involve raising the awareness of society for the better.

Outer Planets crossing the Midheaven seem to have some-thing especially profound to offer in terms of understanding how the social collective works and where it's headed. These planets concentrate on stepping up the evolution of mass consciousness. At the top of our chart, the Tenth House's perspective can become pretty wide-angled. The spotlight is on at least a few of us who feel moved to contribute something of universal worth, even though society may not be ready for or open to our vision. Still, we can become a mouthpiece for these other-worldly planets as we aim to enlighten our community or to world-at-large.

We want to leave our very special mark in society. This can be quite an awesome responsibility, and it's always a challenge to our usual ego-orientation and accustomed ways of handling our life. Are we up to the challenge, considering that sometimes personal sacrifices will be involved? Our ego doesn't like to give up a whole lot in order to reach a goal, yet Neptune urges us to shed undue self-interest when a higher cause is at stake.

CAREER UNCLEAR

In most cases, Neptune conjunct the Midheaven begins a low-key, internal process whereby we re-evaluate our professional direction. Yes, there's a degree of confusion about the direction of our career, and perhaps we've been feeling inner rumblings that are more thann vague moodiness. We wonder if this could this just be a symptom of the changeable economic times in which we live. Perhaps it's merely a case of boredom with a Tenth-House role that we've dutifully played out, seemingly forever. Unconsciously, however, we know that we must expand our perspective, while letting go of any mishandled parts of our professional past, if we are to realize any inner peace. We are not self-contented at this time, and we will need to put our finger on just what's missing in our lives, which is something that's not easy to establish.

Usually our uneasiness has little to do with any apparent lack of success on a worldly basis, because we could currently be seen as quite accomplished in the eyes of society. Perhaps we've fulfilled our role very well and are being rewarded. Still, there's a lack of true fulfillment that troubles us. None of this hits us like a ton of falling bricks (that's a Uranus or Pluto reaction). Still, an unsettled feeling can quietly erode our confidence and our sense of long-range security. We question the ultimate meaning of our life-direction during our private, self-reflective moments.

Two scenarios really grab Neptune's attention. The first is a career that stifles our potential—this career was once a safe choice, but typically hasn't been creatively challenging enough lately, and it's now slowly suffocating us. The second is struggling in a career that has been wrong from the start, an impractical choice we made due to escapist needs and self-delusion. We've either bitten off more than we can chew, or are psychologically ill-equipped for what this career entails. The career itself can even be damaging to our soul-growth, and any rewards to be had involve too much of a psychological struggle to be worthwhile.

Other scenarios exist. However, Neptune will weed out what is defective, so the bottom line is that we cannot continue to live a lie no matter how much fame and acclaim it brings us, and no matter how successfully we can hide our weaknesses or sadness behind the professional mask we wear. There are elements in our career that don't work for us anymore, if they ever did. They must be dissolved so that our energy is no longer trapped by endlessly repeating vitality-robbing activities.

A degree of career claustrophobia is not uncommon, and yet we may deeply wonder what's going to take the place of our long-term commitment. The familiarity of such a vocational pattern still gives us security, but at what expense? We can feel disenchanted with our work during this Neptune transit. However, while we may dream of the perfect escape hatch, we can also suffer from bouts of passivity, leaving at least some of us feeling powerless to change. That's also an illusion, because change is truly in the air. All Outer Planets are intolerant of stagnation—they can't wait to give us a motivational cosmic kick in the pants!

GUIDING LIGHT

Whatever our profession, we may find ourselves more alive and well than ever in our future career endeavors if we go with Neptune's flow in good faith. A degree of trust in a wise and benevolent Universe needs to take the place of any obsession we have with rigid self-management or with attempts to tightly control and limit our performance. We could undergo a change for the better if we'd just stop getting in the way of any Neptunian urge to relinquish what no longer nourishes our deeper self. A new vision may be waiting to be born, but it will require that we steadfastly believe in our talents and creative gifts. These assets may be ready to surface now as never before, yet self-trust and even greater self-love are the keys to our success. We are not stuck on a dead-end road to nowhere, although sometimes, during this transitional stage, it feels as if we are.

What we may yearn to do probably won't seem practical to others at first, and could even appear risky in terms of career stability. Listening to those who are happily bound to conventional Tenth-House values can cause us great confusion and self-doubt. We realize that we no longer have a striving ambition to competitively make it to the top. We don't feel a momentum to move toward anything with sure-footed confidence. If we do, it may be due to compulsive urges stemming from our unconscious. Usually, our objectives are less clear-cut.

We may worry that what we really want to do may look insane to others, who then could begin to doubt our credibility and maturity. How we appear to the world is often a big deal for us in our status-conscious Tenth. Thus, we typically keep our dreams a secret, even as Neptune is whispering in our ear for us to dissolve our personal fears of social criticism. Why not? Often, what we most dread during any Neptune transit rarely comes to pass. It's what we flat-out ignore that could later cause problems. With Neptune, it's typically the less obvious things that trip us up.

Often, Neptune allows things involving our career to fall apart little by little, on their own, chipping away at our sense of loyalty to and security in our company or our chosen field. Such subtle but definite deterioration seems beyond our control. All that we know is that our vital interest in our work is beginning to wane. We could feel indifferent or weary about our job. Of course, while Neptune conjuncts our Midheaven, it opposes our Fourth-House cusp, suggesting deep insecurities at play that make us feel as if our inner foundation is wobbly and collapsible. Something inside of us is ready for a breakdown, especially if we assume that nothing can change outwardly that will improve our lot in life.

AUTHORITY WITHIN

One thing we can commonly experience is having misunderstandings with those in authority. By projecting Neptune onto a boss, we may be confused by his or her lack of clarity, forthrightness, or even honesty. We may not get the structured direction we need or expect. If unclear about our role, we'll need to act as if Mercury is permanently retrograde—since that's how situations currently feel—and learn to ask for concise, straightforward explanations. We should not assume that we *think* we know what those in charge want. It's always the best policy to ask for further clarification when unsure.

In extreme cases, we tend to be overly sensitive, thinking that an employer or the company itself has it in for us for some mysterious reason. With Neptune, our grievances are usually non-specific; we can't prove anything, but we *feel* the bad vibes all around. This could render a few of us suspicious and very anxious, which only negatively affects our job-performance, inviting the criticism we fear. We may not be able to objectively assess our professional situation at this time, because hidden psychological baggage can distort our evaluations. This baggage may be in the form of unfinished business regarding parental rejection or abandonment themes from an unresolved past. Sometimes we are completely unaware of how we are hurting our reputation. It's important for us to realize that our surfacing vulnerabilities and weak spots could sabotage our position or social standing. Maybe this is one way that our unconscious self forces us to break free from a career that no longer inspires us to do our best. However, such self-wounding is not the smartest route to take.

Professional excellence is well supported in the Tenth. Therefore, we'll need to realistically improve our performance and determine what ideals we are capable of attaining. If we are on the right track with Neptune, we could find that our boss is very inspirational and concerned with nourishing and protecting our professional development. A sympathetic employer becomes a dedicated mentor who looks out for us. We, in turn, show healthy levels of devotion and respect. The association seems heaven sent, but Neptune can also slip in an element of hidden sacrifice. Our boss may later resign (due to illness?) or be transferred to another department, leaving us with a feeling of abandonment.

Perhaps the company for which we work is not as sound as we've been led to believe. Chronically poor management is usually at fault. The business may have to close its doors because it's not generating enough money to keep it afloat, no matter how great its intentions. This leaves workers scrambling for new employment. We should look at our current position as just a stepping stone to something better, something that lets more of our inner self shine and be recognized. During this transit, we shouldn't get too attached to our present company and our current role in it.

If we learn how to turn within and give attention to our inner sense of authority, we can navigate amid turbulent waves stirred up by this transit, knowing that things are temporarily shaky and uncertain for a reason. Eventually, the choppy waters will calm down, once we learn to trust the self-illuminating power of change. Remember, we have a dream that could turn out to be a reality, as long as we don't hang on to obsolete ways of operating due to insecurity and self-doubt. When things fall apart around us and then dissolve for good, some of us will learn that we have been unrealistic in the pursuit of our career goals. Our dreams in the Tenth need a degree of practical application, because this is still a very worldly house that demands tangible results. Things must be workable in the Tenth if they are to remain standing.

MAKING PEACE WITH DAD

In some instances, Neptune in the Tenth signals letting go of a parent, usually our father, due to conditions that we cannot alter or heal. These typically involve situations that have taken root long ago, such as chronic health condition that now is reaching its inevitable conclusion. Facing up to sad life endings, while dealing with feelings of loss and regret, can be quite Neptunian. Death may be one way this works out, but there's also divorce, or the complication of a father who runs away from the family, disappears mysteriously, goes to prison, loses his sanity or his memory, or becomes deeply inaccessible due to depression. All of these patently downbeat manifestations suggest that some of us cannot make close contact with our dad for some reason; he cannot be reached, but it's not our fault. Neptune is trying to help us to resolve any feelings of guilt we may harbor. We are to let go of him, at least at the psychological level.

If Neptune removes this family member from our life, we'll have to put focus on the further development of the internal father function of our psyche. In short, we learn how to best parent ourselves by setting down the personal guidelines needed to succeed in life. We establish our own limits and learn to better define exactly who we are and what we are qualified to do in this world. Our structure comes from within. Our father may no longer be around to assist, *or* damage, our ambitions and aspirations. We will no longer be able to seek his permission or fear his disapproval; the acceptance we want will have to come from within. When a parent is removed from the picture like this, the Cosmos is telling us that we are ready to grow up and embrace our autonomy, even though, with Neptune, we can be drawn to surrogate father figures. We'll need to reclaim whatever strengths we've projected onto this parent, because it's now our turn to live them out consciously by turning our aspirations into reality. Neptune can mean being haunted by unfinished business; therefore, we should try to work through our psychological dynamics with our father while he is still alive.

Not everything at this time is dramatic and heavy with the father-child relationship. If we were blessed with a loving and accessible father, this Neptune transit can make the bond we share even closer. Our dad may be in a phase where he wants more of his softer nature to connect with others. He also may be ready to allow for his emotions to flow, as a humanitarian or an artistic side emerges. Making a living in the material world is no longer the only thing that captures his attention. Taking time for spiritual unfoldment becomes equally as important. Often, that can simply mean that he needs to enjoy more moments alone in his world of imagination. Our role is to be as supportive as possible of our father's unfolding dreams, although providing him with a little common sense when needed, because few Neptunian dreams succeed when they ignore certain realities.

NEPTUNE/SATURN TRANSITS

IDEAL REALITY

Transiting Neptune contacting our natal Saturn is not all that hard to figure out, but it's often difficult to undergo. We'll need to loosen up our customary responses to our Saturn, especially if we've been too stiff and regimented in the past, or too concerned with being correct about "the way things really are." Saturn can fixate on its set view of reality, allowing for no other alternatives, especially those of credibility-damaging Neptune. This planet is now ready to invalidate a few of our long held (mis)assumptions about our world, especially if our outlook has become too narrow and short-sighted because of them.

Easing Saturn into a relaxed, non-defensive mode helps this planet to better receive Neptune's flowing energies. It's not easy for Saturn to slip into something silky and comfortable when it's been so used to doing everything in its rugged, scruffy work clothes. In fact, Neptune may seem like a seductively undermining threat to this earthy, no-nonsense planet. Besides, Saturn's not readily charmed by style without substance or by promises seldom delivered. On the other hand, Saturn seems spiritually undernourished to Neptune and in great need of a heaping plate of "soul" food. Neptune wants to fatten up Saturn with a fuller experience of ultimate being—and that requires going beyond the world of physical tangibilities and applied logic.

Natal Saturn shows how and where we need to be grounded and stable throughout our lives, particularly on the material level. It also describes where we are typically insecure and sometimes over-structured in order to compensate for our inner doubts. Here, our head typically rules our heart. Pragmatic self-preservation usually becomes our goal, even as our emotional needs take a back seat. In some cases, a few of us unwisely resist adequate Saturnian development and end up floundering throughout life—we're disorganized, unfocused, and much too dependent on others to build our own practical, worldly structures. People in charge take on *our* responsibilities, leaving us with less autonomy. We can suffer from an immaturity that keeps us uncomfortably bound to authority figures who forever enforce their rules on us. However, Saturn usually bears down hard on those who desperately need to recognize appropriate boundaries and then learn to work productively within those limits. Clear and sensible self-definition is important to Saturn. We can't afford to walk around clueless about ourselves and naive about the ways of the real world.

ANTI-GRAVITY

Hard-to-define Neptune doesn't care much for limits. It won't allow itself to be confined by the illusionary assumptions of dense, physical "reality." Although sharp-edged Uranus and time-bomb Pluto are ever ready to shatter and destroy limitations, Neptune would rather ignore limits or pretend that they don't exist—and in Neptune's boundless world, they really *don't* exist. Neptune urges us to reflect on the needlessly self-imposed restrictions that we over-emphasize at the expense of our ego-transformative development. Saturn is usually too preoccupied with material survival to think much about the uplifting elements of the intangible realm of spirit. Society doesn't reinforce such "spiritual" interests unless they're packaged in the dogmatic terms of sanctioned religions, typically with too much emphasis on Saturnian restrictions and penalties (i.e., the immutable laws of God and the consequences of sin). Neptune is now trying to give Saturn an extended vision of limitless human potential, free of the obstacles that our mind normally perceives.

However, Saturn is far less faith-oriented than Jupiter, a planet that Neptune usually has little trouble convincing of otherworldly possibilities. We have a greater tendency to resist Neptune's unfamiliar territory during this transit in favor of ego-direction and conscious control. Saturn, as our ego's security guard, has been on duty as long as we can remember. Our resistance to Neptune at this time often distorts the overall picture and encourages fearful responses. Self-doubt may plague us. However, even Saturn needs to periodically expand its strategies so that we can grow. Neptune tries to provide dreams that we'll be tempted to make workable.

Neptune knows that Saturn is excellent at manifesting form, due to its organizing power and its consistent application of focus and effort. Neptune alone lacks such skills, although it sometimes gets lucky at making things miraculously "just happen" by using its visualization techniques. Neptune has something inspiring that it wants us to make tangible now, *if* we are first willing to loosen our seat belt and turn on the anti-gravity machine. Can we learn to get off the ground for a while and float in the air, letting the wind's currents take us where they wish? Can we make ourselves as light as a feather in the breeze?

The transiting trine and the sextile encourage us to be more flexible in changing our current life structures. Saturn's natal house shows us where changes are most needed. We'll probably alter and adjust things carefully and gently. We don't blindly rush into anything, but will approach matters thoughtfully, almost contemplatively, and with reasonable hope. Sometimes, with the trine, we don't have to do anything except to be receptive to effortless change. The sextile prompts us to make small alterations in areas that stimulate our mind and that alert us to our ongoing potential. In this case, the potential lies in a fertile imagination that is able to reframe our perceptions in ideal ways.

Harnessing Vision

Regardless of the aspect in question, we are urged to better harness our mix of vision and worldly experience at this time. A dream we've nurtured internally now has a better chance to come true. Neptune is trying to give us a marvelous new view of how our life could be without those accustomed roadblocks. However, Saturn will slowly size up any situation before committing itself to experimental action. Nothing is to be changed overnight or superficially. The Saturn in us doesn't easily surrender to this ephemeral "vision" thing. We may not be feeling particularly assertive or movement-oriented, which means that we don't vigorously shake things up in our world. Neptune is known for gradual transformations. Any improvements are made with patience and steadfast faith in our goals. This can be a very low-key combination of planets that can quietly change the shape of our lives for years to come.

With tensional aspects involved, transiting Neptune's images often frighten Saturn. We can brood and mistrust our interpretation of situations—true gloom-and-doom artists. We begin to anxiously worry about where to place our faith. Upon whom or what should we depend? Life may take a few incomprehensible detours that disturb our sense of security. Perhaps some long-term conditions finally break down, refusing to work for us again, while people we've trusted mysteriously slip away. All of this can leave us disillusioned and even disgusted with our circumstances in general. Some of us may even sense that we are "losing it," becoming unglued on some level, and we probably *are,* for good reasons that we're just not aware of presently. Things can start to look as disorienting as one of those melting Dali paintings. Our sense of time can be thrown way off. We're vaguely alive and not feeling so well, emotionally speaking.

Some of these symptoms signal the normal growing pains that are to be expected whenever Neptune is working on a particularly stubborn Saturn that refuses to modify or let go of anything or anyone. Fixed-sign Saturns have this problem. The more we generally fear the unknown or the consequences of change, the harder this transit can be on us, especially if it's a square or opposition. As waves of Neptunian energy roll in, we try to fortify ourselves with Saturnian defenses that only make things worse. We can feel very isolated whenever we try to block Neptune, a planet that manages to eventually seep through Saturn's concrete walls in spite of our efforts. We invite the further defeat of our goals and desires, making us feel powerless, until our pain and frustration convince us that fighting Neptune itself is the main source of much of our craziness. We'll need to surrender to our Higher Self and let the transformational games begin.

What's the big deal, anyway, about letting go of whatever has outgrown its purpose in our life? The Outer Planets just don't get it—this human tendency to attach ourselves to anything that deadens our awareness of our spirit. Even Saturn, while trying to pressure us to preserve things that already are in great shape, does not want us to hang on to useless junk that's falling apart. Neptune is simply trying to facilitate this process in ways that it deems painless: practice simple non-attachment. Don't worry, be happy, and realize that bliss is a natural state of consciousness independent of what we possess, or *think* we possess, to appease our insecurity.

However, some of us don't care much for the feeling of walking on slippery ground, especially as the fog rolls in and we suddenly realize we're naked—geez, how'd that happen? Symbolically, that's how we might feel at this point. The pervasive sense of uncertainty about our direction that often accompanies tensional Neptune/Saturn aspects can trouble us, making us feel strangely exposed and vulnerable. This could be a blessing, because we are then urged to use our psyche's radar equipment to guide us out of our confusion. This forces Saturn to open up to subtler dimensions of awareness that it normally would deny.

DREAMS OF SUCCESS

On a more mundane level, career becomes the focus of idealistic yearnings. If our dreams of success in the world are based on self-deceit, our hopes crumble during this period. Half-baked schemes evaporate. We could seem to be in an unparalleled career slump, as we find out the hard way that life won't grant our wishes. Perhaps we've been fooling ourselves for quite a while about our capacities. We've been going down the wrong path, and this can be very depressing to realize. Digging a little deeper into our past history could show that we may not have put in the proper time and effort required by Saturn for reliable, long-lasting success. Often, some of us did not want to start from the ground up to give our talents the solid foundation they needed. During this transit, Neptune drowns the false hopes to which we cling. We can't afford to waste any more time in a futile effort to make this tired dream with broken wings fly.

Of course, it's good to look at what's going on with our Tenth House, and our Midheaven ruler as well. What if Jupiter is involved by transit with our Tenth, for example? Our career may appear to be running quite smoothly on the outside but, internally, we are in a state of conflict should transiting Neptune simultaneously conjunct, square, quincunx, or oppose our Saturn. Our ambitions may be cloudy because our drive for worldly attainment is weaker than usual. It becomes increasingly difficult to maintain a professional image of dedication and dependability. We can be disillusioned by our role, our performance of that role, or even our profession.

To feel more alive and well during this period, we'll have to follow our idealistic urges and determine what we can do to expand our concept of duty. Both planets have a strong social consciousness and want to serve society's greater needs. Neptune is now urging ego-preserving Saturn to become less self-serving in its drive to accomplish and succeed. Saturn insists that we work harder to patiently manifest our dreams and visions. We still need to value the wisdom of timely unfoldment and careful application. We'll also have to temper any urges to prematurely abandon people and situations that don't fit into our emerging but still hazy ideals. The trine and the sextile from Neptune to Saturn normally suggest that these two planets are working eye-to-eye. Although Saturn still doesn't understand Neptune's realm all that well, it does trust this planet's sincerity regarding social obligation. Neptune, however, seems to never completely trust Saturn, thanks to Poseidon's early childhood trauma.

FINISHING TOUCHES

Saturn doesn't go for much emotionalism or melodrama, while Neptune has a hard time with self-discipline and common sense.

This planetary combo suggests that we can behave in very contradictory ways for a while, until we realize that Neptune is showing us where we are to take our consciousness at this time. Our natal Saturn will be responsible for the finishing touches. These two planets must willingly share in the creative solutions that are necessary for us to best grow from this transit. We are to transcend certain elements of our Saturn that have weighed us down in the past, or that have kept us fearful of taking chances. Saturn can be wise about what works in the real world, but it doesn't have all the answers. Neptune doesn't really understand how the practical world operates, but keenly intuits where everything is ultimately headed: that blissful state of oneness in some indescribable dimension where the totality of love manifests as pure numinous light—the stuff nirvana is made of.

For now, Saturn will need to be content with the knowledge that the burden of living can ease up a bit as we allow Neptune to help us to effortlessly manage our tasks and responsibilities— maybe with a little help from angelic forces and other divine agents. We don't have to walk around with heavy weights on our shoulders and a sour-puss expression. Help is always nearby if we can open ourselves to trust in the Universe (cautiously, with the square and opposition). Our spiritual integrity will be tested no matter what the transiting aspect is. Neptune can put the finest attributes of Saturn on a pedestal for the whole world to see and be inspired by. It can give us the solid spiritual lift we need to achieve maximum benefits during this period.

CHAPTER SIXTEEN

NEPTUNE TRANSITING THE ELEVENTH HOUSE

UNIVERSAL CITIZEN

During Neptune's transit of our Tenth, we've probably come to realize that fulfilling materialistic goals is not enough to satisfy our evolving yearnings for deeper and more relevant societal involvement. By moving toward Eleventh-House values, we're one step closer toward that objective, as Neptune immerses itself in even more universal life issues. Worldly attainment and status in the eyes of others become meaningless to Neptune if not balanced by altruism, humane concern, and true compassion for all people. Material ambition can even turn into corruptible power when not backed by ethics and integrity. The Eleventh House is where we get to consider the rights of all people, regardless of how different they are from us—and maybe specifically because they are so different from us!

Transiting the Eleventh, Neptune demonstrates that it truly has a heart of gold. In fact, at this time we have a greater need to idealistically respond to the concept of social freedom. This can be a noble and highly-principled Neptune at work, inspiring us to improve conditions for those who have been held down by society's dehumanizing elements, usually based on class structure.

Neptune persuades us to play the role of an advocate, protecting human, animal, and environmental rights—especially when it's aspecting our natal fire planets, such as Jupiter and Mars (two planets that will fight for a cause no matter how unpopular).

In our Eleventh House, we paradoxically become more individualistic while we also learn to team up with many who share our visions and intellectual ideals. Paradox is no stranger to the Eleventh. We are to contribute something toward the experience of the group dynamic while not losing any sense of who we are, or any of that ego power that we've worked so hard in the Fifth House to create and enjoy. We are to build a sense of community spirit, demonstrating that we're much more than just a member of any social class (Tenth House) or ethnic background and religious affiliation (Ninth House). Rising above the limitations of our social rank or national origin is partly what the Eleventh is about. We explore that vast tableau of less familiar relationships available to us, even if that means breaking away from our family's "roots" and Fourth-House heritage. The Eleventh shows us that there's an amazing assortment of fascinating people to be met, as long as we're willing to let go of any restrictive labels that society has historically put on unconventional people from all walks of life.

GROUP SEDUCTION

In essence, the Eleventh House, from Uranus' perspective, would not wish us to become a colony of programmed androids or clones. In this house, we are to experiment with demonstrating our individualism, as well as how we can still fit in with any organized group that promotes progressive attitudes. This is the house of our futuristic expectations for society. Conformity is not easily supported, unless we draw heavily from this house's Saturnian side, where we "get with the social program" and develop a beehive mentality with comrades united in action to serve the one common cause. However, Neptune is not a planet that pushes for strong individualism. Retaining a separate identity is not something that this planet idolizes. The power of our ego to stand alone, independent of group cohesion, frightens Neptune.

As a result, we may begin this transit with mixed feelings about joining groups, especially those committed to social crusades, both spiritual and political. Neptune could easily tempt us to surrender our sense of self to any collective structure that promises to take care of our needs or do our thinking and reasoning for us. An organization with charismatic leadership can sell us on a better future; that is, if we would just lay down our self-will and follow some utopian dream—while we perhaps also unburden ourselves of our worldly possessions to support this great global vision. We could be told at this point how rotten the rest of this selfish, greedy, oppressive world is—and how such a destructive planet as ours is headed toward its annihilation; its days are numbered! This could also be said from a purely sociological point of view, even if dramatized by much Neptunian religious fervor. It's wise the realize that in our Eleventh and our Ninth, we are subject to the power of propaganda. A cult mentality can spring from these two houses, especially if we throw in a potential reality-distorting Twelfth House.

Feisty Uranus would love to pop up right now and warn us about the dangers of impending mind-control and of surrendering our will to mesmerizing dictators, but sly Neptune has just slipped the old sky god a few knock-out drops in his joltin'-java to keep him quiet for a while. "He's such an crackpot alarmist," says Neptune soothingly to an adoring, entranced crowd of starry-eyed idealists. "We don't need that kind of negativity, now do we?" adds Neptune, while sprinkling a little magic fairy dust to further blur what's really going on.

One danger here is that some of us may associate with those who can seduce us with rhetoric about the need for social "unity" and "solidarity of the people," while foaming at the mouth about "the hidden enemies out there" or "all of the world-wide conspiracies going on behind our backs." After a while, it's too confusing to digest but too scary-sounding to ignore. However, we may meet people who seem to have sincere intentions and who make us feel very welcomed and included. We may feel a strong, emotional connection with them. Still, we'll have to be careful of being sucked into any situation where we lose our autonomy and become a puppet for others to use and manipulate.

This all sounds so dramatic, like something that could never happen to reasonable people like us. Perhaps. On a smaller scale, however, we could find ourselves doing things for a club, a society, or an association that can seem more like missionary work, as we try to enlighten "outsiders" about the beliefs of our group. Neptune often shows us where we may give more than we receive, yet we don't realize it until later, when we're burnt out. We can feel drained from being too serviceable to any membership, although the group may not realize that we're having a problem with establishing reasonable limits for ourselves. We're probably not vocalizing our weariness. During this transit, we will need to let it be known when we're tired of others "volunteering" us to do things, especially the stuff that nobody else wants to touch!

In real-life situations, transiting Neptune will aspect various natal planets in our chart during its passage through this house. This could give us clues about when we could feel genuinely eager to devote ourselves to emotionally moving social ideals. This is when we will happily throw ourselves into some cause with much abandon. We'll also need to know when to pull back, drop out, and not feel at all obligated to be a team player. Remember, Neptune needs periodic silence and seclusion to recharge its emotional batteries—the Eleventh House is just too socially busy for Neptune at times, and lacks the privacy and stillness we need. Should Neptune aspect Mars, for example, we may desire to follow a path of exclusive self-direction (Mars) rather than put our energy into networking, although if Neptune puts Mars into a deep enough trance, breaking away from group-consciousness becomes tricky, because we might feel unreasonably guilty for wanting to be so independently self-involved.

IDEAL FRIEND?

Neptune in the Eleventh House also tries to convince us that there are no real strangers in the world, only friends we have yet to embrace—even pals from past lives that are reappearing at this "karmic" point in time. What could be missing is the necessary ability to be selective in developing new friendships. Neptune wants soul-connection and yearns for bosom buddies, in an abstract way. However, the Eleventh draws people to us who are not to be possessed for long. Freedom-hungry Uranus understands this quite well, which explains why it claims this house as its main turf. If any closer companionship is to be sought, we'll have to go to our intimate Seventh House—not our impersonal Eleventh—to search for those who enjoy an involved union. Acquaintances, colleagues, cohorts, and cronies are all found in our Eleventh House, but not our very best friends in the whole world.

However, Neptune can give us the impression that our friendly associations are more intimate than they really are—especially if we also share ideologies with fellow comrades, club members, or political party affiliates. Neptune will emphasize similarities between people whenever possible, idealizing the lowest common denominators. We run the risk of fooling ourselves about our depth of involvement with acquaintances. We tend to colorize these relationships according to our dreams of perfect alliance, ignoring the contrasting qualities that are less desirable. We can overlook the flaws in others that would make them unsuitable friends. Some of us can even befriend people who do not know how to deal with emotional nurturing. They may be wounded in ways that end up hurting us, or they may be capable of abandoning us during our moment of need—perhaps our worst fear. Even Uranus transiting this house attracts us to people who are guilty of that.

It's not surprising that we attract such confusing types, considering that the Eleventh finds getting in touch with emotional needs a challenge. Here, feelings can be intellectualized rather than experienced first hand. There is something detached about this house and the people it symbolizes. To that, we add Neptune, a planet that can cover up its feelings and play masquerade games. We may be associating with folks who have mastered the art of self-concealment. Their ability to deceive themselves and others is powerful. However, to avoid disillusionment, we, too, see only those qualities in others that uplift us. Thus, we can magnetize people who may eventually fail us and disappoint our greater hopes for the future.

It would be wiser to begin this transit with the understanding that looking for spiritual perfection in people is not the point of our Eleventh-House adventure. Learning tolerance regarding people's differences is the issue. This means viewing personality defects as a natural and very human part of the reality of collective evolution. Also, no one person is to be exclusively adored, worshiped, or deified. This house is an area of democratic opportunity, where everyone has a chance to shine and stand out as special in some way, or even be allowed to be the biggest jerk on the block! In our Eleventh, we experience people who don't follow standard rules of behavior or respond to us in ways that we think they should. If we are too emotionally sensitive around such "imperfect" types, we could feel crushed and disturbed by our interactions with them. We'll need to let the old Uranian sky god in us awaken, because Uranus likes people who show great contrasts in their personalities, and isn't impressed by sainthood.

BEAUTIFUL PEOPLE

It's true that inspiration follows Neptune wherever it goes, waiting for a chance to illuminate our darkness and dispel our fears. During this transit, we could really attract some beautiful souls who know how to make miracles happen in their lives—and they're just dying to tap us with their magic wand and give us a few lessons in practical wizardry. At this time in our lives, we need such enchanting people to help us to envision what our future self could look like, if only we had more faith in who we really are and trust in a loving Universe. Such special agents of Neptune may seem not of this Earth, not all that grounded, and yet something shining in their eyes may reveal a spirit that is alive and oh so well! We may crave to have the same close connection to the Cosmos that they appear to enjoy.

We'll need to retain a bit of emotional detachment as we relate to such charismatic individualists. We're not supposed to become just like them (sorry, Neptune), but they are nevertheless role-models—free souls whose creative lives elegantly blend childlike innocence and old-soul wisdom. Doors open wide for such tuned-in people. They never feel stuck in life, and the key to their success may be adaptability and a positive outlook. They also know how to forgive the past and carry on with their lives in the now. There may be a bit of the gypsy in their souls; they are willing to wander far and wide, if need be, to enrich their spirit and widen their vistas. Meanwhile, they warmly befriend us and allow us to re-evaluate all those good things that we suspect that we have inside, but never were encouraged to bring out—until now.

While we treasure such special friendships, we can't afford to become so closely entwined that we suffocate these individuals with too much attention and awe. They don't want it or need it. Our unconscious dependency could ruin a good thing, even though we're feeling a little addicted and platonically love-struck. Putting total focus on any one individual is not what the Eleventh House supports—get thee to your Seventh or Eighth House, if that's what you want! Themes of diversity, multiplicity, and social experimentation are all encouraged here. We are in need of having a more universal appreciation of people—in fact, of the entire human race. Neptune certainly can encompass the larger social picture, as does the Eleventh. No one person can or should become our whole world at this time.

BIGGER DREAMS

In general, Neptune in the Eleventh means that we are still dreaming those big dreams of universal import, first hatched in our Ninth and tested out in our Tenth. Many others now need to benefit from those dreams. By becoming a social activist, we help to manifest our aspirations in ways that can influence a wider range of humanity. Before some readers think that this all sounds a little too far-fetched or implausible, realize that cyberspace (currently, the internet) already allows our visionary ideas to quickly circulate around the world, creating an immediate impact on large numbers of individuals. Maybe it's a good time to set up our own web page ("Please go heavy on visual content," advises Neptune). We should encourage ourselves to be keenly aware of technological advances during these years, as well as futuristic social trends. This transit supports sci-fi consciousness, UFO sightings, and inter-galactic "whatever." However, we'll also need to appease the basic Uranian-Saturnian dimensions of this house and not go overboard with any elaborate global beliefs regarding the dawning of a new world order. Fierce Eleventh-House, Uranus-inspired individualism must be protected from disappearing into Neptune's cosmic melting pot.

NEPTUNE/URANUS TRANSITS
DAWN OF ENLIGHTENMENT

For those of you who have read *Alive and Well with Uranus*[1] (volume one of this series), you might recall in my Uranus-transiting-Neptune material the threat, "just wait until it's Neptune's turn to do a magical make-over on cocksure Uranus!" Well, that time has come. Again, we have the "Clash of the Mighty Ego-Shakers"—a rare moment when time bends and warps and alien inner worlds collide, resulting in tremendous upheavals in consciousness! We can end up feeling tornado-struck and typhoon-battered by life's fateful quirks. Neptune knows that it often has trouble dealing with sometimes insufferable, "I always know what's true!" Uranus, a planet unconvinced of its alleged intellectual arrogance. "But hey, don't blame the messenger," Uranus argues. "It's just that a boldly told Truth is a hard pill for dreamy idealists to swallow!" Touchy Neptune, now feeling its steamier Poseidon side percolating, suddenly wants to drown this brash, outspoken, crazy genius! Sometimes, that's actually what happens.

During this time, Uranus is being plucked from its detached, mental realm of clear blue sky and, instead, is thrown to the bottom of the cloudy sea of our unconscious, where things never move at lightning speed. It *really* feels odd for Uranus to be held captive in such a hypnotically slow and dreamlike dimension.

Uranus is not used to feeling floaty, nor is it accustomed to having its attention drift aimlessly. It certainly has never been vague about things, until now. It's somewhat out of focus, and that feels strange—imagine Uranus worrying about feeling strange! Of course, Neptune's atmosphere can be surreal even for a sky god known for bizarre tastes.

Something within us at this time is to awaken our need for freer self-expression, although Neptune tries to temper this unfolding process, resulting in less abrupt change and less outright willfulness. It's true that both planets are dedicated to our transpersonal growth. Our ego takes a back seat while our superconscious (Higher Self) takes over the wheel. It's also true that many people have this transit around the same time, making astrologers wonder if such aspects are relevant *only* within an impersonal, generational context, symbolizing a collective, consciousness-raising challenge.

I question that assumption. Before a social movement is to be born, seeds of unrest must begin with one individual, then two, then three...and the numbers keep on growing. Think of a religious reformer like Martin Luther and what followed his single act of defiance. Luther natally had a wide Neptune/Uranus conjunction in Sagittarius. Even think of Jesus and his revolutionary message. An individual first has a vision of social reform or technological innovation that later can result in sweeping progressive changes for the masses. (Microsoft's Bill Gates has natal Neptune square Uranus.) In some cases, especially with Neptune, a logically hard-to-understand wave of energy seems to mysteriously descend on many people at once, with everyone so "touched" tuning in to the same idiosyncratic wavelength that others, baffled, cannot detect.

Dramatic but perplexing fads or crazes that whiz around the world are one result of such energy waves. What else could explain why anyone would have an overpowering urge to dance the "Mashed Potatoes," play "Trivial Pursuit," or buy a "Tickle Me Elmo" doll or "Furby" at jacked-up prices? Whenever a social phenomenon is deemed "all the rage" and an irrational frenzy of interest is spawned, even by artificial means, that's Neptune's collective "madness" at work. It's usually a lot of fun and quite exciting, while the mania lasts.

However, when darker elements of Uranus, Neptune, and Pluto erupt in fury, especially in the area of politics and religion, disturbing collective compulsions such as "ethnic cleansing," religious "inquisitions," and systematic social "witch-hunts" result, stunning and revolting great numbers of people. We certainly wouldn't freely admit to having such persecutory impulses. The same goes for hysterical mob scenes: what sane individual would willingly take personal responsibility for that brand of swept-up craziness? However, such atrocious behavior rears its ugly head from the depths of the collective unconscious from time to time—all indicative of suppressed Outer-Planet energy gone haywire.

Owning Up

In some cases, Outer Planet energy suddenly breaks out and spreads its influence far and wide in a seemingly random, inexplicable manner. Perhaps, in the astrology of the twenty-first century, we'll come to appreciate that a growing number of individualists are able to take in more of what these transcendental planets are all about. My analysis of Neptune/Uranus transits, therefore, details the potential of this planetary mix on an individual basis. Much of it, sounding marvelously metaphysical, is not very practical to live out *continuously* in today's materialistic world. Both planets can be very ethereal in their experimental dealings with physical-plane realities. Saturn finds Neptune and Uranus to be quite maladjusted and frighteningly unstable, especially when they join forces. Of course, some would say that being locked up in a small, windowless room for twenty-four hours with a notorious control-freak like Saturn could *really* be a terrifying experience!

It should be noted that, individually, we are not going to experience the full range of Neptune/Uranus transits. Each of us will not even undergo the same series of aspects that others encounter. In this case, we might want to study the so-called "minor" aspect phases, such as the transiting semi-square and the sesqui-square, to see if they offer any insight into our ongoing life patterns. My grandmother had transiting Neptune conjunct her natal Uranus in Sagittarius when she was in her mid-seventies, at a time when widowhood helped to usher in a new social lifestyle that she ended up loving—she learned about the value of joy-producing friendships outside of her close-knit family and became more independent as a result. Even her wardrobe got jazzier and up-to-date, thanks to her Uranian awakening.

I probably will never experience that conjunction in this lifetime: I get to have Neptune forming an upper (waning) quincunx to my Uranus by age fifty, followed by the upper square when I'm about seventy-eight years old, and, finally, the transiting conjunction, if I'm still alive and kicking butt at the age of 115 years—actually, it's unlikely that I'll be able to kick anything at that point! Neptune/Uranus transits may seem impersonal, but they also have their own individual aspect-cycles within a life span that not everybody shares equally.

STRANGE DAYS

So, what to expect? This seems like a silly question to ask regarding these two highly unpredictable forces. Life in general at this time can begin to look strange to us, which is not necessarily a "bad" thing. Our social environment may show signs of growing instability—in the name of what some call progress—with old structures being torn down and new ones built up. This is not in a dramatic, Plutonian manner, especially during the Neptune/Uranus trine. Still, our old stomping grounds may suddenly appear different and disorienting to us, depending on our age and our attitude toward radical change.

Such transits could be read from a sociological perspective. We may perceive current cultural shifts in values and behavior to be alienating and disturbing, especially during the transiting opposition years, although some societal stirrings may perfectly symbolize sweeping changes that are, perhaps, going on within us as well. Our psyche is in a state of revolution, shaking up its own status quo. If we are still unconscious of our Uranian urge to be free from rigid social programming, much of this transit's ability to break down and reinvent reality is first projected onto the world at large. Things around us are in a state of continual flux and disruption. Sometimes it can be downright exciting and futuristic. (The Internet began to captivate the public's imagination during the transiting Neptune/Uranus conjunction in 1993.)

At some point, we'll have to go within and realize that Neptune can now illuminate our pathway to Uranus, making this planet more appealing than ever. We may finally be waking up to its fuller potential. We may also, surprisingly, find ourselves very future-oriented, curious about flirting with different lifestyles that allow for greater freedom of self-expression. How far we go with this depends on the amount of Saturnian baggage we still carry from the past. Saturn can be quite a doubting Thomas, squelching our pipe dreams left and right, and insisting that we be strictly reality-based and concrete with our goals.

In contrast, Neptune and Uranus can have us live happily inside our heads, where we merely play around with abstract possibilities that we don't expect to actually live out. Some of us are much too conformist in temperament to make revolutionary changes. Maybe we enjoy exposing ourselves to thought systems (via books or workshops) that speak of awakening any psychic or spiritual gifts we possess. It would be a thrill to read someone's aura, we speculate, or have prophetic visions. However, as far as altering the real social structures that we personally spent years establishing, few of us will act in ways that jeopardize stability. A Neptune/Uranus transit is usually more talk than action, more dreaming than doing, more yearning than achieving. Meanwhile, a few of us may walk around in a state of "divine" discontent. We can feel like ET, wanting to phone home!

Should the transit be a square or an opposition, Uranus can be very restless for change, yet Neptune is not offering clear, reliable options. Parts of us can feel in turmoil as we long to escape from mundane pressures. Some of the escape routes we could choose invite further chaos if we are unrealistic from the start about making changes. We could also go down dead-end roads that certainly don't justify all of the instability we managed to stir up. We'll have to apply a little common sense during this transit, drawn from potentials shown by other parts of our chart, because Neptune/Uranus combinations are not easily grounded in material reality. They present an idealism that can inspire us to better ourselves and the world, but that also may fail to suggest a sensible game plan. It's as if we are making up the rules as we go along. Well, we are!

Psychic Awakening?

Astro-texts typically emphasize the level of psychic power possible in these transits. This may happen because Neptune, in theory, can help to remove the mental barriers that have stopped us in the past, due to doubts or fears, from tapping into our Uranian intuition. Neptune is an alluring influence. During these transits, we may be very curious about how to contact our Higher Self and/or invisible planes of existence. How to become more spiritually aware fascinates us now. We might want to learn techniques that assist our unfoldment along these lines. Some of us could even find that our ESP spontaneously awakens at some point during this transit. Neptune glamorizes Uranus' ability to simply know things due to sudden flashes of insight.

Even if only four out of every hundred people who experience a Neptune/Uranus transit at the same time become psychically aroused, we could be one of those awakened four. Perhaps many of the other ninety-six just feel the urge to go visit a good psychic or clairvoyant! A few of us might opt to enter therapy to sort out any internal chaos and try to figure out our current peculiar, inner states. Whatever the case, odd synchronistic events make many of us wonder about the true nature of time and space, and about the mysteries of the Universe. We start to question whether there is more to Life than meets the eye—and we may not even care what others think about our "crazy" pursuits and wild-eyed theories.

THE RIGHT CHANNEL

It's important to realize that these transits do not occur very often. By pulling out a ephemeris that covers planetary positions for a century, we could easily pinpoint the times we'll have Neptune transiting our Uranus during the context of a reasonable life span. There won't be many such periods on our list. However, realizing how uncommon these transits are may help us to put any interpretations in perspective. These rare moments in time may come and go without too much fanfare, because both planets operate freely on unconscious levels. If our natal Uranus aspects a few of our personal planets—such as the Moon, Mars, Mercury—we are already able to more directly use our Uranian energies. A Neptune transit, therefore, becomes more accessible to our waking self. Its symbolism is not restricted to the bigger world around us. We're able to create personal experiences that test out these astrological principles for ourselves.

Channeling this unusual planetary mix may not be easy. Nothing mainstream or ordinary is suggested here. We can't work out such awesome forces by going shopping or by watching hours of TV, unless we're watching continuous reruns of *The Twilight Zone!* In fact, we'll need to conjure up an all-around atmosphere that tries to take us to the "Outer Limits," or even "One Step Beyond." Anything involving a heavy usage of imagination and fantasy may be helpful, because Neptune and Uranus are eager to work out creative solutions that prevent us from feeling too Earth-trapped. Artistic outlets supported by this transit are the usual routes: drama, dance, painting, and music. Now we can include a new electronic medium—digital-art. In fact, "virtual reality" would be a fantastic way to experience these transits—just not while driving or operating heavy machinery.

It's good to make sure that we have made peace with our Saturn before we crank up the volume of our Outer Planets. If we have, we've earned our mental and emotional stability. Our ego is durable and flexible enough to handle such otherworldly power. Neptune transiting our Uranus is a swell time to consider the enormous implications of being a pure spirit temporarily housed in a physical body and using a mind that's merely renting a brain to attend to various earthly maintenance chores. These two planets are trying to convince us that we are, indeed, quite alive and well and ready for a ride on the mothership. Don't forget to bring an extra pair of space goggles—and, please, leave the beeper at home!

NOTE

1 Bil Tierney, *Alive and Well with Uranus,* Llewellyn Publications, St. Paul, MN, 1999.

CHAPTER SEVENTEEN

NEPTUNE TRANSITING THE TWELFTH HOUSE

PEACE AT LAST?

The Twelfth House is home for Neptune, by now a world-weary and sometimes bewildered planet that tried its best to cope with uninspiring circumstances of earthly life during its tour of the eleven previous houses. Much of what Neptune witnessed didn't make a lot of sense. "Why does the ego always insist on being so stubborn, choosing to do things the hard and selfish way?" Neptune asks. Much of how others saw us handling Neptune in action was misunderstood. Neptune tried to bring love and light into the picture, when possible, uplifting the human spirit, which nonetheless generated the cynicism of a few skeptics—those who play hardball with their fixed interpretation of reality.

Now Neptune can take off its make-up, even its clothes, and get off its sore feet for a while. It's finally in a safe space, a place of sanctuary and soul renewal. This means that Neptune can put a lot of its energy into just being its old, limit-dissolving, wondrous self, with no more masks or costumes to wear. The pressure is off to perform feats of Neptunian magic for the difficult, unappreciative material world. Now begins the process of dematerialization and going back to the original source of all Being—our ultimate journey.

Actually, there are a few final stages to undergo before Neptune can fall into its deep state of cosmic sleep—that brief but blissful hibernation in total unconsciousness before a new cycle of self-realization begins again in the First House. There are some loose ends to wrap up, some unfinished business to put to rest. We are embarking on a long period of reflection regarding where we have been and what we have done to make this life experience more inspiring for ourselves and for others. How much compassion have we shown? How generous have we been with our time and energy to those in real need? Did we take the task of soul-searching seriously? If not, we will now. Did we, instead, make others sad or crazy? Have we destabilized situations in insidious ways? Is our life now in shambles? Are we lost to ourselves?

Sometimes, this transit coincides with a confusing period in which a few of us psychologically break down due to years of dysfunctional behavior or distorted views of our life situation. Perhaps, during this planet's Eleventh-House experience, some of us retreated from healthy group involvement to become social misfits, loners who now cannot meaningfully connect with people. Instead of beautiful visions for reforming the world, we may have developed a bleak, twisted outlook centered around the meaningless chaos of living. We've become fear-based and suspicious of the intent of others. Our desire is to withdraw from social activity and be left alone for good.

If this is so, Neptune now will have us fall apart at the seams so that we can eventually rid ourselves of our inner demons and of whatever else haunts or alienates us. We are in a purposeful state of needed disintegration. During our lives, many of our rejected, abandoned psychological parts sink to our Twelfth's dark, underwater caverns. They hide out, undetected, for years, slowly draining us. Neptune is now ready to throw light and understanding onto this shadow-infested material.

STRIP-SEARCHED

At this time, we must learn to deal with hidden pain and unspoken grief, unburdening ourselves of all that has weighed down our soul. Here, the ego is strip-searched and, while in such a state of naked vulnerability, we are less able to remain defensively detached from the source of our inner wounds. This drawn-out process takes many years to unfold. Thankfully, Neptune's action can be gentle and unpressured. Neptune lives in a timeless dimension, so there's no big rush. Forgotten images, now surfacing and made conscious, need to be recognized as real and potent. We will best heal by forgiving ourselves and others for past transgressions and failures. We cannot afford to hold on to ancient injuries that drain our life-force and poison our spirit. At some point, we have the option to surrender all such unfulfillment to a compassionate, loving Universe that will non-judgmentally absorb our residual darkness in exchange for a glimpse of more-luminous dimensions.

At this time, we can cleanse ourselves of all hurtful or disappointing life experiences that have tainted us emotionally, rendering us sick on some level. Old grudges and hatreds can hide out in our Twelfth House—but Neptune will find them. Humiliations and secret self-loathing may also implant themselves in our Twelfth, but Neptune will sniff those out, too. Remember, Neptune is not wearing any clothes right now, symbolic of a time when we no longer cover up those disturbing truths about ourselves that our soul knows only too well. We cannot escape from ourselves, nor should we, if optimum growth is our goal. At some revelatory turning-point during this transit, we begin to see the light at the end of our tunnel—a brilliant light. We begin to shed all that has prevented us from acknowledging our spiritual goodness and from appreciating our greater worth to the collective—and to ourselves.

However, to get the ball rolling, we'll need to set up a lifestyle or dwell in an environment where we can periodically go within and contemplate our essence. Having quality "quiet time" is a must. This may require that we minimize superfluous social activity. Our inclination is to cocoon ourselves and keep the harsh external world at bay. We'll need more silence and less external flux and mundane busyness. Who are we, *really*, once we have let go of most of our family and societal conditioning?

This is an opportunity to find out first hand, as we begin to peel back the layers of our psyche. Neptune is that small voice inside of us that assures us, in states of serenity, that we are more than the superficial labels that others have given us. This period permits us to dig deep into ourselves in order to reclaim our most valuable qualities: the divine elements of our nature—the spark of Divinity within.

BEYOND SOCIAL STRUCTURE

Neptune has just finished its assignment in our Eleventh House, so we probably have become very responsive to humanitarian goals, assuming that we haven't taken the malcontent, lone wolf route that bypasses human involvement altogether. We've shown an interest in collective dreams for the future and have realized that we cannot exist solely for ourselves, insulated from society's greater concerns. We've learned to reach beyond our immediate ego desires toward a world of vaster human connection. Hopefully, we've also learned to be more discriminate and realistic about the crusades and inclusive social causes to which we seek to dedicate ourselves. Maybe critics are now calling us "bleeding heart liberals," but that only prepares us for the final touches to be attended to in our Twelfth.

Social dreams common to the Eleventh House are usually adopted from an intellectual stance, perhaps as a result of a theoretical model of collective idealism. That's the Aquarius/Uranus approach: an enlightened but cerebral overview of the human condition and where it's headed—or where it should be headed (Saturn co-rulership)—provided that everyone cooperates and shares equally in realizing the universal ideal. The Eleventh tries to do what's best for all people in an egalitarian sense. Transiting Neptune in that house can glorify social harmony, with individuals willingly sacrificing for the sake of group welfare. It's all very upbeat in expectation, with much faith put into our mind's powerful ability to solve every problem. The Eleventh often takes a high-tech, scientific route to improving society. However, this is still an impersonal interpretation of humanity from a primarily "air" perspective. There's a potential to be emotionally detached and uninterested in unifying people on deeper levels.

However, in the Twelfth, all former efforts toward greater social integration prepare us for the ultimate reality of Oneness, the total merging of all consciousness through the annihilation of separative existence. We can take our social dream one step further. The fundamental similarities between all people, regardless of their status, capture our attention. How are members of the human race commonly linked? Both Neptune and the Twelfth understand that, while we are not all "equal" on the surface, we nevertheless are undifferentiated on the inner planes of being. Even on the surface, we all bleed alike and cry the same tears. It's obvious that a lesson in empathy becomes part of this transit, because that's not something that the more emotionally removed, Eleventh-House experience, by itself, necessarily teaches us.

CHARITABLE HEART

It's always good to be aware of our upcoming astrological transits. It puts us ahead of the game, to know what the general mood might be like when Neptune moves through our Twelfth. Perhaps we can find ways to consciously evoke this experience rather than passively wait to see what manifests; this allows the knowledge to empower us. At this time, volunteer work can be good for us, especially when we're at the transition point where Neptune moves from our Eleventh to our Twelfth—a time when we may not be ready to forego Eleventh group involvement in favor of personal solitude. Using a 1° orb, Neptune crossing back and forth over the cusp could take about eighteen months, in some cases. Both Neptune and the Twelfth hold a special place in their hearts for the underdog, the social outcast, the disenfranchised, or anyone else who is unfairly rejected by society. Some of us may find ourselves drawn to working behind-the-scenes to benefit the lives of people such as the poor and the homeless, or anyone wounded by the harsh realities of life.

If we cannot physically become involved in such social assistance, we at least find ourselves more willing to support charitable organizations and activist groups that quietly work for humanity's social betterment, for ecological sanity, and for the protection of the defenseless, including animals and their rights. If Neptune is forming transiting squares and oppositions, our compassion may be at an all-time high, and yet our judgment could be clouded by emotionalism and by the hidden agendas of others. That's when we can unknowingly contribute funds to groups that are not what they appear to be. We can get ripped off. Televangelistic financial scandals of recent times would fit the Neptunian dilemma here: duped in the name of (misplaced) religious devotion and caught up in the glamorous charisma of the "spiritual" leader. Should we find that we want to do good works in society, we will now have to use better judgment when trying to fulfill our urge to give and sacrifice. Once again, where's our natal and transiting Saturn?

WHEN SPIRIT CALLS

What about our spiritual needs? Furthering dynamic growth of any kind is not a Twelfth-House theme, because we're are at the end of a developmental cycle. We're winding down and starting to turn within. This implies a cessation of any assertive drive to continue building structure in our lives, even spiritual structure. Opportunities to seek well-defined spiritual paths are more active in our Ninth. Pushing for worldly achievement is to be less emphasized in this house, especially if our ego is still attached to the results of our efforts. For instance, what if transiting Saturn is also going through our Fifth—a transit describing a time to work at polishing up our ego-presentation in the world? Natal charts are often full of ongoing contradictions, with energies tugging us in different directions. Every planet seems to have its own "special-interest" campaign. In the above example, we'll have to find out how to accommodate our attention-demanding Saturn transit while still respecting visionary Neptune's need to release our ego's tight grip on us—not an easy task.

The Twelfth House operates by creating an environment conducive to reflecting on the fruits of our former efforts to spiritualize ourselves. We don't have to struggle here to be what we already are deep down inside. We simply have to embrace our inner being, experience it, and validate ourselves on a soul level. How to do this *effortlessly* is what Neptune is to teach us. We'll need to learn how to surrender ourselves *to* ourselves in the most expansive way possible. This involves a matter of complete trust in something greater than our ego, suggesting that chronic fears and insecurities will have to dissolve in the Twelfth for us to actualize such self-illumination. It's important that we find the quality time needed to refocus on our spiritual reality while in peaceful environments that allow us to be meditative.

We are able to experience a wide spectrum of psychic talents and otherworldly phenomena with Neptune in this house, even when natally found here. All of these sometimes extraordinary intuitive abilities show us the illusionary nature of time and space. This should teach us a thing or two about the underlying boundlessness of reality. Because we can break those mental barriers that both the ego and our waking consciousness create, we are able to tap into things normally hidden. Matter is not as solid as it appears to be, nor is spirit is as nebulous and remote. However, a degree of reason is a must when having these internal experiences, so that we don't become completely lost in Neptune's clouded waters. We're not to lose all perspective concerning earthbound existence—our Sixth House is opposite our Twelfth for a stabilizing reason. However, too much Sixth-House focus is to be avoided, because we'll find ourselves working too hard to be "spiritually correct," or else we'll over-analyze our transcendent experiences and risk fragmenting instead of unifying our consciousness.

We are to gently bring spirit-based awareness into the physical plane, rather than obliterate earthy experience entirely (at least, while we're still functioning in our body). This does not mean that we cannot have an occasional, mystical attunement during which we lose all sense of physical form and only perceive consciousness as pure light. These intoxicating but brief experiences probably serve as reminders of the Greater Reality that lovingly holds everything together that exists. While meditation is to be encouraged, it's not everyone's cup of tea. Others forms of stillness and quietness help us to enter Neptune's soul-enriching world—perhaps taking a contemplative walk alone on the beach or in the woods can stimulate our inner center.

Deep sea divers are aware of the otherworldly silence of Neptune's ocean depths. Where do we have too much noise in our lives? Are we over-thinking or talking up a storm, usually about petty, insignificant matters that momentarily take on more importance than they should? Maybe we'll find our inner sanctuary by writing poetry, painting, weaving, working the potter's wheel, or absorbing ourselves in music. Some kind of involvement with the arts and with the process of creating beauty from "nothing" can, in itself, become our meditation. Even dancing and feeling the flow of our body rhythms can entrance us. We'll need to give Neptune suitable outlets of fluid expression that transport us to inner realms of amazing possibility.

NEPTUNE/NEPTUNE TRANSITS
DREAMS FOR SALE

Transiting Neptune infrequently aspects itself in the course of a life time, but such "life-cycles" are usually experienced by most people around the same age. The ones that seem to stand out are the transiting square, quincunx, and opposition. However, the semi-square, the sextile, and the trine phases all offer us different insights. All of these phases can be *very* subtle, giving us the impression that nothing is really going on—but that's typical for Neptune. These transits don't readily translate into dynamic situational events, at least not in any cut-and-dried way. It also takes a special refinement of consciousness to sense Neptune's unfoldment. Many of us are not paying internal attention to this process and therefore may seem to be uninfluenced. Still, we can evoke the power of Neptune's cycles more consciously by putting ourselves in touch with this planet's ability to better synthesize experience, once we emotionally open up to reality's more subtle levels. Much seems to depend on our age and the situational opportunities at hand.

NEPTUNE SEMI-SQUARE NEPTUNE (AGES 19–21)

This period is a time of the dawning of young and innocent adulthood. The sense of invincibility in our early twenties is partly due to the Neptune mystique, the illusion that we'll never grow old and be trapped by stale, limiting routines. Such invincibility is also aided by the Uranus square Uranus transit around age twenty-one—an aspect that makes us feel fully in charge of ourselves and immune to behavioral restrictions imposed by society. The tensional pattern of this semi-square is mildly stimulating, and brings Neptunian urges a bit more to the forefront. The idealism that feeds our youthful dreams, plus the great expectations we have about making it on our own, tie in with faith in ourselves at this time. This can also be the beginning of a permissive stage, subtly tempting us to abandon Saturnian common sense in favor of the glamour of freedom and independence from any symbolic form of parental control. We can indulge in a lot of impractical interests.

This could also be a time when some of us seek out and attempt to merge with an ideal "other." Unconsciously desiring perfection, some of us yearn for a relationship that will sweep us off our feet. We also want involvement in outer-world conditions that elevate our feelings and make our spirit soar. However, vagueness of direction and indecision about future commitments can plague this transit, resulting in temporary uncertainties. Our options usually depend on the limits of the social environment in which we live. Some of us without a self-determined direction may flounder, with no relevant goals in sight.

In an economy that's not doing very well, this transit can make us feel very shaky and hopeless. We may keep everything tentative until our direction becomes clear. This can be a poor time for marriage or raising a family, regardless of the emotional high we're on from our relationships. Later on, usually during the Saturn Return, we may realize that we married young partly to escape from parental structure. However, while this semi-square is active, we're convinced that true love motivates us, and nothing else. This is obviously a time when we'll need to address a few blind spots, even though the semi-square doesn't provoke a crisis of self-confrontation as does the transiting square.

NEPTUNE SEXTILE NEPTUNE (AGES 26–28)

In this period, we may feel that we're starting to see the light. In a subtle manner, our vision and understanding of our deeper needs increases. Although the previous semi-square cycle fed illusions of ideal relationships—including the assumption that our "will" alone will magically help us to secure our heart's desire—this phase serves as a reliable internal support system, functioning in the background. Still, more pressing concerns are dictated by the upcoming Saturn Return. Neptune, in theory, can aid us in our inner realization of what we *could* be, once we dissolve our ties with any self-blinding elements of our less-enlightened early twenties.

Regardless of surface conditions at this time, transiting Neptune is trying to help us to sense that it is all right to be discontent with our world and to want more for ourselves. Neptune urges us to expand our potential at any point in its life-cycle. Any changes in our mundane circumstances, even disappointing ones, are actually working for our highest spiritual good, because sextile phases are opportune times to grow along new lines of interest. This could be a time to learn about self-compassion, forgiving ourselves for our dumbest mistakes during this decade. We are also in a state of consciousness where we can better tap into the fruitful expression of our imagination, resulting in more creative solutions in our lives. A more ideal image of ourselves is now ready to take form in the world. Unconsciously, we're just waiting for the Saturn Return to help us to put an end to a host of other self-limiting views and behaviors.

NEPTUNE SQUARE NEPTUNE (AGE 42)

This cycle occurs during the highly popularized and often misunderstood "mid-life crisis" years. Any square aspect in general tends to highlight issues that demand of our attention. A resolution is needed. The Neptune square to itself is probably the most critical aspect of its life cycle that we'll get to experience in our lifetime. It's associated with much of the growing disillusionment that we can feel with our current life pattern. In our attempt to sort out what is real to our true needs versus what is illusionary, we can become confused. This Neptune phase describes the emotional discontentment of the mid-life years. Buried feelings and forgotten yearnings may now emerge from our unconscious depths, needing our nurturance and understanding. We should acknowledge them now, rather than further suppress or deny their existence.

Things could prove painful for those of us who would rather ignore inner conflicts, although that's hard to do at this time. Getting in touch with such energies, made more powerful due to their suppression, can be rejuvenating when given suitable outlets for release. Self-compassion is also a must to help us offset any fleeting feelings of being a failure or an impostor who shows to the world an image that doesn't honestly depict our internal state of affairs. We can feel unreal to ourselves at this point, wearing a social mask that has, for so long, protected our inner vulnerabilities, but has also kept the outer world at a safe distance. The tightness of this rigidly worn mask now suffocates us. With Neptune's help, the mask is ready to slip off and melt. This allows us a chance to perceive the hidden features behind the facade—features that reflect our ideal facets and the reality of our spiritual identity.

This transit implies that it's best for us not to resist any self-transcendent changes taking place inside of us. We can be in a metamorphic period, similar to that of a butterfly emerging from its dark cocoon in all its radiant beauty and lightness. However, before any spiritual transfiguration can take place, we must examine our motivations with complete self-honesty. We'll have to draw on our inner resources to find the strength and the courage needed to do this, because society has not conditioned us to undergo such intense self-appraisal. It is typical that some of us can feel alone and cut off from outside support systems when attempting to do this. This "dark night of the soul" feeling is perfectly normal and appropriate for this phase. We can suffer more when we remain in a fog regarding our real nature by clinging to former attachments that we should have long outgrown. When blocked, Neptune fails to provide us with the psychological lubrication needed, thus keeping our ego-structure dry and brittle. This makes us vulnerable to emotional calcification in our later years.

Life is telling us that we can no longer seek ideal security from sources out there in the world. It will have to come from within if it is to be trusted. As we begin to illuminate those previously unlit parts of ourselves, this transit will seem less dark and threatening. Throwing light on our shadows is the best way to completely dissolve them. This "lower" square (waxing phase) Neptune transit inspires us to establish a new, inner foundation based on values more universal than society has offered.

NEPTUNE TRINE NEPTUNE (AGE 55)

This transit occurs shortly before transiting Uranus trines itself. This can be a peak expansion period in which we can sense spiritual renewal and self-blossoming. We have another opportunity to feel free and unhampered when exploring newer dimensions of our life, and with a more mature sense of innocence, as paradoxical as that sounds. Simultaneous Neptune and Uranus trine phases indicate a time when we can feel at peace with ourselves. This is a natural time to open up to the non-material side of our existence. Even if we have been receptive to our soul-needs earlier in our lives, now we perceive we are transforming according to a more ideal but realistic self-image.

We may also have the proper emotional and mental framework in which to re-cultivate special abilities we once abandoned due to other, diverting reality concerns. We can now relax and feel more content with self-insights gained. This can be positive, affirmative, and confidence-boosting. How far we allow ourselves to go depends on how well we can re-structure ourselves during our Second Saturn Return (usually at ages fifty-seven to fifty-nine). We may even be inspired to dream new dreams about how we will function during our upcoming, post-retirement years. This is the right time, however, to start envisioning an ideal plan for living out our golden years.

NEPTUNE QUINCUNX NEPTUNE (LATE 60S)

We experience this cycle at a time when Uranus also sextiles itself, Jupiter sextiles itself, and Saturn trines itself. Although Neptune's phase could prove disorienting and confusing for more calcified personalities (we probably blew that last Saturn Return and became meaner and grumpier), the backup support from these, concurrent phases should help us to make the emotional adjustment required for a healthy psychological break with our past.

This can also be a time for spiritual adjustments, in which we more deeply reflect on memories of our former growth cycles, both the bitter and the sweet. Discrimination, typically a quincunx theme, is not easily achieved at this stage of life, because our recollection of the past can be faulty and distorted. However, life now requires that we not get too attached to past impressions or attempt to relive them in our heads. Instead, we are to let go of non-productive recollections and other memories that are negatively charged with hostile, unresolved feelings. The more creative types at this time will not get hung up on self-pity or personal remorse. To do so could jeopardize our health and render us less functional—without any future dreams to shoot for.

NEPTUNE OPPOSING NEPTUNE (AGE 82)

This second most significant life-cycle for Neptune occurs just before our Uranus Return. This is a prime time for a fuller awareness concerning illusions that we have experienced during our lifetime. Many false assumptions about ourselves, others, and the world in general were necessary during those times when we gave them our greatest emotional energy. Realizing this, much—if not all—can be forgiven. We do not have to live out the remaining years of our life feeling defeated, dejected, and unfairly victimized. Our illusions eventually helped us to learn more about the nature of our real self in an in-depth, compassionate manner. They served a higher purpose.

At this phase, we can experience many reversals of emotional attitude. Matters that we had assumed to be unfortunate are now seen as blessings in disguise, while those which we once highly regarded as most important to the fulfillment of dreams now appear less magical and meaningful. Former distortions to which we clung with blind determination can clarify themselves at this phase, making it easier for us to let go of them once and for all. The opposition's potential for fostering total awareness helps us to dissolve a lot of emotional baggage.

We can also make peace with all troublesome life patterns of our past, once we have acknowledged that everything that happened to us or through us was for our own greatest spiritual good. Never once did we actually fail in any experience but, instead, had a chance to grow closer toward the God within. This allows us to begin the process of withdrawal into our inner world in a state of serenity and tranquil self-acceptance. For some of us, this becomes a time in which our spiritual comprehension of the unity of all life is at a peak. The culmination of this transit can result in true self-illumination. It's time to surrender our will and our ego to the greater cosmic flow until death. This will facilitate our soul's transition into the next dimension that awaits.

GOODBYE FOR NOW

I hope that you have enjoyed reading *Alive and Well with Neptune,* volume two of my *Alive and Well* trilogy. If you haven't already done so, I strongly advise you to read volume one—*Alive and Well with Uranus*—in which we rocket to exciting mental heights of awareness and learn to make life-altering breakthroughs that free up our sense of self. Finally, in volume three—*Alive and Well with Pluto*—we probe our most profound depths so that we can tap into a hidden power base that can rejuvenate our soul and transform our lives. Happy journeying!

BIBLIOGRAPHY

I am listing the titles of some books that either cover information about Neptune transits, or that describe the nature of Neptune at length. This certainly is not a complete list of available titles; I tried to select books that are not out-of-print and therefore hard to find. Happy Reading!

NEPTUNE

Greene, Liz. *The Astrological Neptune and the Quest for Redemption.* York Beach, ME: Samuel Weiser, 1996.

Paul, Hadyn. *Visionary Dreamer: Exploring the Astrological Neptune.* Dorset, England: Element Books Limited, 1989.

Waram, Marilyn. *The Book of Neptune.* San Diego, CA: ACS Publications, 1989.

All Outer Planets

Ashman, Bernie. *Roadmap to Your Future*. San Diego, CA: ACS Publications, 1994.

Arroyo, Stephen. *Astrology, Karma, and Transformation*. 2nd Rev./Expanded Edition. Sebastopol, CA: CRCS Publications, 1993.

Forrest, Steven. *The Changing Sky*. 2nd Edition. San Diego, CA: ACS Publications, 1999.

Greene, Liz. *The Outer Planets and Their Cycles*. 2nd Edition. Sebastopol, CA: CRCS Publications, 1996.

Hand, Rob. *Planets in Transit*. Atglen PA: Schiffer Publishing, Ltd., 1980.

Marks, Tracy. *The Astrology of Self-Discovery*. Sebastopol, CA: CRCS Publications, 1985.

Rodden, Lois. *Modern Transits*. Tempe, AZ: AFA, 1978.

Rudhyar, Dane. *The Sun Is Also a Star—The Galactic Dimension of Astrology*. New York, NY: E.P. Dutton & Co., 1975. (Hard to find.)

Sasportas, Howard. *The Gods of Change: Pain, Crisis and the Transits of Uranus, Neptune, and Pluto*. New York, NY: Arkana—Viking Penguin, Inc., 1989. (This is the only book I'm aware of that gives an in-depth coverage of all three planets in a single volume; I definitely recommend that you have this book on your library shelf.)

Thorton, Penny. *Divine Encounters*. London, England: The Aquarian Press, 1991.

Tompkins, Sue. *Aspects in Astrology*. Dorset, England: Element Books Limited, 1989.

Tyl, Noel, ed. *How to Personalize the Outer Planets: The Astrology of Uranus, Neptune, and Pluto*. St. Paul, MN: Llewellyn Publications, 1992. (This is an anthology presenting the works of seven astrologers.)

MYTHOLOGY

Aldington, Richard and Ames, Delano. *New Larousse Encyclopedia of Mythology*. New York, NY: The Hamlyn Publishing Group Limited, 1978. (Hard to find.)

Bolen, Jean Shinoda. *Goddesses in Everywoman*. New York, NY: HarperCollins Publishers, 1989.

———. *Gods in Everyman*. HarperCollins Publishers, 1989.

Gayley, Charles Mills. *The Classic Myths in English Literature and in Art*. Atlanta, GA: Ginn & Company, 1939; Cheshire, CT: Biblo-Moser, 1991 (paperback edition).

Morford, Mark P. O. and Lenardon, Robert J. *Classical Mythology*. New York, NY: Longman, Inc., 1977.

Richardson, Donald. *Greek Mythology for Everyone: Legends of the Gods and Heroes*. New York, NY: Avenel Books, 1989.

LOOK FOR THE CRESCENT MOON

Llewellyn publishes hundreds of books on your favorite subjects! To get these exciting books, including the ones on the following pages, check your local bookstore or order them directly from Llewellyn.

ORDER BY PHONE
- Call toll-free within the U.S. and Canada, 1–800–THE MOON
- In Minnesota, call (651) 291–1970
- We accept VISA, MasterCard, and American Express

ORDER BY MAIL
- Send the full price of your order (MN residents add 7% sales tax) in U.S. funds, plus postage & handling to:

    Llewellyn Worldwide
    P.O. Box 64383, Dept. K715–3
    St. Paul, MN 55164–0383, U.S.A.

POSTAGE & HANDLING
(For the U.S., Canada, and Mexico)
- $4 for orders $15 and under
- $5 for orders over $15
- No charge for orders over $100

We ship UPS in the continental United States. We ship standard mail to P.O. boxes. Orders shipped to Alaska, Hawaii, the Virgin Islands, and Puerto Rico are sent first-class mail. Orders shipped to Canada and Mexico are sent surface mail.

International orders: Airmail—add freight equal to price of each book to the total price of order, plus $5.00 for each non-book item (audio tapes, etc.).

Surface mail—Add $1.00 per item.

Allow 4–6 weeks for delivery on all orders.
Postage and handling rates subject to change.

DISCOUNTS
We offer a 20% discount to group leaders or agents. You must order a minimum of 5 copies of the same book to get our special quantity price.

FREE CATALOG
Get a free copy of our color catalog, *New Worlds of Mind and Spirit.* Subscribe for just $10.00 in the United States and Canada ($30.00 overseas, airmail). Many bookstores carry *New Worlds*—ask for it!

Visit our website at www.llewellyn.com for more information.

TWELVE FACES OF SATURN
Your Guardian Angel Planet
Bil Tierney

Astrological Saturn. It's usually associated with personal limitations, material obstacles, psychological roadblocks and restriction. We observe Saturn's symbolism in our natal chart with uneasiness and anxiety, while intellectually proclaiming its higher purpose as our "wise teacher."

But now it's time to throw out the portrait of the creepy looking, scythe-wielding Saturn of centuries ago. Bil Tierney offers a refreshing new picture of a this planet as friend, not foe. Saturn is actually key to liberating us from a life handicapped by lack of clear self definition. It is indispensable to psychological maturity and material stability—it is your guardian angel planet.

Explore Saturn from the perspective of your natal sign and house. Uncover another layer of Saturnian themes at work in Saturn's aspects. Look at Saturn through each element and modality, as well as through astronomy, mythology and metaphysics.

1–56718–711–0, 6 x 9, 360 pp.   **$16.95**

Astrology for Beginners
An Easy Guide to Understanding
& Interpreting Your Chart
William Hewitt

Anyone who is interested in astrology will enjoy *Astrology for Beginners*. This book makes astrology easy and exciting by presenting all of the basics in an orderly sequence while focusing on the natal chart. Llewellyn even includes a coupon for a free computerized natal chart so you can begin interpretations almost immediately without complicated mathematics.

Astrology for Beginners covers all of the basics. Learn exactly what astrology is and how it works. Explore signs, planets, houses and aspects. Learn how to interpret a birth chart. Discover the meaning of transits, predictive astrology and progressions. Determine your horoscope chart in minutes without using math.

Whether you want to practice astrology for a hobby or aspire to become a professional astrologer, *Astrology for Beginners* is the book you need to get started on the right track.

0-87542-307-8, 5¼ x 8, 288 pp., softcover   **$9.95**

HEAVEN KNOWS WHAT
Grant Lewi

Here's the fun, new edition of the classic, *Heaven Knows What!* What better way to begin the study of astrology than to actually do it while you learn. *Heaven Knows What* contains everything you need to cast and interpret complete natal charts without memorizing any symbols, without confusing calculations, and without previous experience or training. The tear-out horoscope blanks and special "aspect wheel" make it amazingly easy.

The author explains the influence of every natal Sun and Moon combination, and describes the effects of every major planetary aspect in language designed for the modern reader. His readable and witty interpretations are so relevant that even long-practicing astrologers gain new psychological insight into the characteristics of the signs and meanings of the aspects.

Grant Lewi is sometimes called the father of "do-it-yourself" astrology, and is considered by many to have been astrology's forerunner to the computer.

0-87542-444-9, 6 x 9, 480 pp., tables, charts, softcover $14.95

To order call 1–800–THE MOON
Prices subject to change without notice.

ASTROLOGY FOR THE MILLIONS
Grant Lewi

First published in 1940, this practical, do-it-yourself textbook has become a classic guide to computing accurate horoscopes quickly. Throughout the years, it has been improved upon since Grant Lewi's death by his astrological proteges and Llewellyn's expert editors. Grant Lewi is astrology's forerunner to the computer, a man who literally brought astrology to everyone. This, the first new edition since 1979, presents updated transits and new, user-friendly tables to the year 2050, including a new sun ephemeris of revolutionary simplicity. It's actually easier to use than a computer! Also added is new information on Pluto and rising signs, a new foreword by Carl Llewellyn Weschcke, and introduction by J. Gordon Melton.

Of course, the original material is still here in Lewi's captivating writing style all of his insights on transits as a tool for planning the future and making the right decisions. His historical analysis of U.S. presidents has been brought up to date to include George Bush. This new edition also features a special "In Memoriam" to Lewi that presents his birthchart.

One of the most remarkable astrology books available, *Astrology for the Millions* allows the reader to cast a personal horoscope in 15 minutes, interpret from the readings and project the horoscope into the future to forecast coming planetary influences and develop "a grand strategy for living."

0–87542–438–4, 6 x 9, 464 pp., tables, charts $14.95

To order call 1–800–THE MOON
Prices subject to change without notice.

ASTROLOGICAL TIMING OF CRITICAL ILLNESS
Early Warning Patterns in the Horoscope

Noel Tyl
Foreword by Mitchell Gibson, M.D.
Introduction by Jeffrey Wolf Green

Now, through master astrologer Noel Tyl's work, astrology has a thoroughly tested method with which to understand and anticipate the emergence of critical illness: from the natal horoscope, throughout development, and within the aging process. Astrologers can use Noel Tyl's discovery to work with people to extend life as much as possible, to live a full life, and to do it all with holistic understanding.

Tyl painstakingly researched more than seventy cases to test his patterning discoveries Your analytical skill will be alerted, tested, and sharpened through these very same cases, which include notables such as Carl Sagan (bone cancer), Betty Ford (breast cancer), Larry King (heart attack), Norman Schwarzkopf (prostate cancer), and Mike Wallace (manic depression), and many, many others.

1–56718–738–2, 7 x 10, 288 pp., charts   **$19.95**

To order call 1–800–THE MOON
Prices subject to change without notice.

SYNTHESIS & COUNSELING IN ASTROLOGY
The Professional Manual
Noel Tyl

One of the keys to a vital, comprehensive astrology is the art of synthesis, the capacity to take the parts of our knowledge and combine them into a coherent whole. Many times, the parts may be contradictory (the relationship between Mars and Saturn, for example), but the art of synthesis manages the unification of opposites. Now Noel Tyl presents ways astrological measurements—through creative synthesis—can be used to effectively counsel individuals. Discussion of these complex topics is grounded in concrete examples and in-depth analyses of the 122 horoscopes of celebrities, politicians, and private clients.

Tyl's objective in providing this vitally important material was to present everything he has learned and practiced over his distinguished career to provide a useful source to astrologers. He has succeeded in creating a landmark text destined to become a classic reference for professional astrologers.

1–56718–734–X, 7 x 10, 924 pp., 115 charts $29.95

THE HOUSE BOOK
The Influence of the Planets in the Houses
Stephanie Camilleri

What gave Marilyn Monroe, John Lennon, John F. Kennedy and Joan of Arc their compelling charisma—could it be that they all had planets in the Eighth House? Find out why someone with Venus in the Fifth may be a good marriage partner, and why you may want to stay away from a suitor with Uranus in the Second.

Now you can probe the inner meaning of the planets in your chart through their placement in the houses. *The House Book* provides a solid base for students of astrology, and gives advanced astrologers new ways of looking at planet placement.

The author culled the similarities of house qualities from 1,500 different charts in as intensive and as scientific a method as possible. The most important feature of this book is that each description was written from the perspective of real charts with that location, without referencing preconceived ideas from other books. In some places, the common wisdom is confirmed, but in others the results can be very surprising.

1-56718-108-2, 5 ³/₁₆ x 8, 288 pp., softcover   **$12.95**

To order call 1–800–THE MOON
Prices subject to change without notice.

ASTROLOGY: WOMAN TO WOMAN
Gloria Star

Women are the primary users and readers of astrology, yet most astrological books approach individual charts from an androgynous point of view. *Astrology: Woman to Woman* is written specifically for women, by a woman, and shows that there *is* a difference in the way men and women express and use their energy. It covers every facet of a woman's life: home, family, lovers, career, and personal power.

Whether the reader is new to astrology or an old pro, there are new insights throughout. Those of you who don't know what sign their Moon is in or which planets are in their seventh house can order a free natal chart from Llewellyn that will tell you everything you need to know to use this book.

Discover what's at the heart of your need to find a meaningful career, understand your inner feminine power, own up to your masculine self, uncover your hidden agendas, and much more.

1–56718–686–6, 7 x 10, 464 pp.   **$19.95**

To order call 1–800–THE MOON
Prices subject to change without notice.

PLUTO, VOL. II
The Soul's Evolution Through Relationships
Jeffrey Wolf Green

From the great mass of people on the planet we all choose certain ones with whom to be intimate. Pluto, Vol II shows the evolutionary and karmic causes, reasons, and prior life background that determines whom we relate to and how.

This is the first book to explore the astrological Pluto model that embraces the evolutionary development and progression of the Soul from life to life. It offers a unique, original paradigm that allows for a total understanding of the past life dynamics that exist between two people. You will find a precise astrological methodology to determine the prior life orientation, where the relationship left off, where the relationship picked up in this lifetime, and what the current evolutionary next step is: the specific reasons or intentions for being together again.

In addition, there are chapters devoted to Mars and Venus in the signs, Mars and Venus in relationship, Mars and Pluto in relationship, and Pluto through the Composite Houses.

1–56718–333–6, 6 x 9, 432 pp., softcover   **$17.95**

To order call 1–800–THE MOON
Prices subject to change without notice.

WHEN PLANETS PROMISE LOVE
Your Romantic Destiny Through Astrology
Rose Murray

(Formerly *When Will You Marry?* Now revised and expanded.) Never before has an astrology book so thoroughly focused on timing as a definitive factor in successful romantic partnerships. Written in language the beginner can easily follow, *When Planets Promise Love* will engage even the most advanced student in search of love. Identify what you need in a partner and the most favorable times to meet him or her based on transits to your natal chart. Then learn how to compare your chart with that of a potential mate. This premier matchmaking method is laid out step by step, starting with the basics through fine tuning with Sun-Moon midpoints, chart linkups, and Arabian parts. Confirm with exactness whether or not someone is "the one!"

Includes a 50% off coupon for a marriage year chart.

1–56718–477–4, 6 x 9, 256 pp. **$12.95**

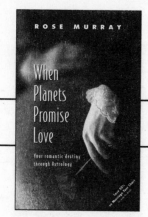

INSTANT HOROSCOPE PREDICTOR
Find Your Future Fast
Julia Lupton Skalka

Want to know if the planets will smile favorably upon your wedding day? Wondering when to move ahead on that new business venture? Perhaps you're curious as to why you've been so accident prone lately. It's time to look at your transits.

Transits define the relationship between where the planets are today with where they were when you were born. They are an invaluable aid for timing your actions and making decisions. With a copy of your transit chart and *Instant Horoscope Predictor* you can now discover what's in store for today, next month, even a year from now.

Julia Lupton Skalka delivers an easy-to-use guide that will decipher the symbols on your transit chart into clear, usable predictions. In addition, she provides chapters on astrological history, mythology, and transit analyses of four famous people: Grace Kelly, Mata Hari, Theodore Roosevelt, and Ted Bundy.

1–56718–668–8, 6 x 9, 464 pp., softcover   **$14.95**

ASTROLOGY FOR WOMEN
Roles & Relationships
Edited by Gloria Star

Despite the far-reaching alterations women have experienced
collectively, individual women are still faced with the challenge
of becoming themselves. In today's world, a woman's role is not
defined so much by society's expectations as by the woman herself. This book is a first look at some of the tasks each woman
must embrace or overcome. Ten female astrologers explore the
many facets of the soulful process of becoming a whole person:

- Jan Spiller—The Total Woman
- Demetra George—Women's Evolving Needs: The Moon
  and the Blood Mysteries
- M. Kelley Hunter—The Mother-Daughter Bond
- Carol Garlick—Daughter's and Fathers: The Father's Role
  in the Development of the Whole Woman
- Barbara Schermer—Psyche's Task: A Path of Initiation
  for Women
- Gloria G. Star—Creating Healthy Relationships
- Madalyn Hillis-Dineen—On Singleness: Choosing
  to Be Me
- Ronnie Gale Dreyer—The Impact of Self-Esteem
- Kim Rogers-Gallagher—Who Should I Be When I Grow
  Up?
- Roxana Muise—The Sacred Sisterhood

1–56718–860–5, 5 ³⁄₁₆ x 8, 416 pp., charts, softcover $9.95

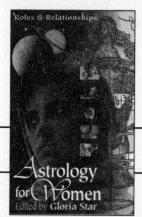